The Fine Art
of Literary Mayhem

MYRICK LAND

A Lively Account of Famous Writers & Their Feuds

LEXIKOS

san francisco

The Fine Art of
Literary
Mayhem

Second edition, revised

Published in 1983 by
Lexikos
703 Market Street
San Francisco, California 94103

Cover design and chapter titles by Bill
Prochnow. Text design by Ernest Reichl.
Text set in Fairfield with Palatino and Goudy
Old Style by Turner & Brown, Inc. Printed on
55-pound Emerson, covers 80-pound Strath-
more Americana. Printed and bound by
Cameron belt press by Banta Co.

Manufactured in the United States of America.

Acknowledgments and permissions appear
on pages 270–73.

Library of Congress Cataloging in Publication Data

Land, Myrick, 1922–
    The fine art of literary mayhem.

    1. Literary quarrels. 2. Authors—Biography.
I. Title.
PN165.L3   1983   809 [B]   82-49332
ISBN 0-938530-11-9

83 84 85 86 87 5 4 3 2 1

Contents

5

Preface

THE often-troubled lives of great writers had intrigued me for years, but not until I began my research on this book in the early 1960s did I realize how many of them had become embroiled in complex feuds with other writers.

A few of these encounters had been written about before, but many of them had never been closely examined in print. The last book-length treatment of a wide range of literary feuds had appeared more than a century before, and many of the most revealing and dramatic relationships between noted writers had occurred in the years since that book's publication.

Once I began my work, I was able to obtain accounts of twentieth-century feuds from writers who were involved in them or had witnessed them.

W. Somerset Maugham, far less mellow than one might expect of a man in the closing years of a very long life, offered me a final scorching estimate of his one-time friend, Hugh Walpole.

Aldous Huxley, obviously disappointed by what he saw as the failure of his last novel, still took the time to answer my questions about the strange relationship between D.H. Lawrence and his lost disciple, John Middleton Murry.

Norman Mailer responded quickly to a series of queries about the feuds that grew out of his published "evaluations" of his contemporaries. He later joined me in persuading the very genteel publisher of the hardcover edition of *The Fine Art of Literary Mayhem* that it was permissible to use the word "ass" in print without bringing out the censors. (Mailer seemed first amused, then outraged, when an editor suggested that the word could be printed "a——.")

Those who saw themselves as victims of the Mailer evaluations helped me round out the account of this literary free-for-all by offering their evaluations of Mailer and their reactions to his unusually candid criticism. Vance Bourjaily, Gore Vidal, Calder Willingham, Herbert Gold and William Styron each contributed valuable details to the chapter, "Norman Mailer Challenges All the Talent in the Room."

The help I received from many others, including distinguished scholars who reviewed several of the chapters, is acknowledged on pages 270–73. Here I wish to thank my wife, who quietly rescheduled our lives to make certain that, whatever happened, there would always be time available for the book, and Alan Magary and Tom Cole, who have given my favorite book a second life.

*The Fine Art
of Literary Mayhem*

Once again
to Barbara

Notes on a Fine Art.

READING *Fear of Flying* by Erica Jong "is like being locked in a lift with a woman who tells you her life story twice over, rapes you, and stops you from reaching for the Emergency button."

That comment by the British critic Jonathan Raban in *Encounter* illustrates a form of literary mayhem that can be traced back for centuries—the savage assault on anyone who has the audacity to publish a book.

The most unrestrained attacks have usually been directed at writers who succeed in reaching an enormous audience. When Leon Uris published *Topaz*, reviewer Anthony Boucher wrote in *The New York Times Book Review*:

Mr. Uris is flagrantly unable to construct a plot, a character, a novel, or a sentence in the English language—and he takes 130,000 words to display his incompetence.

Often a writer whose first work is received with special enthusiasm by reviewers faces a startling change if his subsequent novels seem to rise automatically toward the top of the bestseller list. James A. Michener's *Tales of the South Pacific* brought him general praise, but that early warmth dissipated as the size of his first printings increased. When he published his 865-page novel *Chesapeake* in 1978, a *Newsweek* reviewer offered the magazine's readers two suggestions:

> My best advice is don't read it; my second best is don't drop it on your foot.

Herman Wouk experienced a similar change in the attitude of many reviewers toward his work. *Caine Mutiny* received almost unanimous approval, but the temperature dropped precipitously when he published *Youngblood Hawke*, a novel obviously based on the life of Thomas Wolfe:

> Wouk has borrowed almost everything from Wolfe but his cuff-links.
>
> *—Time*

> Sometimes [Wouk] plods so doggedly that you begin to admire him more for his stamina than for his story-telling.
>
> *—Commonweal*

> The characters (including those diluted from Wolfe's books) are constructed with the knit-browed, honest concentration of a child working with a Mecano set...[The] ideas that are expressed are the utterances of a tapioca mind.
>
> *—The New Republic*

Popular storytellers such as Uris, Michener, and Wouk have been traditional targets for critics since the publication of the earliest novels. Some reviewers seem to watch eagerly for the first sign that these public entertainers are faltering, and their reviews indicate their genuine pleasure in revealing the deficiencies of such popular favorites. But novelists who are usually treated with respect by both reviewers and fellow writers can also experience a sudden change in the way their work is received.

The gallery of victims of this phenomenon is impressive:

> Public libraries have little old ladies of all ages and both sexes who ask for something to take their minds off the headlines. [Truman Capote's] *The Thanksgiving Visitor* is it.
> *—Library Journal*

> John Updike makes all his characters sound like adulterous literature professors.
> —Gene Lyons

> Nothing happens in [Joseph Heller's] *Something Happened.* No one, not even Heller, can stand Bob Slocum, the central character.
> —John Gardner

> [Much] of Joyce Carol Oates' recent prose output has been an unpruned orchard of high gothic romance . . . Sound, not sense, is Miss Oates' strength.
> —David Bell, *Saturday Review*

> If you read [James Jones] long enough, you'll be ashamed to be sober and out of jail.
> —Edmund Fuller

> Tom Wolfe's *The Right Stuff* is about the first American astronauts, and it is not a great example of "New Jour-

nalism." Like all Wolfe's writing, it is not a great example of anything. If Wolfe described Judgment Day he would make it sound like July the Fourth in the Hamptons.

—Penelope Mortimer, *New Statesman*

The cruelest thing anyone can do to [Philip Roth's] *Portnoy's Complaint* is to read it twice . . . The basic structural unit . . . is the skit, the stand-up comedian's shuffle and patter that comes to a climax with a smashing one-liner.

—Irving Howe

The disrespectful tone of many of these comments about some eminent twentieth-century writers demonstrates the accuracy of Paul Gray's observation: "Fame has a way of ruining a writer's reputation."

But if one or two of these novelists needs reassurance after reading a condescending or hostile review of his work, he may find it by searching through records of some past reviews. Reviewers now long-forgotten set themselves up as judges of Theodore Dreiser, Ernest Hemingway, William Faulkner, and F. Scott Fitzgerald—and rendered such pronouncements as these:

The commonplaceness of the story is not alleviated in the slightest degree by any glimmer of imaginative insight on the part of the novelist.

—*Boston Transcript*

The book being reviewed: *An American Tragedy* by Theodore Dreiser.

His characters are as shallow as the saucers in which they stack their daily emotions, and instead of interpreting his material—or even challenging it—he has been content merely to make a carbon copy of a not particularly significant surface of life in Paris.   —*Dial*

The book being reviewed: *The Sun Also Rises* by Ernest Hemingway.

If any theory of esthetics leads to justification of such a book as this . . . [the normal reader] is tempted to say, better send theory to the devil and join the naive majority who feel that the novelist should practice somewhat the same restraint on his imagination as is expected of him in his conduct.   —A.R. Thompson, *Bookman*

The book being reviewed: *Sanctuary* by William Faulkner.

The Great Gatsby by F. Scott Fitzgerald, now universally recognized as a masterpiece, was greeted by these comments:

The Great Gatsby is not a good book.

—*The Independent*

What has never been alive cannot very well go on living, so this is a book of the season only.

—*New York Tribune*

A little slack, a little soft, more than a little artificial, *The Great Gatsby* falls into the class of negligible novels.

—Springfield *Republican*

These twentieth-century reviewers and writers are continuing a tradition of overstatement (and frequent misjudgment) that can be traced back as far as ancient Greece.

Aristophanes called his great fellow-playwright Euripides a "cliche anthologist" and a "maker of ragamuffin manikins," and devoted some twenty years to attacks upon the writer of some of the world's great plays. Ben Jonson spoke sourly of William Shakespeare's failure to revise some of his lines. Edmund Waller said of John Milton's *Paradise Lost*, "If its length be not considered a merit, it hath no other." During the same century Andrew Marvell started to dissect the work of one of his fellow writers, but then broke off abruptly. He should continue, he said, so the public could at last see just what a scurvy creature he was carving up, but he felt compelled to halt because of "the offensiveness of the scent and fouling of my fingers."

In the eighteenth century, Jonathan Swift was less reticent in examining the defects of Sir Richard Steele. The author of *The Spectator* might, Swift conceded, become a reasonably good writer if he first overcame a few weaknesses. He would have to begin paying a little more attention to grammar, learn something about "the propriety and disposition of words,"—and, incidentally, "get some information on the subject he intends to handle."

In the nineteenth century, Thomas Carlyle, in refusing even to meet Algernon Swinburne, remarked that he did not wish to know anyone who was "sitting in a sewer and adding to it." As a man who did not believe in masking his feelings, Carlyle described the philosopher Herbert Spencer as "the most unending ass in Christendom," and bequeathed to posterity an acid word portrait of Charles Lamb:

". . . insuperable proclivity to gin, in poor old Lamb," he wrote. "His talk contemptibly small, indicating wondrous ignorance and shallowness, even when it was serious and good-mannered, which it seldom was . . . ghastly make-believe or wit; in fact, more like 'diluted insanity.' "

Yet Carlyle himself did not escape unscathed. The elder
Henry James, summing up but not quieting down the fiery
Scot, said, "... same old sausage, fizzing and sputtering in
his own grease."
The tone of the attacks on such now-revered figures as
William Wordsworth seems surprising with the passage of
time. The critic Francis Jeffrey was outraged by the appearance of Wordsworth's long poem, *The Excursion,* in 1814. He
called the poem "a tissue of moral and devotional ravings,"
and said that because of its "hubbub of strained raptures and
fantastical sublimities... it is often difficult for the most
skillful and attentive student to obtain a glimpse of the
author's meaning..."
Jeffrey then rendered his verdict on the poet himself:

> The case of Mr. Wordsworth, we perceive, is now mani-
> festly hopeless; and we give him up as altogether incurable
> and beyond the power of criticism.

The *Literary Gazette* was even more unrestrained in its
assault on Percy Bysshe Shelley when reviewing *Prometheus
Unbound:*

> [It] is little else but absolute raving; and were we not
> assured to the contrary, we would take it for granted that
> the author was lunatic—as his principles are ludicrously
> wicked, and his poetry a melange of nonsense... the
> stupid trash of a delirious dreamer... maniacal raving.

This kind of extravagantly worded response to both poetry
and fiction was exhibited in France when an editor asked
Alphonse Daudet to write an article saluting Emile Zola upon
the completion of the twentieth and final volume of his series
of novels about the Rougon–Macquart family.

"If I were to write that article," Daudet told the editor, "it would be to advise Zola, now that the family-tree of the Rougon–Macquarts is complete, to go and hang himself from the highest branch."

The younger Henry James was another frequent victim of contemptous comment. Mark Twain once observed that if he were given a choice between reading one of James's later novels or of burning in Dante's Inferno, he would not hesitate before jumping into the flames. And H. L. Mencken, one of the greatest practitioners of casual literary mayhem, labeled James "an idiot, and a Boston idiot, to boot, than which there is nothing lower in the world. . ." Furthermore, he observed, James had known nothing "about women or men or animals or writing" and "could no more write a good book than Bishop Manning can dance a jig. . ."

In the twentieth century writers have often dismissed their fellow craftsmen with a few ill-tempered words, as we have seen. A notable example was Dorothy Parker's treatment of a particularly saccharine book by A. A. Milne. Writing under her *New Yorker* by-line "Constant Reader," Ms. Parker paused dramatically in her review to announce:

> Tonstant Weader fwowed up.

Later when Truman Capote was asked his opinion of Jack Kerouac, who never looked back after committing words to paper, he said:

> That's not writing—that's typing.

Nelson Algren managed a neat double scalping when dealing with two of his most prosperous fellow novelists, Sloan Wilson and Herman Wouk:

If *The Man in the Gray Flannel Suit* married *Marjorie Morningstar* on my front porch at high noon, I wouldn't bother to go to the wedding.

This high-spirited name calling, which is diverting to almost everyone except the victim, has been a feature of literary life for centuries. But along with these brief hit-and-run attacks there have been many prolonged feuds involving major novelists, poets, and playwrights, and the most dramatic of these are chronicled in this book.

Aristophanes' twenty-year campaign against Euripides has a modern counterpart in Max Beerbohm's thirty-year war against Rudyard Kipling—an obsessive one-sided feud that deserves brief examination because of what it reveals about the compulsive nature of this phenomenon.

Beerbohm, who had met Kipling and had found him considerate and friendly, nevertheless felt a strange, almost lifelong compulsion to attack and deride him. One of Beerbohm's comments about Kipling, who was sometimes criticized for the coarseness of his language, was a speculation over whether the name "Rudyard Kipling" was actually a pseudonym used by a woman writer. "A lady who writes fiction reveals her sex clearlier through her portrayal of men than through any other of her lapses," Beerbohm noted with unusual savagery. "And in . . . Kipling's short stories . . . men are portrayed . . . from an essentially feminine point of view."

The astonished and deeply hurt Kipling remained silent, and Beerbohm then turned to parody in a story entitled "P.C., X, 36" and signed: "By R*D**RD K*PL*NG." The story featured a police constable named Judlip, who speculated about himself and the universe in a passage that could easily have appeared in some of Kipling's cruder stories without seeming out of place:

"Wot am I? A bloomin' cypher. Wot's the sarjint? E's got the Inspector over 'im. Over and above the Inspector there's the Sooperintendent. Over above 'im's the old red-tape-masticatin' Yard. Over above that there's the 'Ome Sec. Wot's 'e? A cypher, like me. Why?" Judlip looked up at the stars. "Over above 'im's We Dunno Wot . . ."

Still unchallenged by his victim, Beerbohm proceeded to caricature Kipling as a favorite of the tasteless British public, and in *The Second Childhood of John Bull*, he let "John Bull" address Kipling directly in these words:

"Yes, I've took a fancy to you, young feller. 'Tain't often I cottons to a Pote, neither, 'Course there's Shakespeare. 'E was a wonder. 'E was . . . 'Swan of Avon' *I* calls 'im. Take 'im for all in all we shall not look upon 'is like again. And then there was Tennyson—'im as wrote the ode to Bala-clavy. 'E was a mastermind too, in his way. So's Lewis Morris. Knows right from wrong like the palm of 'is 'and, and ain't afraid to say where one begins and t'other ends. But most potes ain't like that. What I say is, *they ain't wholesome.* Look at Byron! Saucy 'ound with 'is stuck-up airs and 'is stuck down collars and 'is oglin' o' gals. But *I* soon sent 'im to the right about. *'Outside'* said I, and out 'e went. And then there was that there friend of his, went by the name o' Shelley, 'ad to go too . . . Drowned hisself in 'a I-talian lake, and I warrant that was the fust bath 'e ever took. Most of 'em is like that—*not wholesome* . . . You're different, you are: don't give yourself no 'aughty airs, and though you're rough (with your swear-words and your what-nots), I will say as 'ow you've always bin very civil an' respec'ful to myself. You're one o' the right sort, you are . . ."

When S. N. Behrman was interviewing Beerbohm for his *Conversation with Max*, he led the conversation around to this strange crusade against Kipling. Beerbohm seemed to prefer to speak of other things, but after a few moments he made an extraordinary confession about his one-sided literary battle.

"You spoke to me of Kipling. When first I met him, in Baltimore, he received me so nicely. He was charming. And later... so sympathetic, so kind. And then—you know—his books kept coming out, and occasionally I was asked to review them. I couldn't, you know, abide them. He was a genius, a very great genius, and I felt that he was debasing his genius by what he wrote. And I couldn't refrain from saying so. It went on and on. Friends of his and mine kept telling me that he was so pained and shocked by what I wrote, but I couldn't stop. You know, I couldn't stop. As his publication increased, so did my derogation. He didn't stop; I *couldn't* stop. I meant to. I wanted to. But I couldn't."

After a pause, Beerbohm continued:

"After that meeting in Baltimore, I saw him twice. Once in a hansom. I was in another hansom, and we passed each other in the Strand. He saw me and he knew that I had seen him. But as the hansoms passed, we each of us averted our eyes. Then, some years later, I saw him again, in White's Club. There was a table between us, and, looking across it, over the heads of the diners, I caught his eye. He was looking at me. I wished to get up. I very much wanted to go over to him and to say, 'Mr. Kipling, I admire you. I admire your very great genius. If I have written harshly of you, it is because I do not believe you are living up to the possibilities of your genius.' I so much wished to do this. But I didn't. Why didn't I do it? Why didn't I unbend? Why did I go on persecuting him? And now he is dead and it is too late."

Unlike the silent Kipling, other victims of such assaults have been quick to counter-attack, and the result has been a number of feuds that rumbled on for decades.

Why have so many famous writers devoted so much of their time and energy to these prolonged literary battles? There is no single answer, but most of the feuds examined here seem to develop from such causes as these:

Envy: William Makepeace Thackeray, living off the meager payments made to magazine writers, watched sourly as crowds fought over the latest installment of Charles Dickens' current novel. Even after Thackeray's own books gained considerable popularity, he was always conscious of the far greater sales enjoyed by Dickens. This shadowed his life and created the climate that led to their prolonged alienation.

Jealousy: Bernard DeVoto saw a whole group of writers achieving both critical and popular success while his own attempts at fiction were treated with derision by reviewers. Far from being humbled by his own limitations, DeVoto set out to tell Ernest Hemingway, John Dos Passos, William Faulkner, Thomas Wolfe, and Sinclair Lewis how to write novels. Most of them ignored him—but Lewis responded, and the result was one of the fiercest literary battles of the twentieth century.

Pride: Young Ernest Hemingway made an indelible impression on many other writers, including several who were already world-famous. Most of them were not only generous in praising his work but went to considerable trouble to help him on his way to wider recognition. Rather than expressing gratitude for the unselfish assistance he had received, Hemingway seemed determed to prove that he had made his way without assistance. Sooner or later he publicly denounced most of those who had first recognized and proclaimed his genius.

Antagonistic personalities: D. H. Lawrence detected fairly early some unappealing characteristics in John Middleton Murry, but despite repeated, often bitter, clashes, their relationship lasted for seventeen years. At the very end, Lawrence observed: "[We] belong in different worlds... Even when we are immortal spirits, we shall dwell in different Hades."

Genuine literary differences: Henry James saw the young H. G. Wells as a worthy disciple, a lively and vigorous writer who might contribute to the development of a new kind of novel. Then, as one crude, hastily written manuscript after another was rushed into print by Wells, James was first puzzled, then troubled, then outraged. When James finally began to express his criticism strongly, the brash young Wells responded with mockery. The dramatic change in the relationship between these two writers could have served as the basis for one of Henry James' memorable short stories.

While each of the causes for literary quarrels I have listed can be discovered in the chapters offered here, it would be foolish to try to fit each of these feuds into a neat category. The disputes are complex, and labeling them does not completely explain them.

The encounters do help reveal something about figures ranging from Samuel Johnson and Alexander Pope to Norman Mailer and Edmund Wilson. Most of the people who appear in this book had great gifts; some were markedly querulous, while others were capable of unexpected kindness; most at times could be petty, and some were occasionally near madness.

Here, then, are stories of the feuds that seem worth recounting because of the view they give us of the often troubled, sometimes angry, occasionally happy, sometimes repentant men and women who have also been some of the world's most famous writers.

The cantankerous DR. JOHNSON Battles a Lord~~and some commoners.

NEVER in the history of English letters has there been a more dedicated participant in the literary feuds of his day than the great and cantankerous Dr. Samuel Johnson, who stomped noisily through eighteenth-century London, demolishing arguments and smashing reputations with enormous vigor and gusto. Usually his verbal abuse was enough to smite the unworthy, but sometimes the impatient Doctor resorted to physical violence. ("There is no arguing with Johnson," the novelist, Oliver Goldsmith, said, "for when his pistol misses fire he knocks you down with the butt end of it.") Once, when a waiter used his dirty fingers instead of the proper tongs to drop a lump of sugar into the Doctor's tea, Johnson tossed the glass through the window and was about to do the same with the waiter, when a friend appeared and calmed him. On another occasion, the manager of a theater had placed a chair on a side stage especially for Dr. Johnson's use. Another man, finding the seat empty, sat in it, and then made the unpardonable error of failing to relinquish it to its rightful holder. Faced with this effrontery, the powerful Dr. Johnson simply picked up the chair, with the man still in it, and threw both chair and occupant into the pit.

As the Doctor grew older and a trifle more mellow, some of his friends suspected that the stories of his violent temper were becoming exaggerated. A woman once asked him to tell the background of his widely reported battle with the bookseller, Tom Osborne. Johnson, she had heard, had knocked down Osborne in the latter's library, using as the weapon his own famous—and hefty—dictionary.

"There is nothing to tell, dear lady," Johnson replied, quite forthrightly, "but that he was insolent and I beat him, and that he was a blockhead and told of it, which I should never have [told] . . ." And then the crusty old littérateur added with some satisfaction: "I have beat many a fellow, but the rest had the wit to hold their tongues."

Yet the victims of Samuel Johnson's physical beatings were relatively fortunate, for they soon recovered. It was those who suffered abuse from the great Doctor's tongue and pen who were the really luckless ones. Like the enemies of Alexander Pope, these unfortunates were etched in acid for generations yet unborn. Although Johnson himself did not publish his attacks, they were widely quoted while he was alive and preserved in print by biographers after his death. For example, all the accomplishments of Lord Chesterfield, the author of the famous *Letters to His Son* and one of the great public figures of Johnson's day, have been cast in shadow by

Johnson's devastating comment about those same elegant letters. Said the not always elegant Johnson: "they teach the morals of a whore, and the manners of a dancing master." Chesterfield left to the world a description of a huge, slovenly, ill-mannered man who, though not named in Chesterfield's letter, was undoubtedly Johnson. Of this man, he said, "His figure (without being deformed) seems made to disgrace or ridicule the common structure of the human body. His legs and arms are never in a position which, according to the situation of his body, they ought to be in, but constantly employed in committing acts of hostility upon the Graces." He then described the noted scholar's disconcerting behavior at the dinner table. He "throws anywhere but down his throat whatever he means to drink; and mangles what he means to carve. Inattentive to all the regards of social life, he mistimes and misplaces everything."

Johnson barely stopped to notice such insults. He was too enjoyably occupied in uttering his own pronouncements upon the people and the questions that aroused his interest, his temper, or his prejudices. It was at "The Club," an informal organization with nine members that met every Monday evening at the Turk's Head tavern in London, that he perfected the inimitable style he used later in expressing his thoughts on an endless variety of subjects.

When someone mentioned His Majesty's rebellious colonists in North America, Johnson commented with asperity: "Sir, they are a race of convicts, and ought to be thankful for any thing we allow them short of hanging." Asked to compare the talents of the poets Samuel Derrick and Christopher Smart, he replied: "Sir, there is no settling the point of precedency between a louse and a flea." When a pompous tradesman asked him to compose a funeral sermon for his daughter, who, her father said, was always modest in the presence of her inferiors, Johnson said that he considered the trait very laudable, but added: "It might not be so easy to discover who the lady's inferiors were." And once, when Boswell noted that drinking drives away care and then asked Johnson: "Would not you allow a man to drink for that reason?" the Doctor replied crustily: "Yes, Sir, if he sat next *you.*"

One of the great Doctor's most prolonged battles was with a famous poet of his age, Charles Churchill. The now almost-forgotten Churchill's work attracted attention partly because of its assaults upon public figures. And, naturally, the fabulous, vociferous, and frequently smug Dr. Johnson was one of his earliest targets. Giving Johnson the satirical name of "Pomposo," in his poem *The Ghost,* Churchill tried to demolish him in typical eighteenth-century heroic couplets:

> . . . insolent and loud,
> Vain idol of a scribbling crowd,
> Whose very name inspires an awe,
> Whose every word is sense and law;
> For what his greatness hath decreed,
> Like laws of Persia and of Mede,
> Sacred through all the realms of Wit,
> Must never of repeal admit;
> Who, cursing flattery, is the tool
> Of every fawning, flattering fool;
> Who wit with jealous eye surveys,
> And sickens at another's praise;
> Who, proudly seized of learning's throne,
> Now damns all learning but his own;
> Who scorns those common wares to trade in,
> Reasoning, convincing, and persuading,
> But makes each sentence current pass
> With puppy, coxcomb, scoundrel, ass . . .

For good measure, Churchill also threw in a reference to Johnson's generally acknowledged ugliness, with the following lines:

Features so horrid, were it light,
Would put the devil himself to flight.

Naturally, these lines did not please Johnson, but he was not to be outdone. When his most loyal follower, the biographer, James Boswell, ventured to express an opinion that Churchill, though "a rough, blunt fellow," was also "very clever," the Doctor disagreed. Churchill's poetry was, he said, enjoying "a temporary currency, only from its audacity of abuse, and being filled with living names . . ." But he predicted that it "would sink into oblivion."

Then, when Boswell, with some reason, asked Johnson whether he considered himself "quite a fair judge" of Churchill, the good Doctor drew himself up to his full height and delivered a characteristically "impartial" judgment.

"Nay, sir," said Johnson, "I am a very fair judge. He did not attack me violently till he found I did not like his poetry; and his attack on me shall not prevent me from continuing to say what I think of him, from an apprehension that it may be ascribed to resentment. No, Sir, I called the fellow a blockhead at first, and I will call him a blockhead still."

Only once did Dr. Johnson go down in defeat under Churchill's attacks, and that time the ignominy was understandable, for Churchill had found a particularly vulnerable spot to probe. Dr. Johnson had announced the completion of a long-promised edition of Shakespeare for publication in 1756. The Doctor had, in fact, collected advance deposits from a number of subscribers. Yet, each year, publication was postponed, and the impatient subscribers began to wonder whether they would live long enough to read the book. The long delay offered the irrepressible Churchill another excuse for attack:

> He for subscribers baits his hook,
> And takes your cash; but where's the book?
> No matter where; wise fear, you know,
> Forbids the robbing of a foe;
> But what, to serve our private ends,
> Forbids the cheating of our friends?

Johnson, as usual, published no reply to this public attack. But there was little he could have said, for it was not until nine years after the promised date that the monumental work finally appeared, and not only had he spent all the money he had collected but he was also forced to confess that he had lost the list of his subscribers.

In his battle with the Scottish poet, James Macpherson, however, the bombastic Dr. Johnson emerged the undisputed victor.

In the 1760's Macpherson presented to the world some "epics," which he claimed to have discovered in remote parts of Scotland. He had taken great pains, he said, in translating these "epics" from the old Erse language into English.

The most ambitious of these spurious works were offered by Macpherson as *The Poems of Ossian*. Ossian was a legendary Scottish warrior-poet whom Macpherson called "the Homer of the Highlands." And as proof of Ossian's genius, Macpherson now offered to the public these "long-lost" works —in three expensive volumes.

Fellow Scots eagerly acclaimed Macpherson's discovery. Here, at last, was tangible evidence that their bleak land had been a northern Greece, in which civilization and literature had flourished as far back as the third century after Christ.

But Dr. Johnson, who held a low opinion in general of Scottish literature, past as well as present, was not convinced. He immediately suspected Macpherson of attempting to pass off some of his own rather crude and uninspiring prose poems as the work of Ossian, and, with his usual directness, he demanded that Macpherson produce the original Erse manuscripts.

When the Scotsman produced vague excuses instead of original documents, Johnson loudly denounced him as a fraud. And when the unfortunate Mr. Macpherson still underestimated his opponent by writing a threatening letter, the great Doctor replied mercilessly:

"I received your foolish and impudent letter. Any violence offered me I shall do my best to repel; and what I cannot do for myself, the law shall do for me. I hope I shall never be deterred from detecting what I think a cheat, by the menaces of a ruffian. . . .

"I thought your book an imposture; I think it an imposture still. For this opinion I have given my reasons to the publick, which I here dare you to refute. Your rage I defy. Your abilities . . . are not so formidable; and what I hear of your morals inclines me to pay regard not to what you say, but to what you shall prove."

Then, completely undaunted, he concluded with a very generous offer to his demolished opponent. "You may," he wrote, "print this if you will."

Perhaps the gentlest and best-natured of Johnson's encounters involved his close friend Thomas Percy, an industrious clergyman of uncertain literary taste who had achieved considerable fame by publishing a collection of ballads entitled *Reliques of Ancient English Poetry*. Johnson had encouraged Percy to collect the materials for the *Reliques,* and he even wrote the dedication for the work. Although Percy told his readers that he had added a few lines here and there and had done a bit of editing of these "ancient ballads," he did not manage to make clear just how extensive these changes were. Not until after his death was it discovered that some of his poems were not only of doubtful age and authenticity, but that some were also twice as long as the original. Fairly typical of Percy's "discoveries" was the ballad entitled "Lady Isabella's Tragedy." The tragedy begins when Lady Isabella's cruel stepmother sends her innocent stepdaughter into the kitchen with instructions to tell the master cook to dress a "faire and milk-white doe" for dinner. In Percy's version of olde English, of which a few sample verses suffice, the treachery increases with each stanza.

Thus Lady Isabella

> . . . streight into the kitchen went
>   Her message for to tell;
> And there she spied the master-cook
>   Who did with malice swell.

Quoth the girl:

> Nowe, master-cook, it must be soe,
>   Do that which I thee tell:
> You needes must dresse the milk-white doe,
>   Which you do knowe full well.

But the master cook, well coached by the conniving stepmother, has other plans:

> Then streight his cruell bloodye hands
>   He on the ladye layd;
> With quivering and shaking stands,
>   While thus to her he sayd:

> Thou art the doe that I must dresse;
>   See here, behold my knife;
> For it is pointed presently
>   To ridd thee of thy life.

Enter the hero, in the form of an honest scullion boy:

> O then, cried out the scullion-boye
>   As loud as loud might bee;
> O save her life, good master-cook,
>   And make your pyes of mee!

> For pityes sake do not destroye
>   My ladye with your knife;
> You knowe she is her father's joye,
>   For Christes sake save her life.

Though the bloody scene itself is not described, the treachery is accomplished by the cook:

> I will not save her life, he sayd,
>   Nor make my pyes of thee,
> Yet if thou dost this deed bewraye [betraye],
>   Thy butcher I will bee.

> Now when this lord [the father] he did come home
>   For to sit downe and eat;
> He called for his daughter deare,
>   To come and carve his meat.

> Nowe sit you downe, his ladye sayd,
>   O sit you downe to meat;
> Into some nunnery she is gone;
>   Your daughter deare forget.

Then solemnlye he made a vowe,
  Before the companie:
That he would neither eat nor drinke,
  Until he did her see.

O then, bespake the scullion-boye
  With a loud voice so hye;
If now you will your daughter see,
  My lord, cut up that pye:

Wherein her fleshe is minced small,
  And parched with the fire;
All caused by her step-mother,
  Who did her death desire.

The ballad ends "happily," with the stepmother burning at
the stake, the master cook left "in boiling lead to stand," and
the noble scullion boy inheriting the lord's estate.

When Percy brought out another book entitled *The Hermit of Warkworth*, which was his own acknowledged adaptation of a singsong ballad, presented with a solemn introductory note, Dr. Samuel Johnson was no longer ready to applaud him. He felt such modern imitations of ancient forms were silly, and he demonstrated just how easily this kind of simple-minded verse could be tossed off, in order to convince his good friend Percy that concocting such false "reliques" was hardly necessary. A dozen equally good verses could, he said, be written in a few minutes. And in a few minutes he did indeed dash off three Johnsonian "ballads," each cleverly parodying Percy's style. Wrote Johnson:

'The tender infant, meek and mild,
  Fell down upon the stone;
The nurse took up the squealing child,
  But still the child squealed on.

And:

> I put my hat upon my head
> And walked into the Strand
> And there I met another man
> Who's hat was in his hand.

And:

> I therefore pray thee, Renny dear,
> That thou wilt give to me,
> With cream and sugar soften'd well,
> Another dish of tea.

> Nor fear that I, my gentle maid,
> Shall long detain the cup,
> When once unto the bottom I
> Have drunk the liquor up.

> Yet hear, alas! this mournful truth,
> Nor hear it with a frown;—
> Thou canst not make the tea so fast
> As I can gulp it down.

In the year 1746, Johnson signed a contract to write his dictionary of the English language and made a characteristically rash pledge to deliver the manuscript long before he could possibly finish it. Thus it was that he met the most famous and most powerful of his adversaries, Philip Dormer Stanhope, Fourth Earl of Chesterfield.

A friend, stunned by the magnitude of the task Johnson had so lightly undertaken, and skeptical of his ability to finish it in three years, reminded the good Doctor that forty members of the French Academy had required forty years to compile a dictionary of the French language.

"Sir, thus it is," replied the unconcerned Johnson. "This is the proportion. Let me see: forty times forty is sixteen hundred. As three to sixteen hundred, so is the proportion of an Englishman to a Frenchman."

Yet, though he was not troubled by the size of the project he had set for himself, he nevertheless recognized the practicality of obtaining a patron—as was the custom of the day—who could make it possible for him to devote his complete energies to the dictionary by giving him financial aid. And so, he was happy to take the advise of one of his publishers, Robert Dodsley, who suggested that Johnson make some subtle overture to Lord Chesterfield, who was noted as a patron of the arts.

The result was that Johnson sketched out a plan for the dictionary, dedicated it flatteringly to the Earl, and asked a friend to present this outline to Chesterfield.

Shortly after that, Chesterfield invited Johnson to call upon him.

But the meeting of these two men of letters was doomed from the beginning. The fastidious Lord Chesterfield was understandably repelled not only by the forthright Johnson's lack of ceremony but also by his somewhat grotesque appearance. In addition, and most unforgivably, the good Doctor, as Chesterfield later confessed to a friend, displayed his typical lack of respect for the opinions of his betters. Said his Lordship:

"He disputes with heat indiscriminately, mindless of the rank, character, and situation of those with whom he disputes."

It was only as a token of his own fine feeling for the fitness of things that Lord Chesterfield at the end of this first meeting presented Johnson with ten pounds. Now it was Johnson's turn to be offended. So small, in fact, did Johnson consider the amount that, from that moment on, he avoided mention-

ing it in his own accounts of the feud with his intended
patron. But his later calls on Lord Chesterfield were to prove
even more irritating to the irascible Doctor. Often, he was
forced to sit for hours in the Chesterfield antechamber, his
great haunches resting uneasily on the dainty furniture, his
famous temper just barely under control, as he watched fops
and idlers precede him to the inner sanctum.

Then came the day when, after a particularly long and uncomfortable wait, Johnson saw the door open and out came
the man whom he regarded as perhaps the worst poet laureate
England had ever had, Colley Cibber. Outraged, the good
Doctor stomped out of the antechamber, never again to return.

Now, no longer asking or expecting any help from Chesterfield, Johnson faced the daily drudgery of his work for seven
years, piling manuscript page on top of manuscript page, without one penny from his hoped-for patron.

Then, as the publishers in 1754 at last prepared to offer his
monumental dictionary to the public, Johnson learned to his
surprise and dismay that an enthusiastic article about the
work had appeared in a periodical called *The World,* and
that a second would follow in the next issue.

Both articles had been written by Lord Chesterfield!

"I think the publick in general, and the republick of letters
in particular, are greatly obliged to Mr. Johnson, for having
undertaken, and executed so great and desirable a work," the
long-silent patron now told all literary London. "Perfection
is not to be expected from man: but if we are to judge by the
various works of Johnson already published, we have good
reason to believe, that he will bring this as near to perfection
as any man could do. The plan of it, which he published
some years ago, seems to me to be a proof of it. . . ."

To Johnson it seemed that Chesterfield was endeavoring

unjustly to share the credit, despite his seeming modesty. The article continued:

"It must be owned, that our language is, at present, in a state of anarchy, and hitherto, perhaps, it may not have been the worse for it . . . many words and expressions have been imported, adopted, and naturalized from other languages, which have greatly enriched our own. . . . The time for discrimination seems to be now come. Toleration, adoption, and naturalization have run their lengths. Good order and authority are now necessary. But where shall we find them, and at the same time the obedience due to them? We must have recourse to the old Roman expedient in times of confusion, and chuse a dictator. Upon this principle, I give my vote for Mr. Johnson, to fill that great and arduous post, and I hereby declare, that I make a total surrender of all my rights and privileges in the English language, as a free-born British subject, to the said Mr. Johnson, during the term of his dictatorship. Nay more, I will not only obey him like an old Roman, as my dictator, but, like a modern Roman, I will implicitly believe in him as my Pope, and hold him to be infallible while in the chair . . ."

The good Doctor was understandably unimpressed by this sudden elevation to both dictatorship and the Papacy. To his friend, David Garrick, he said:

"I have sailed a long and painful voyage round the world of the English language, and does he [Chesterfield] now send out two cockboats to tow me into harbour?"

Now, in another attempt to show "his own fine feeling for the fitness of things," Chesterfield sent to Johnson as an emissary a minor poet named Sir Thomas Robinson. But this fellow, although adept at flattery, was not equipped to deal with the wounded Dr. Johnson.

Sir Thomas praised Johnson effusively and declared that

were his own circumstances other than they were, he himself
would settle five hundred pounds a year on Johnson.

But the Doctor was not to be taken in, and the ensuing conversation between the two has been recorded for posterity by
one of Johnson's biographers, Sir John Hawkins:

" 'And who are you,' asked Johnson, 'that talk thus liberally?'

" 'I am,' said the other, 'Sir Thomas Robinson, a Yorkshire
baronet.'

" 'Sir,' replied Johnson, 'if the first peer of the realm were
to make me such an offer, I would shew him the way downstairs.' "

Thus, having regally rejected a hypothetical five hundred
pounds a year from the blundering Sir Thomas, Johnson
wrote directly to Chesterfield.

The letter has long been regarded as a masterpiece.

"I have been lately informed, by the proprietor of the
World," the great lexicographer began, calmly enough, "that
two papers, in which my Dictionary is recommended to the
publick, were written by your Lordship. To be so distinguished, is an honour, which, being very little accustomed to
favours from the great, I know not well how to receive, or in
what terms to acknowledge."

The Doctor then mentioned his first meeting with Chesterfield—a meeting which, he said, had been made "upon some
slight encouragement." And he continued: ". . . I was over-
powered, like the rest of mankind, by the enchantment of
your address . . ."

But subsequent visits had been far less enchanting, he now
admitted, recalling those endless waits in the crowded antechamber.

". . . I found my attendance so little encouraged," he
pointed out, "that neither pride nor modesty would suffer me
to continue it. When I had once addressed your Lordship in

publick, I had exhausted all the art of pleasing which a retired and uncourtly scholar can possess. . . ."

Drawing himself up to his full literary stature, the great
lexicographer declared:

"Seven years, my Lord, have now past, since I waited in
your outward rooms, or was repulsed from your door; during
which time I have been pushing on my work through difficulties, of which it is useless to complain, and have brought
it, at last, to the verge of publication, without one act of assistance, one word of encouragement, or one smile of favour.
Such treatment I did not expect, for I never had a Patron
before. . . .

"Is not a Patron, my Lord, one who looks with unconcern
on a man struggling for life in the water, and, when he has
reached ground, encumbers him with help? The notice which
you have been pleased to take of my labours, had it been
early, had been kind; but it has been delayed till I am indifferent, and cannot enjoy it; till I am solitary, and cannot im-
part it; till I am known, and do not want it. . . ."

"I should have imagined that Lord Chesterfield would have
concealed [such a letter]," a friend of Johnson's publishers
said, when told that Chesterfield was showing Johnson's now-
famous letter to his callers.

"Poh!" said the publisher, "do you think a letter from
Johnson could hurt Lord Chesterfield? Not at all, Sir. It lay
upon his table, where any body might see it. He read it to me;
said, 'this man has great powers,' pointed out the severest passages, and observed how well they were expressed."

Although Chesterfield seemed proud of the letter, Johnson,
as his biographer James Boswell has noted, later developed "a
remarkable delicacy" about it. Yet, characteristically, he was
still to have the final say in the feud. When no less a person-
age than a bishop of the Church of England requested a copy

of the letter, the good Doctor was quick to seize the opportunity.

"No, sir"; he replied very grandly to the bishop's request. "I have hurt the dog too much already."

But he was still critical of Lord Chesterfield's hypocrisy and his artificial manners. When Chesterfield counseled his illegitimate son on how to behave in society in his *Letters to His Son,* Johnson read the posthumously published missives carefully and then uttered his devastating comment. The letters, he said, "teach the morals of a whore and the manners of a dancing master." It was, perhaps, the most famous of all his insults.

Even in death the great lexicographer was the cause of one final literary feud. For almost before his funeral sermon was spoken, a dispute erupted over the question of who was best fitted to write the story of his stormy life—despite the later fame of the great Johnson biographer, James Boswell.

At first, the natural choice seemed to fall not on Boswell at all, but on Sir John Hawkins, who had not only known Johnson during his years of both obscurity and fame, but had also been designated by Johnson himself as his literary executor.

The Hawkins-Boswell feud began when a group of London booksellers approached Hawkins to ask him to accept the task of writing the official biography. As a result, Hawkins was subjected to one of the most concentrated assaults any author has ever endured—with the final blows being struck by Boswell.

Some of the attacks on Hawkins could be traced to his own extraordinarily unattractive personality. Even Johnson, who considered himself one of Sir John's few real friends, had once said: ". . . as to Sir John, why really I believe him to be an honest man at the bottom: but to be sure he is penurious, and he is mean, and it must be owned he has a degree of brutality, and a tendency to savageness, that cannot easily be defended."

And, on another occasion, Johnson had told of Sir John's insistence upon being excused from paying his share of the expenses of a club to which they both belonged: "We all scorned him and admitted his plea. . . . Hawkins was a most *unclubable* man!"

Now Johnson's death gave to George Steevens—who was nicknamed "The Asp" and who was one of Sir John's most dedicated enemies—a long-awaited opportunity to strike publicly and repeatedly against Hawkins.

"It is evident from the Conduct of the late Dr. Johnson," Steevens contended, "that he designed Mr. Boswell for the sole Writer of his Life. Why else did he furnish him with such Materials for it as were withheld from every other Friend? . . . Little indeed did he suppose that a Person whom he had made one of his Executors would have instantly claimed the Office of his Biographer . . ."

After dismissing as "trifles" any documents to which Hawkins might have access as Johnson's executor, Steevens then made a few observations concerning the mind and materials with which the rival, Boswell, had been endowed. "The Value of Mr. Boswell's Intelligence," he wrote, "is unquestionably ascertained. It must be genuine, because received from the Deceased."

He continued: "It must be copious, as it is the Result of Enquiries continued through a Period of more than twenty Years. It must be exact, because committed to Paper as fast as communicated . . ." And he challenged Sir John to "prove the Authenticity and Consequence of his Materials in a Manner as satisfactory to the Publick. The Publick may then judge between our rival Biographers . . ."

So violent did the feud become that Sir John, who was admittedly penurious, was even accused of charging to the deceased Johnson's estate the cost of hiring a coach, as well as of appropriating Johnson's watch and cane for his own personal use. And when Sir John's biography finally did appear in March, 1787, one Sir Herbert Croft predicted that "Boswell, and Co. will torture the poor Knight, half an inch at a time, to literary death"—a prediction almost immediately substantiated, for, though the book received some favorable reviews, Hawkins was soon drowned in a flood of eloquent invective. Not only was he charged with carelessness, incompetence, and malevolence, but one reviewer even called him the "assassin of Johnson's memory."

In the early pages of his own biography of Johnson, James Boswell was later to add *his* criticism of Hawkins' *Life*—and at length.

"Since my work was announced," Boswell wrote by way of introduction, "several Lives and Memoirs of Dr. Johnson have been published, the most voluminous of which is one compiled for the booksellers of London, by Sir John Hawkins, Knight, a man, whom, during my long intimacy with Dr. Johnson, I never saw in his company, I think but once, and I am sure not above twice."

Then, point by point, Boswell proceeded to tear apart Hawkins' entire work. It was unfortunate, he said, that Hawkins' lack of perception kept him from appreciating "the finer and less obvious parts of Johnson's character." Since he realized that some readers might consider Hawkins' access to the diaries and personal papers of Johnson a great advantage, Boswell next observed:

"His [Hawkins'] being appointed one of his [Johnson's] executors, gave him an opportunity of taking possession of such fragments of a diary and other papers as were left; of which, before delivering them up to the residuary legatee, whose property they were, he endeavoured to extract the substance."

Then he added, seemingly settling the matter for all time: "In this he [Hawkins] has not been very successful, as I have found upon a perusal of those papers, which have been since transferred to me."

With such questions out of the way, Boswell then offered a few comments upon Hawkins' style and his organization of such bits of information as he had managed to gather:

"Sir John Hawkins's ponderous labours, I must acknowledge, exhibit a *farrago*, of which a considerable portion is not devoid of entertainment to the lovers of literary gossiping; but besides its being swelled out with long unnecessary extracts from various works, . . . a very small part of it relates to the person who is the subject of the book; and, in that, there is such an inaccuracy in the statement of facts, as in so solemn an authour is hardly excusable, and certainly makes his narrative very unsatisfactory."

Yet, according to Boswell, it was not even in this failing that Hawkins' worst fault as a biographer lay. For, he quickly added:

". . . what is still worse, there is throughout the whole of it [the book] a dark uncharitable cast, by which the most unfavourable construction is put upon almost every circumstance in the character and conduct of my illustrious friend; who, I trust, will, by a true and fair delineation, be vindicated from the injurious misrepresentation of this authour . . ."

As far as Dr. Samuel Johnson is concerned, such a monumental feud over his biography would probably have pleased him enormously. For it meant that the cantankerous old man's irascible spirit continued, long after death, to influence the literary world he had dominated for so many decades.

As for the Hawkins biography, it was a failure. For one

hundred and seventy-four years it remained out of print, while edition after edition of Boswell's *The Life of Samuel Johnson* appeared in both England and the United States.

Yet, according to at least one outstanding Johnson scholar, Hawkins' *The Life of Samuel Johnson, LL.D.* deserved to become a standard work, despite the abuse of its contemporary critics, and, very recently, an edition of the work was published, and received respectful attention from reviewers. However, Hawkins' second chance had come far too late. Though some copies of the new edition found their way to library shelves, the general public continued to think of James Boswell as *the* biographer of Johnson.

The literary mayhem committed a century and three-quarters ago had long since determined which of the accounts of Johnson's life was destined to live.

Mr. Pope confers immortality upon the unworthy

MR. COLLEY CIBBER.

RARELY in the long history of literary mayhem have two writers quarreled against a more bizarre background than the court of George II in early eighteenth-century England. George, who was German-born and spoke very little English, had the responsibility of approving the appointment of an English poet laureate. For him, it was enough if his laureate composed odes in a singsong rhythm suitable for setting to equally undistinguished music. If one of his poets had accidentally written a good ode, he would hardly have known it.

Yet, since even an empty honor is better than none at all,

three different poets competed for the privilege of writing the annual tributes to George and his consort, Queen Caroline. For a time, each of these candidates insisted upon intoning an ode in celebration of Caroline's birthday. As a result, the suffering of Caroline, who did understand English and also had some feeling for poetry, must have been intense.

It was under these circumstances that, in 1730, a buffoon who possessed no literary talent, and who bore the improbable but alliterative name of Colley Cibber—pronounced Kolley Kibber—became the official poet laureate of England. And thus it was, too, that the name of Cibber, which might otherwise have been properly forgotten by posterity, was immortalized in line after stinging line by the great Alexander Pope.

In a curious way, the preposterous Colley Cibber has managed to emerge as one of the most appealing of all victims of recorded literary feuds. Clearly, he was a wretched poet. But just as clearly, he was so self-confident that public ridicule did not disturb him, and he would, on occasion, even counterfeit satires against himself. Friends often brought him copies of Pope's satirical verses or of the parodies others wrote of his foolish odes and asked him to read them aloud—in public. ". . . and to do my doughty antagonists justice," he recorded in his memoirs, "I always read them with as much impartial spirit as if I had writ them myself."

The beginnings of Colley Cibber's career were almost as improbable as his later elevation to the post of laureate. As a young apprentice actor, he had first gained notice in a drama starring the famous Thomas Betterton, for managing to spoil the only scene in which he had lines to speak.

Cibber had appeared on stage to deliver a message to Betterton. But, terrified by the audience as well as by the imposing older actor, he had muffed the speech.

"Who is the young man who made the blunder?" Betterton inquired at the end of the performance.

"Master Colley," the prompter told him.

"Master Colley!" Betterton said. "Then forfeit him."

"Why, sir," the prompter said, "he has no salary."

"No?" Betterton replied. "Why then put him down [for] ten shillings a week and forfeit him five."

After such an unlikely start toward success in the theater, Colley Cibber's rise in the literary world proved equally incredible. No sooner had he gained some fame as a low comedian than he decided to become a playwright, and, though he had few original ideas, he became adept at taking scenes from other people's plays and rewriting them. Furthermore, he was delighted to notice that his borrowings either went undetected or else were shrugged off. He was even able to take scenes from two of Shakespeare's plays, add a few of his own awkward lines, and present this theatrical goulash profitably.

When the playwright William Congreve saw Colley Cibber's first farce, he shrewdly observed that there were many things *like* wit in it, but no wit. But audiences were less critical. Soon, in fact, the untalented young playwright became one of London's most popular writers of bedroom farce. In many of his plays, the characters seemed to be living licentiously for four acts; then, in the fifth and final act, the author would reveal a supposedly unsuspected relationship which made their actions moral and proper. In one of his most popular comedies, for example, the widow's apparent lover turned out to be her long-lost husband. In defense of his method, Cibber argued that he had managed to keep the action "lewd for four acts."

After a few years as a playwright, the future poet laureate became an actor-manager, and one of his productions was a witty farce by John Gay entitled *Three Hours after Marriage.*

It was this production which led to Cibber's first collision with Alexander Pope.

Many explanations have been offered for the great Alexander Pope's extraordinary bitterness toward the world and most of its inhabitants. In the first place, he suffered from being short of stature. Secondly, he looked, as one biographer has described him, "like a crippled wren . . ." Then, too, his health was so poor that he once complained his entire life had been one "long illness." And, as historians have noted, he was handicapped by the fact that he was a Roman Catholic in a country which at the time regarded—and treated—Catholics as potential traitors.

Whatever the reasons, however, Pope was one of the great "haters" in the history of English literature, and the range of his hatreds was awesome. When a scholar once took the time to list Pope's *major* enemies—that is, the people whom Pope denounced at least twice in his verses—the grand total came to sixty-three. And one of his victims, in drawing up a list of the poet's chief targets, was forced to begin the roll call in the manner of a minister of protocol:

> "1. Almighty God
> 2. The King . . ."

Toward the bottom of this list, in order of importance, though he belonged at the top because of the number of times he had been negatively mentioned, was the name of Colley Cibber.

Pope was twenty-eight years old and Cibber was forty-five when their feud began, and the cause is easy to trace. Although he would not acknowledge it publicly, Pope had contributed some characters and lines to Gay's *Three Hours after Marriage,* including a character named Plotwell who was an unmistakable caricature of Cibber. Cibber, good-natured as always, agreed to play the part of Plotwell.

The project seemed off to a promising start.

But, to Pope's dismay, the same audiences that supported and applauded Cibber's own farces hissed *Three Hours after Marriage* off the stage. Some of the spectators were so enraged by the production that they wrote pamphlets denouncing it.

To the sensitive Pope, as well as to John Gay, such a reception of their work seemed a gross indignity. But Cibber, who had lived with the vagaries of theater audiences for years, accepted the public verdict calmly, and began staging a revival of a perennial favorite of the day, *The Rehearsal.* The character he played in this revival traditionally made some comment about contemporary matters, and in this role Cibber now made reference onstage to the disastrous fate of *Three Hours after Marriage.*

That night, Pope was in the audience, and was not amused. As Cibber later recalled, he "came behind the scenes, with his lips pale and his voice trembling, to call me to account for the insult, and accordingly fell upon me with all the foul language that a wit out of his senses could be capable of . . . choked with the foam of his passion . . ."

But Cibber was not intimidated by the four-foot, six-inch poet.

He told Pope that his threats would merely insure the repetition of the same lines about *Three Hours after Marriage* at every performance of *The Rehearsal.* The next night, when Pope sent John Gay to the theater in the hope that Gay might seem a greater physical threat, the indiscreet Cibber, in one of the few violent actions of his career, punched Gay in the nose

before the guards separated them and took the angry playwright out.

In 1718, Colley Cibber again aroused Pope's temper by
adapting Molière's *Tartuffe* into an anti-Catholic diatribe
under the title *The Non-Juror*—the term "non-juror" being
commonly used in describing English clergymen who avoided
taking the oath of allegiance to the Protestant Hanoverian
dynasty. Nor did it profit Cibber in Pope's eyes when George
II awarded the author a two-hundred-pound honorarium in
recognition of his services to the House of Hanover for writing *The Non-Juror*. From that date until his death twenty-
six years later, Pope was to focus much of his censorious attention on the insignificant Cibber. He composed satirical
verses about him, mocked him at length in the *Art of Sinking
in Poetry,* and mentioned him unfavorably five times in the
first edition of *The Dunciad.*

But this was only the beginning of Pope's assault on Cibber. The subsequent feud was destined to take on a far
greater intensity and bitterness after the buffoon had attained
the eminence of poet laureate to the court of George and
Caroline—an appointment that astonished even Cibber's
closest friends.

In 1730, a drunken parson named Laurence Eusden, who
happened also to be poet laureate of England, died. Although
Pope was acknowledged even by his enemies to be England's greatest living poet, everyone realized that his religion
would exclude him from consideration for the honor. The
three most likely candidates seemed to be a literary critic
named John Dennis, a Shakespearean scholar named Lewis
Theobald, and a self-taught peasant named Stephen Duck,
whose poetry had attracted the attention and the patronage
of the Earl of Macclesfield.

Of the three, Duck was undoubtedly the most talented poet. He could write with genuine feeling of the life of a thresher, and even today a passage on the death of a child in one of his poems remains somber and moving. But it was a different note in his work which probably accounted for his strong appeal to those closest to court. In a land where poverty was common, it was comforting for the rulers to find an impoverished peasant expressing such thoughts as these:

> Contented Poverty's no dismal Thing.
> Free from the Cares unwieldy Riches bring . . .

> That steady Man is worthy of our Praise,
> Who in Distress, or pinch'd with Hunger, says,
> Let Poverty, or Want, be what it will,
> It does proceed from God, therefore's no Ill.

On September 11, 1730, a few months before Eusden's death, the Earl of Macclesfield had read some of the works of the "Thresher-Poet" to Queen Caroline in the drawing room at Windsor Castle. And the Queen had expressed her pleasure with the lines that emphasized the good fortune of Duck and his fellow threshers. The lines read:

> Give Martial Camps and Kingly Courts to them
> Who place their only Bliss in fleeting Fame;
> There let them live in golden Chains of State,
> And be Unhappy, only to be Great.
> But let us in our Native Soil remain,
> Nor barter Happiness for sordid Gain . . .

> This we prefer to Pomp, and formal Show,
> Which only serves to varnish o'er our Woe.

The Queen showed her favor by awarding Duck a pension of thirty pounds a year. And, at Eusden's death, some newspapers reported that the "Thresher-Poet" was now certain to become poet laureate, a post which carried with it two hundred pounds a year and, in addition, an annual butt of sack.

But Duck was to experience ill luck at this point. While the appointment was still under consideration, his wife died, and he was forced to remain away from London when he should have been present to press his advantage. It was at this crucial moment that the London newspapers began to speculate regarding a new and unexpected candidate: Colley Cibber. The already hostile Pope was freshly aroused.

Immediately, the *Grub Street Journal* published a satirical poem by Pope. The missing letters of the proper names were well-known to the *Journal's* readers.

> Shall royal praise be rimed by such a ribald,
> As fopling C[ibbe]r or attorney T[heobal]d?
> Let's rather wait one year for better luck;
> One year may make a singing swan of Duck.
> Great G—! such servants since thou well canst lack,
> Oh! save the salary and drink the sack!

It was, in fact, so difficult for many to believe the clown Cibber was under serious consideration as laureate that in November, 1730, when his appointment was rumored by a part of the London press, the *Journal* declared the report false. It was only after the preposterous selection was officially announced by the Duke of Grafton that the editor of the *Journal* was able to voice the general surprise and indignation:

> By guessing who would have the luck
>   To be the b[irth]day fibber,
> I thought of Dennis, Theobald, Duck,
>   But never dreamt of Cibber.

Now, Cibber, being duly appointed, went to work, and soon produced his first ode. Here are two verses from this initial effort:

> Ye grateful Britons bless the year,
>   That kindly yields increase,
> While plenty that might feed a war,
>   Enjoys the guard of peace;

> Your plenty to the skies you owe,
>   Peace is your monarch's care;
> Thus bounteous Love and George below
>   Divided empire share. . . .

No verses could have been more widely mocked. They were parodied in almost every coffee house in the city of London.

When a poem defending Cibber appeared in a newspaper, many people simply assumed that Cibber had written the poem himself. Actually, however, it had been written by one of his friends. The matter was settled only when Cibber wrote a reply to his own defense.

Under the name of "Francis Fairplay," he submitted this mockery to the *Whitehall Evening Post*. It read:

> Bring thy protected Verse from Court
>   And try it on the Stage;
> There it will make much better Sport,
>   And set the Town in Rage.

> There, Beaux and Wits and Cits and Smarts,
>   Where Hissing's not uncivil,
> Will shew their Parts to thy Deserts,
>   And send it to the Devil.

In time, the novelist and playwright Henry Fielding, who shared Pope's contempt for Cibber, was even parodying the poet laureate's odes in a play entitled *The Historical Register*. The most telling of Fielding's lines were:

> This is a day, in days of yore,
> Our fathers never saw before;
> This is a day, 'tis one to ten,
> Our sons will never see again.
> Then sing the day,
> And sing the song,
> And thus be merry
> All day long.

But by far the most witty attack against Cibber now came from his old enemy, Alexander Pope. Since Pope's lines summed up the entire situation, they were widely quoted. Wrote Pope:

> In merry Old England, it once was the Rule,
> The King had his Poet, and also his Fool.
> But now we're so frugal, I'd have you to know it,
> That Cibber can serve both for Fool and for Poet.

In public and good-natured self-defense, Cibber replied: "If I am the King's Fool, now, Sir, pray, whose fool are you?"

The preposterous situation was more than Alexander Pope could bear, especially since the clown Cibber seemed not at all to mind Pope's assaults on him. In this frame of mind, Pope, in 1735, bemoaned the seeming uselessness of his previous attacks against the poet laureate. The lines appeared in the *Epistle to Dr. Arbuthnot*:

> Who shames a Scribbler? break one cobweb thro',
> He spins the slight self-pleasing thread anew:
> Destroy his fib, or sophistry—in vain!
> The creature's at his dirty work again,
> Throned in the centre of his thin designs,
> Proud of a vast extent of flimsy lines. . . .

More spitefully, he bluntly added to these lines the fillip which he hoped would hurt the high-riding Cibber most:

> Whom have I hurt? has Poet yet or Peer
> Lost the arch'd eyebrow or Parnassian sneer?
> And has not Colley still his lord and whore?

Now the mark hit home, though, since the wise Cibber still seemed to ignore even this insult, Pope could not at first be sure of his effect. Then, in 1742, Cibber at last replied, by publishing a pamphlet that bore the cumbersome title of *A Letter from Mr Cibber to Mr Pope, Inquiring into the Motives that Might Induce Him in His Satyrical Works, to be so Frequently Fond of Mr Cibber's Name.*

The first pages of the pamphlet were remarkably gentle and good-natured. Modestly, Cibber made it clear that he did not consider himself a major literary figure. He wrote, he said, "more to be Fed than to be Famous." It was not he who had insisted upon treating himself as an important man by frequently introducing the name of Cibber into so many satires of the day. With a modesty that was not entirely false, he raised the question of whether a man so lacking in distinction as himself was worth the constant attention of the greatest poet of the age. Perhaps, he suggested, Pope meant to pay him a compliment in acknowledging that most of the people of England at least knew who Colley Cibber was, whether or not they admired him.

Then, quite suddenly, the pleasant tone of *A Letter from Mr Cibber to Mr Pope, etc.* vanished.

"And has not Colley still his lord and whore?" Cibber now inquired, rhetorically.

To the charge that he had enjoyed the patronage of lords and the company of whores, he quite frankly pleaded guilty. But, he noted, the same accusation could be made against many other literary figures. As a matter of fact, he observed, even Mr. Pope, the great translator of the epics of Homer, could be included in this group.

Whereupon Mr. Colley Cibber made one of the most sensational revelations in the history of literary mayhem.

". . . I must own," wrote Mr. Cibber, addressing Mr. Pope directly, "that I believe I know more of *your* whoring than you do of *mine;* because I don't recollect that ever I made you the least confidence of *my* amours, though I have been very near an eyewitness of *yours.*"

He then told a story calculated to prove extremely embarrassing to his antagonist.

One evening, as Cibber recalled, a young nobleman had "slyly seduced the celebrated Mr Pope . . . to a certain house of carnal recreation near the Haymarket . . ."

Wrote Cibber:

". . . [the noble lord] proposed . . . to slip his little Homer, as he called him [Pope], at a girl of the game, that he might see what sort of figure a man of his size, sobriety, and vigor (in verse) would make when the frail fit of love had got into him . . ."

According to Cibber, the girl who served them tea at this establishment "happened to have charms sufficient to tempt the little-tiny manhood of Mr Pope into the next room with her . . ." Then, for some time the young nobleman and Cibber himself waited in the outer room.

Later on, according to his account, Cibber began to worry

about the great poet's safety. And, he said, it was fortunate that he had done so. For "... without ceremony," Cibber now wrote, "[I] threw open the door upon him [Pope with the girl], where I found this little hasty hero, like a terrible tomtit, pertly perching upon the mount of love!"

The scene, according to the poet laureate, demanded a hero. And, in a day when the health hazards of London low-life were all too well known, Cibber described to readers his thoughtful act of rescuing the great but frail poet from imminent danger:

"... I fairly laid hold of his heels," he wrote, "and actually drew him down safe and sound from his danger. My lord, who stayed tittering without in hopes the sweet mischief he came for would have been completed, upon my giving an account of the action within, began to curse and call me an hundred silly puppies for my impertinently spoiling the sport; to which with great gravity I replied, 'Pray, my lord, consider what I have done was in regard to the honor of our nation! For would you have had so glorious a work as that of making Homer speak elegant English cut short by laying up our little gentleman of a malady which his thin body might never have been cured of? No, my lord! Homer would have been too serious a sacrifice to our evening merriment!' ..."

So, Cibber mockingly concluded: "Now as his Homer has since been so happily completed, who can say that the world may not have been obliged to the kindly care of Colley that so great a work ever came to perfection?"

When a friend asked Pope if he had seen the pamphlet, the translator of Homer tried Cibber's own tactics: he shrugged off the entire matter by replying that, although he had a copy, "God knows when I shall read it ..." Later, too, following Cibber's past example, he even showed Cibber's *Letter* to some friends and told them that reading such pamphlets was his "diversion." Then, in order to demonstrate exactly how lightly he took such attacks, he began reading the *Letter* aloud to them. But, unfortunately, he was not as successful as was his rival in such tactics, for one of the friends present reported that Pope's face was "writhen with anguish" when he came to the most revealing part of the pamphlet.

A few weeks later, when a London newspaper published an artist's conception of the scene in the "house of carnal recreation," at which a wizened Pope was supposedly rescued by the high-minded Cibber, the victim's anguish increased.

Although Cibber's satirical story about Pope had undoubtedly been exaggerated, there was apparently enough truth in it to prevent Pope from denying it flatly. Instead, he was now forced to seek his revenge by republishing a 1728 work in revised form. In the earlier edition of *The Dunciad*, the scholar, Lewis Theobald, who had infuriated Pope by pointing out that the poet's edition of Shakespeare's plays was riddled with errors, had been crowned "prince of Dulness." Now, in 1743, Pope replaced the name of Theobald with that of Colley Cibber, and he kept the poet laureate under constant fire throughout the long poem.

He made a concentrated assault on Cibber's intelligence early in *The New Dunciad* by describing Cibber's agony in composing even nonsensical verse. Wrote Pope:

> Swearing and supperless the hero sate,
> Blasphemed his gods the dice, and damn'd his fate;
> Then gnaw'd his pen, then dash'd it on the ground,
> Sinking from thought to thought, a vast profound!
> Plunged for his sense, but found no bottom there,
> Yet wrote and flounder'd on in mere despair.

Then Pope paid his respects to the poet laureate's odes and plays:

Round him much Embryo, much Abortion lay,
Much future Ode, and abdicated Play;
Nonsense precipitate, like running lead,
That slipp'd thro' cracks and zigzags of the head . . .

He also noted Cibber's penchant for borrowing other men's lines and ideas for his dramas:

Next o'er his books his eyes began to roll,
In pleasing memory of all he stole;
How here he sipp'd, how there he plunder'd snug,
And suck'd all o'er like an industrious bug.

And, to round out the portrait, the angry Pope called Cibber a fop, a rake, a dunce, and a snob.

The battle had ended, with Pope the victor. For Cibber, who had by this time endured at least a dozen major public attacks from Pope, now contented himself with expressing his curiosity as to why the great Pope had devoted so much time to "snapping and snarling" at him and other men of his day.
"What have you gained by it? . . ." Cibber inquired of Pope. Then he answered his own question with:
"[You have gained a] Victory over a parcel of poor Wretches that were not able to hurt or resist you, so weak it was almost Cowardice to conquer them . . . [To] make . . . Revenge the chief Motive of your writing your Dunciad, seems to me a weakness that an Author of your Abilities should rather have chosen to conceal . . ."
Then he made a startlingly accurate prediction.
"The very lines you have so sharply pointed to destroy them," he told Pope, "will now remain but so many of their Epitaphs, to transmit their Names to Posterity . . ."
And so it has proved for Cibber himself. His plays lie un-

disturbed in the dusty stacks of a few libraries. His years as an actor-manager are mentioned in a few histories of the theater. His preposterous odes have long since been forgotten. But any reader of the work of Alexander Pope is reminded again and again that a buffoon named Colley Cibber once lived; and even for those who find Pope's heroic couplets wearying, there can be no escape from sometimes hearing the clever lines which have become Colley Cibber's epitaph:

> In merry Old England, it once was the Rule,
> The King had his Poet, and also his Fool.
> But now we're so frugal, I'd have you to know it,
> That Cibber can serve both for Fool and for Poet.

"I BEG YOU TO FORGET MY EXISTENCE" cries the Gentle IVAN TURGENEV.

THE relationship between a lender and a borrower is always a particularly delicate one, and over the centuries a widely recognized gentleman's code has been developed to guide both the debtor and the creditor if they hope to remain friends. In such a relationship it is best, as the scholar Edward Hallett Carr has observed, for the lender to refrain from reminding the borrower of his debt, and it is also wisest for the borrower to show not even the slightest hint that he suspects the lender is capable of reminding him of his embarrassing obligation.

In the entire history of literature, few writers have had more opportunities to master the finer points of this code than did the erratic Russian genius Fëdor Doestoevski. Yet rarely has any writer displayed so little skill in practicing the code—and least of all when, during one of his frequent periods of desperate financial need, Doestoevski turned to the gentle Russian novelist Ivan Turgenev for help.

Turgenev was a wealthy landowner, an agnostic, and a man who found life in Western Europe far more congenial than life in Czarist Russia. Doestoevski was a far different sort. He was a religious mystic, long accustomed to poverty, who felt an almost fanatical love for everything Russian. Yet, despite these differences, the two writers had managed to maintain a semblance of friendship for two decades. Then Doestoevski's behavior when he borrowed one hundred German thalers from Turgenev eventually led to so open a break between the two men that, finally, the kindly Turgenev was driven to write in sheer desperation one of the most pathetic sentences in Russian letters:

". . . I beg you," wrote Turgenev, ". . . to forget my existence. . . ."

But all this happened long after Turgenev had been involved in a series of literary feuds. In fact, he might equally well have written these same pathetic words earlier to the paranoic Russian novelist, Ivan Goncharov—whose dark suspicions were to trouble him for so many years—or to the great but difficult Leo Tolstoi, who in *his* feud with Turgenev went so far as to challenge him to a duel. For at the end of each of these unsettling encounters, it was Turgenev's custom to withdraw into himself in defeat, a puzzled look on his kind face and a baffled but injured tone to his voice.

Early in life Turgenev had developed the custom of confessing that he was wrong (even when he was right), and thus retreating from any harsh and unpleasant scene. As a boy he had learned the futility of trying to oppose any whim of his iron-willed mother, an enormously wealthy woman who was also a natural tyrant.

Not until 1838 did Turgenev, then nineteen years old, assert himself with his mother. Apparently with the hope of escaping from her control, he managed to convince Mme Turgenev that he should go to Germany to study at the University of Berlin. And, within a few hours after he had taken this first move toward independence, he was involved in an inglorious incident that his enemies—including Doestoevski—were to cite against him as long as he lived.

Before his departure, Mme Turgenev came down to St. Petersburg from the huge family estate near Moscow to see him off on the steamship *Nicholas I*. Though Ivan was a tall, broad-shouldered youth, his mother treated him as if he were a child. She arranged for a private Mass to be said for his safety, and warned him repeatedly against playing cards with strangers. Finally, having taken over all the details of his sailing, she saw her boy aboard ship, said good-bye—and then fainted dead away soon after she had watched the ship, with her Ivan aboard, moving out to sea.

During the first hours aboard the vessel, the obedient Ivan remembered his mother's warning and stayed away from the smoke-filled salon where the gamblers had already gathered. But, as always, he found it difficult to curb his curiosity, and in the evening he made his way to the forbidden area. Soon, one of the gamblers asked if Ivan would like to join the game.

In a high, thin voice that was never to grow deeper, Turgenev replied:

"No, I can't. I promised my mother I wouldn't."

The contrast between Turgenev's powerful body and his shrill voice made the men laugh. Stung, the proud and sensitive Ivan disregarded his solemn promise. He accepted a chair offered by the men and in the first few hands he was fortunate enough to enjoy a run of beginner's luck.

Then, as was so frequently the case for Turgenev, his luck was suddenly reversed. As he watched the stack of gold coins in front of him grow higher, a woman passenger burst into the room shouting, "Fire!"

In the panic that followed, few of the men on the *Nicholas I* behaved heroically, but there could be no doubt Ivan Turgenev managed to seem not only a coward but, worse, a fool. Terrified by the noise, the disorder, and the smoke, he rushed from one sailor to another, screaming in his shrill voice words that Doestoevski was to recall years later during their feud:

"Save me!" pleaded the distraught Turgenev. "I am my mother's only son!"

". . . why," asked his always critical mother, when she was informed of the incident, "do they tell this only about you? That you are a *gros monsieur* is not your fault, but! that you are a coward—which the other passengers could not help noticing in their panic—that has left a stain on you, if not of dishonour, then of *ridicule*—you must admit."

Although his mother said that an author was little better than a clerk, since both were paid merely for soiling paper, Turgenev also held stubbornly to his early decision to become a writer. And, by 1847, he had become the author of some pleasant little sketches.

It was as a sketch-writer that he was introduced in that year to Ivan Goncharov, a phlegmatic civil servant whose first novel, *An Ordinary Story,* had just been published and had been acclaimed by both the critics and the public.

Soon, the two men were meeting frequently to read their works to each other. Goncharov, who was six years older than Turgenev, would listen politely as Turgenev read from a sketch on which he was working; and the younger author would, in turn, listen while the famous novelist read long sections from his own projected works. They continued this practice as the years passed and as Turgenev's reputation grew with the publication of *A Sportsman's Sketches* and his first novel, *Rudin*. During this period, Goncharov continued to think of Turgenev as a minor literary figure and, apparently, saw in him no threat to his own secure place in Russian literature.

Turgenev, however, had during this same period come to feel that his earlier work did not indicate the range of his talent, and, approximately a decade after his first meeting with Goncharov, he decided to write a much more ambitious novel than *Rudin*.

Following his established custom, he then asked Goncharov to give his opinion of the manuscript.

Never a demonstrative man, Goncharov listened quietly—perhaps even a little moodily—as Turgenev read to him part of this new novel, which was later to be published as *A Nest of Gentlefolk*. But this time, quite unexpectedly, Goncharov interrupted to make a strange request. Would Turgenev, he asked, eliminate one scene he had written for his novel? He would appreciate it, Goncharov said, since the dialogue in that scene paralleled rather closely a conversation he had previously read to Turgenev from his own long-projected novel, *The Precipice*.

Goncharov's request was the first open expression of a deep and irrational jealousy that was inevitably to lead to a series of clashes. But the perplexed, though obliging, Turgenev, unaware of this fact, shrugged his massive shoulders and acquiesced to the older writer's request, hoping that this would end the matter.

It was, however, by no means the end. *A Nest of Gentlefolk* appeared at almost the same time as Goncharov's laboriously composed work, *Oblomov*. And now the latter's hostility toward Turgenev increased enormously, for both the critics and the public gave more attention to *A Nest of Gentlefolk* than to *Oblomov*. The suddenly overshadowed Goncharov wrote an angry letter to Turgenev. In it, he accused Turgenev of simply scratching the surface of life, while he himself was, he said, exploring unknown depths. When Turgenev published his next novel, *On the Eve*, Goncharov accused him of stealing the entire plot of this new book from his own still-unfinished *The Precipice* and charged that character after character in Turgenev's new novel bore a remarkable resemblance to those which had first appeared in his own manuscript!

No longer able to avoid an unpleasant confrontation of a type he hated, Turgenev now decided on the only possible course. He asked three writers who were acquainted both with Goncharov and himself to consider the accusation and to make a report on their findings. In March, 1860, this privately constituted literary court convened, each member having read many pages of manuscript produced by the hard-working Goncharov.

The result was that Turgenev was exonerated of the charge of plagiarism. And yet, as the years passed, Goncharov's morbid jealousy continued to increase.

Soon Goncharov's behavior took the unmistakable form of paranoia. Before he was finished, this obsessed man was to accuse Turgenev of carving four novels out of his own long-delayed *The Precipice*, and of offering other sections of it to a German writer and two French novelists. According to Goncharov, even Gustave Flaubert's great *Madame Bovary* contained much material from *The Precipice* given to him by Turgenev!

In a document entitled *An Extraordinary Story*, which has never been translated into English but has been summarized by the scholar Avrahm Yarmolinsky, Goncharov recorded his accusation.

"Having thus robbed his friend," Goncharov charged, "the

conscienceless wretch [Turgenev] organized an immense conspiracy designed to keep him informed of whatever Goncharov wrote or planned or uttered, with a view to interfering with the latter's work at every turn.

"The unhappy victim [Goncharov himself] could never be sure that during his absence from home, his manuscripts were not being copied by one of Turgenev's thousand agents; moreover, his conversations were reported verbatim and his letters regularly opened. Indeed . . . Turgenev was living abroad, first, in order to conceal his literary impotence from his compatriots, and, second, in order to be able to dispose of the stolen goods, as well as to see that nothing by Goncharov should be translated into a Western language."

And one day, upon seeing Turgenev in a St. Petersburg park, Goncharov actually ran after him, shouting: "Thief! Thief!" until the abashed Turgenev fled in horror.

The strange affair with Goncharov had actually been an unfortunate collision with a totally irrational man. But the feuds through which Turgenev was to suffer with his literary peers, Tolstoi and Doestoevski, were to be more subtle battles.

Ivan Turgenev first became aware of the talent of the younger Count Leo Tolstoi when he happened to read *The Story of My Childhood* in the Russian magazine *Sovremennik*. ". . . this is a real talent . . .," he wrote to the editor of the magazine. "Tell him—if he should be interested—that I salute him, bow to him, and applaud him. . . ."

Tolstoi returned the salute by asking one of his relatives to search out Turgenev and give him the greetings of a young admirer.

The two men finally met in November, 1855.

With unusual enthusiasm, Turgenev wrote to a friend about his new acquaintance. "Just think of it! Tolstoy has been staying with me over two weeks. . . . You can't imagine what a fine and remarkable fellow he is. . . ." Then he added: "I've conceived a strange affection for him, which has something paternal about it."

And Tolstoi spoke with equal warmth of Turgenev.

Yet, even in these early meetings, there were some difficult moments. When Turgenev and other writers held a special dinner in memory of the famous Russian critic, Vissarion Belinski, whom Turgenev had worshiped, Tolstoi asked the members of the solemn group whether they could be sure the man they were honoring hadn't been "a son of a bitch." On another occasion, when Turgenev complained of suffering from bronchitis, the unsympathetic Tolstoi replied coldly that bronchitis was an imaginary disease.

In 1857, Turgenev was living in Paris, and Tolstoi journeyed there to visit him. After they had spent many days together, Tolstoi wrote in his journal: "On leaving him [Turgenev], I cried. I don't know just why. I love him very much. He has made—he will make a new man of me."

By this time, however, Turgenev was not so sure about *his* feeling for Tolstoi. The days in Paris had been marred by several disputes, and they troubled him.

"In spite of all my efforts, I can't get close to Tolstoy," he wrote to one friend. "He's built too differently from me. Whatever I love, he doesn't, and vice versa. In his presence I feel embarrassed, and it is probably the same with him. . . ." But with characteristic fairness, he added: "He will develop into a remarkable person, and I shall be the first to admire and applaud him, at a distance."

After another year had passed, Turgenev was even more certain of their basic incompatibility.

"I am through with Tolstoy . . . ," he wrote then. "We are poles apart. If I like the soup, I am certain Tolstoy will hate it—and vice versa."

Yet the two men still admired each other, and each of their clashes was followed promptly by a warm reconciliation. Thus, when the poet Afanasi Fet invited both of them to visit his new estate in May, 1861, both accepted. And they made the journey to their host's home together.

After enjoying an elaborate dinner that first day at the Fet estate, Turgenev and Tolstoi stretched out in leisurely fashion on the lawn with the host and looked up at the sky, talking easily about farming and books. And Turgenev was still feeling pleased with the way the evening had gone when he came down for breakfast at eight o'clock the next morning.

Mme Fet asked him to sit at her right, while Tolstoi took the seat at her left, and the conversation was light and untroubled until Mme Fet turned to Turgenev with a question.

Was he, Mme Fet asked, satisfied with the English governess he had recently employed to care for his daughter Pauline?

Yes, Turgenev replied, the governess was an excellent woman. Just recently she had proved how very conscientious she was by asking him exactly what sum he wished Pauline to contribute to charity.

And now, added the pleased father, "She insists that my daughter should visit the poor and take their worn clothes home to mend them with her own hands."

At this moment, Tolstoi, who was extraordinarily contentious during this period of his life and particularly enjoyed provoking arguments with the usually calm and unruffled Turgenev, interrupted his fellow novelist.

"You think that's a good thing?" he asked in a challenging voice, for he had actually come to consider Turgenev something of a hypocrite.

"Yes," said Turgenev. "The girl gets in close touch with actual want."

"And I think," shouted Tolstoi, "that a starched miss stepping squeamishly into a poor man's lodgings is an abomination. A dressed-up girl holding dirty stinking rags in her lap takes part in an insincere theatrical scene."

The gentle Turgenev was astonished. He looked pleadingly at his antagonist.

"I beg you not to say that," he requested.

The words served only to enrage the already annoyed Tolstoi. "Why shouldn't I say what I think?" the younger writer demanded; and by the time the alarmed host was able to intervene in the hope of changing the subject, the two friends had gone too far to turn back.

"So you think I'm bringing up my daughter badly?" Turgenev asked.

As Fet later reported, the poor fellow's nostrils dilated as he spoke.

"I meant what I said," Tolstoi replied, "and without being personal I simply expressed my thoughts."

Then, bitingly, he added a remark guaranteed to infuriate Turgenev, whose daughter had been born of a liaison with one of his mother's servants.

"If she were your legitimate daughter," Tolstoi said, "you would educate her differently."

"If you keep on talking like that," shouted Turgenev, rising from his chair, "I'll slap your face!"

But he then put his hands to his head and rushed from the room, instead.

A few minutes later, having regained his self-control, he returned. After apologizing to Mme Fet for the unpleasant scene, he muttered a few vague words of regret to the glowering Tolstoi.

The two men left the estate in separate carriages.

Tolstoi went to Novosyolki, the nearby estate of Fet's brother-in-law, and, still seething, wrote immediately to Turgenev demanding a written apology which he could then show to the Fets. He said a return message would reach him more quickly at Bogoslovo, the post station near Novosyolki. He would wait at Bogoslovo until he had received a reply, he told Turgenev.

Now began a series of farcical errors that could have led to a tragedy—perhaps even the death of Turgenev or Tolstoi.

Upon receiving Tolstoi's note, Turgenev sat down at once to write a conciliatory reply, characteristically accepting the full blame for the scene at the Fet estate.

". . . I insulted you without any positive provocation on your part and [ask] your pardon," he wrote. And he added: "What happened this morning showed clearly that any attempt to bring about friendly relations between such incompatible natures as yours and mine is quite useless . . ."

He asked one of his servants to rush this apology on its way, but, with his nerves still unsettled by the quarrel, overlooked Tolstoi's instructions to deliver the message to Bogoslovo. Instead, he addressed it to Novosyolki.

In the meantime, the impatient Tolstoi, annoyed by a night-long wait at the bleak post station of Bogoslovo, dashed off a second note to Turgenev, challenging him to a duel. He meant a real duel, he said—to the death. And, while awaiting Turgenev's reply, Tolstoi sent for his dueling pistols.

Then, while the second message was on its way to Turgenev, Tolstoi received the long-delayed reply to his first note. Since it was conciliatory, Tolstoi sent it on to the Fets, indicating to them that he found the apology satisfactory.

It was, however, too late to stop the servant who was on the way to Turgenev with Tolstoi's challenge. And when that note reached poor Turgenev, he was baffled. He assumed that Tolstoi had already received his abject apology, and, dejectedly, sat down to write another letter to the young author he admired.

He believed there was nothing he could add to what he had already written, Turgenev now wrote.

"I say in all sincerity that I would gladly stand under your fire in order to wipe out my truly insane words. That I spoke as I did is so foreign to my habits that I cannot ascribe it to any other cause than irritation, due to the extreme and constant antagonism of our views. . . . I consider it my duty to repeat that in this matter you were right and I was wrong."

The self-accusing tone of this note brought another communication from the proud Tolstoi. "You are afraid of me," Tolstoi wrote him, "but I scorn you and do not want to have anything to do with you." A few weeks later, still filled with contempt for the older writer, he wrote in his diary: "Final break with Turgenev. He is an utter scandal, but I think with the passing of time I shall surrender and forgive him."

Three months later, Tolstoi went even further than he had predicted. He wrote to Turgenev, who was abroad, humbly asking for Turgenev's forgiveness. But this missive was delayed, and in the intervening period Turgenev had heard reports that Tolstoi was showing his own earlier letter of apology to friends as proof of Turgenev's cowardice.

In an about-face, the angry Turgenev wrote to Tolstoi, challenging *him* to a duel "upon my return to Russia next Spring, . . ."

When Tolstoi's apologetic letter finally reached him, Turgenev withdrew the challenge. But his feelings toward the other man could never again be the same.

In January, 1862, he wrote with remarkable restraint to his old host, Fet. Clearly, he had struggled painfully toward the proper solution, and he had at last found it.

". . . You can write [Tolstoi] or tell him (if you see him)," he wrote Fet, "that I, without making speeches or playing with

words, like him very much, respect him, and follow his career
—*from a distance,* but that everything appears different when
we are near each other.

"What is to be done?" he asked, rhetorically.

Then he stated his solution:

"We ought to live as though we existed upon different
planets or in different centuries."

And for almost seventeen years, the two famous novelists,
whose estates were in the same part of Russia, managed to
achieve exactly this difficult feat. It was not until the end of
this long period of time that the eminent Tolstoi, who had
reached that spiritual period of his life in which he decided to
ask the forgiveness of all those he had wronged in his younger
days, approached Turgenev in the hope of a reconciliation.
But, though the two men did then declare their friendship,
the earlier warmth was irretrievably lost. For somehow, both
men still realized rather hopelessly that Turgenev had been
right about their basic incompatibility many years before when
he had observed: "If I like the soup, I am certain Tolstoy will
hate it—and vice versa."

It would seem that few men could have been better condi-
tioned by experience than Turgenev for the buffeting he was
to endure in his most disastrous feud—that with Fëdor Doestoevski. Yet, his fellow novelist's erratic behavior, together
with the delicacy of the borrower-lender relationship, proved
too much for even this warier Turgenev.

The two had first met in 1845, at the beginning of their
literary careers, but the dispute which made them enemies did
not begin until 1865, when both were living in Germany.

At that time, as usual, Doestoevski was in financial trouble.

Absolutely certain that he had discovered a reliable system
for winning at roulette, the author of *The Gambler,* as well as
of greater novels, had managed to lose all his money in the

casino at Wiesbaden, and, having borrowed small sums from casual acquaintances, had proceeded to gamble away those amounts, too. Convinced that it was he who had failed the system rather than the system that had failed him, he had even pawned his watch to obtain a few more thalers—and this amount had also vanished at the gaming tables.

In desperation, Doestoevski then wrote to Turgenev, who was living in Baden Baden, begging for a loan of one hundred thalers. Making no attempt to conceal his reason for needing the money, he told Turgenev:

"You are much more understanding than the others, and therefore morally it's easier for me to turn to you."

But at that time Turgenev did not happen to have one hundred thalers readily available to lend to Doestoevski, however understanding he was about the situation. Though he was one of the two heirs to an estate that was worked by five thousand recently freed Russian peasants, he was an absentee landlord with no talent at all for managing his properties, and because of his weakness, he was victimized and plundered by his unfaithful stewards. Thus, he did not find it convenient to make the requested one-hundred thaler loan, but he did send half the amount. And, in turn, Doestoevski promised to repay the sum within a month.

Doestoevski made such promises frequently, with no intention of keeping them. But for a time after the loan was made, both men were abroad, which reduced the probability of any embarrassing meetings between the debtor and the creditor.

In 1867, however, fate at last caught up with the dilatory borrower.

By this time, Doestoevski had further refined his system at the roulette table; and, after a considerable investment for research, he was more certain than ever that he had at last discovered the one infallible method of winning. Furthermore, even though he knew that Turgenev was living in Baden Baden, he now chose to test his theory at the famous casino there.

One day in the casino, Doestoevski happened to run into the paranoic Ivan Goncharov, who had also developed a mania for gambling. Goncharov told Doestoevski he had heard that Turgenev had walked through the casino one afternoon and had seen the feverish Doestoevski huddled over a roulette table. According to Goncharov, Turgenev had read enough about gamblers to know that they did not like to have their attention diverted while playing, and thus, said Goncharov, Turgenev had purposely passed by without greeting Doestoevski.

Now Doestoevski had no choice. Now that his creditor knew of his presence in Baden Baden, he felt he must pay Turgenev a courtesy visit. Though he put off the embarrassing chore for three days, he finally decided to get the visit over with, and, on Wednesday, July 10, 1867, he reluctantly made his way to Turgenev's house on Schillerstrasse.

He had long worried over his financial plight, and it is possible that during his walk to Turgenev's house he brooded over the differences between his own harried existence and the life of ease and comfort which Turgenev enjoyed. Only recently, the new Mme Doestoevski had actually had to pawn her only skirt so the couple would have enough money with which to buy food. The fact that the skirt was pawned because Doestoevski had gambled away all the money he could earn, borrow, or beg did not seem to impress him. But he was impressed by the fact that Turgenev lived and traveled in comparative luxury.

It so happened that recently, too, Turgenev had published a new novel, *Smoke*, which had been so coldly received by the critics that the author had been moved to write to an editor:

"It seems to me that at no time has anyone been so unanimously cursed as I have been for *Smoke*."

Doestoevski had read and also detested *Smoke*.

Thus it was that, upon his arrival at Turgenev's house, Doestoevski had hardly more than greeted his benefactor before he launched into a furious attack upon Turgenev's new book. The writer, said Doestoevski, had insulted every Russian by portraying his countrymen as lazy and confused and indecisive!

When the startled Turgenev tried to defend his novel, his guest shouted that the book ought to be "burned by the public executioner."

The beleaguered Turgenev, realizing that he was once again at the mercy of a near-madman, said later that he "listened in silence to . . . this tirade."

But Doestoevski had not finished. He now took it upon himself to inform Turgenev that his long absence from Russia had made it impossible for Turgenev to understand what was going on in his native land. He suggested that Turgenev buy a telescope and use it to study Russian life from the comfort of the German spas he so clearly preferred.

According to Doestoevski's version of the incident, these remarks at last aroused Turgenev. In fact, Doestoevski later claimed, Turgenev finally lost his temper, and replied that "If Russia sank through the ground, that would be no loss to mankind. . . ." Furthermore, the fanatically religious Doestoevski later reported, Turgenev even confessed openly to being an atheist!

It seemed to Doestoevski that such remarks should be preserved for posterity. They would, he decided, prove to future generations that this writer, who considered himself a spokesman for the great Russian nation, was not only a shameless anti-Russian but also a dangerous and Godless man.

Seething, he rushed from the house on Schillerstrasse. Soon Doestoevski's new wife, who was one of the first Russian stenographers, was making detailed shorthand notes on his version of what had taken place, and a few weeks later Doestoevski himself set down for posterity a more dramatic rendering of the conversation in a long letter to a friend in Russia.

In due time, a copy of Doestoevski's letter reached the office of the editor of the historical review, *Russian Archives,* with instructions that it be held for twenty-three years—until 1890 —and then made public as an historic document. Some time later, Turgenev heard about the curious epistle and wrote to the editor of *Russian Archives* in his own defense:

"He [Doestoevski] sat with me no more than an hour," explained poor Turgenev, "and retired after having relieved his heart by ferociously abusing the Germans, myself, and my latest book. I had neither time nor desire to argue with him. . . . I treated him as I would a sick man.

"The arguments which he expected from me must have presented themselves to his deranged imagination . . ."

He then made his own plea to posterity.

"Doubtless," he wrote, "in 1890, neither Mr. Doestoevski nor I will engage the attention of our compatriots any longer, and if we are not wholly forgotten, we shall be judged not by one-sided denunciation, but by the results of our whole lives and work. . . ."

The dispute dragged on for years. In 1871, Turgenev wrote to a friend regarding Doestoevski's accusations.

"It would be out-and-out slander," Turgenev pleaded, "if Dostoevsky were not a madman, which I do not doubt in the slightest. Perhaps it all came to him in a dream. But, my God, what petty, dirty gossip!"

But by this time Doestoevski had discovered a new method of attacking Turgenev. The method: a cruel lampooning of his victim in Doestoevski's novel, *The Possessed*.

Many readers of this Doestoevski work were soon to realize that the character of Karmazinov* in the novel was based on Turgenev. Like Turgenev, Karmazinov talked in a "squeaky voice, though he uttered each word with a soft cadence and agreeable gentlemanly lisp." Again, like Turgenev, Karmazinov was a famous Russian novelist who preferred to spend most of his time in Germany and Western Europe. And in one passage of the novel Doestoevski cruelly caricatured Turgenev's excessive and widely known concern over the safety of his manuscripts.

"'. . . you have my manuscript,'" Karmazinov says to Pyotr Stepanovitch in a scene from *The Possessed*. " 'Have you read it?' "

" 'Manuscript? Which one?' " Pyotr Stepanovitch asks.

"Karmazinov was terribly surprised.

" 'But you've brought it with you, haven't you?' He [Karmazinov] was so disturbed that he even left off eating and looked at Pyotr Stepanovitch with a face of dismay.

" 'Ah, that *Bonjour* you mean. . . .'

" '*Merci*.'

" 'Oh, all right. I'd quite forgotten it and hadn't read it; I haven't had time. I really don't know, it's not in my pockets . . . it must be on my table. Don't be uneasy, it will be found.'

" 'No, I'd better send to your rooms at once. It might be lost; besides, it might be stolen.'

" 'Oh, who'd want it? But why are you so alarmed? Why, Yulia Mihailovna told me you always have several copies made

---

* The name is based on a French word sometimes used in Russia to mean "crimson." In this manner Doestoevski inferred that Turgenev sympathized secretly with the radicals: the Reds.

—one kept at a notary's abroad, another in Petersburg, a third in Moscow, and then you send some to a bank, I believe.' " 'But,' " says Karmazinov, " 'Moscow might be burnt again and my manuscript with it. No, I'd better send at once. . . .' "

The readers of *The Possessed* were understandably amused at Turgenev's foibles, especially when, later in the novel, Karmazinov reads a part of this same *Merci* aloud at a literary fête, with a sort of melancholy condescension. The subject, as Doestoevski satirizes it in *The Possessed* is—well—"Who could make it out?" Writes Doestoevski: "It was a sort of description of certain impressions and reminiscences. But of what? And about what?" He continues: "Though the leading intellects of the province did their utmost during the first half of the reading, they could make nothing of it, and they listened to the second part simply out of politeness."

Finally, as Karmazinov drones on, paying no attention to the restless audience, a loud voice is heard from the back row, shouting: " 'Good Lord, what nonsense!' " Others begin muttering their agreement with the heckler. Writes Doestoevski, with obvious satisfaction: "The great genius had completely lost touch with his Fatherland . . ."

At various points in *The Possessed*, Doestoevski managed to lampoon Turgenev's mannerisms, his works, and even his inglorious behavior in early youth aboard the *Nicholas I*. He also portrayed the defenseless Turgenev as a political dilettante. And, of course, Turgenev recognized himself in the character of Karmazinov. He also realized that the story read at the literary fête was a parody of one he had long ago allowed the then eager and far younger Doestoevski to publish in a short-lived magazine edited by him. In his own defense Turgenev now wrote to a friend

". . . F.M. Dostoevski's conduct has not astonished me in the slightest; he hated me even when we were both young and at the beginning of our literary careers, although I have in no way deserved his hatred. But they say that groundless passions are the strongest and the most prolonged. . . . Dostoevski has permitted himself something worse than a parody; he has presented me, under the name of Karmazinov, as a secret sympathizer of the Nechaev party. [Sergei Nechaev was a revolutionary disciple of Bakunin who ordered the murder of one of his fellow conspirators on November 25, 1869.] The strange thing is that he chose to parody the one story ["Phantoms"] I had placed in the magazine edited at one time by himself—a story for which he showered me with letters of gratitude and praise.

"I have kept those letters. It would be amusing to print them! But he knows that I will not do it. I only regret that he is using his undeniable talent to satisfy such vile emotions; evidently he does not care about debasing his talent as a pamphleteer . . ."

Yet the final irony was still to come, and perhaps in this one instance it was actually Turgenev who was at fault.

In 1876, eleven years after Doestoevski had borrowed the fifty thalers from Turgenev, he finally paid off the debt. Unfortunately, however, Turgenev at this point suffered a lapse of memory. He was able to recall that Doestoevski had asked him for one hundred thalers back in 1865. But he did not remember that he had loaned Doestoevski only half the requested amount. And now, since he was abroad when Doestoevski's payment arrived, he asked his friend Aleksandr Fedorovich Onegin to deliver a receipt for fifty thalers to the sender, and simultaneously to ask Doestoevski when it would be convenient for him to pay the other fifty thalers which he believed were still owed to him!

Onegin accepted this delicate assignment and dropped by to see Doestoevski.

The insulted debtor, muttering angrily, searched through piles of old letters, manuscripts, and papers. Finally, he pulled out a crinkled document to prove the amount of the debt. As a result, Onegin, feeling that he had been placed in an extremely embarrassing position, wrote a bitter letter to Turgenev, accusing him of cowardly behavior. The reply from Turgenev came a few days later. In a way, it was the most pathetic letter of Turgenev's life.

"Upon receiving your letter," he wrote Onegin, "I rummaged through my entire correspondence, and at last found the subjoined letter of Mr. Doestoevski's. The fact is that I had loaned him not 100 thalers as I thought, but 50. I shall be obliged to you if you would remit to him this letter together with the receipt, in lieu of the receipt I had sent him through you as the intermediary.

"I shall not conceal from you," he went on, "that you have hurt me more deeply than anyone else has ever done . . . believing me capable . . . of cowardly behavior, you should not have hesitated to decline taking on the errand in the first place. Or you might have supposed that my memory had betrayed me, that I was mistaken about the sum (as was the case), and then, how could you have failed to warn me, to tell me to look through my papers again? Instead, after a hesitation that I find offensive, you did not hesitate to cast the insult in my face. (All I can do is to hope you did not realize the magnitude of its force.)

". . . I beg you," he concluded in sheer despair, "—and this will not surprise you at all—after you have fulfilled my last request (that is to say, the exchange of receipts), to forget my existence. . . ."

Mr. THACKERAY & MR. DICKENS BECOME Embroiled in a very victorian Feud.

IN 1845, when William Makepeace Thackeray was thirty-four years old, the editor of *The Edinburgh Review* wrote the following letter to a friend in London:

"Will you tell me . . . whether you know anything of a Mr. Thackeray, about whom Longman has written me, thinking he would be a good hand for light articles? . . . One requires to be very much on one's guard in engaging with mere strangers. In a Journal like the *Edinbro'*, it is always of importance to keep up in respect of names."

When Thackeray learned of this letter, it was simply one more bitter reminder of his relative obscurity after eight years of hard work as a writer. For, although he had published travel books, contributed regularly to *Punch*, and written reviews and articles for any magazine ready to meet his modest fees, he was aware of the fact that few people even knew his name and that most of those who read his magazine and newspaper pieces considered him little more than a casual scribbler.

Such neglect had already soured Thackeray on both editors and readers alike, so much so that when a friend who also hoped to become a contributor to magazines sent him two stories for criticism, Thackeray promptly returned them with a discouraged—and discouraging—note. Wrote the disgruntled Thackeray:

"It is not because a story is bad or an author a fool that either should not be popular nowadays, as you and I know, who see many donkeys crowned with laurels, while certain clever fellows of our acquaintance fight vainly for a . . . reputation."

At this time the man who was to become one of England's most successful novelists was forced to spend much of his time reviewing the books of writers who were achieving far wider notice and earning far more money than he. Though some of his reviews were calm and balanced and he even bestowed his enthusiastic approval upon some books, it is not surprising that other of his comments were damning, leading frequently to quarrels that sometimes rumbled on for years.

One early victim of Thackeray's critical pen was a writer named R.H. Horne, who has long since returned to the obscurity which both he and Thackeray were trying to escape. In 1844, the luckless Horne published a ponderous volume entitled *A New Spirit of the Age*, and the editor of the *Morning Chronicle* turned the book over to the increasingly disillusioned Thackeray for review.

The rather long critique began in a deceptively quiet and benevolent manner:

"There is an easy candour about Mr. Horne," Thackeray wrote, "which ought to encourage all persons to deal with him with similar sincerity. He appears to us to be generous, honest, in the main good humoured . . ."

Then the tone changed abruptly:

"But having awarded the 'New Spirit of the Age' praise so far," he now wrote, "the critic finds himself at a loss for further subjects of commendation . . . For it is not only necessary that a man should be a perfectly honest and well-meaning individual, but that he should have something novel, or striking, or witty, or profound [to say], to make his works agreeable or useful to the world. Thus, to say that 'Shakespeare is a great poet,' that 'hot roast beef is an excellent food for man, and may be advantageously eaten cold the next day,' that 'two multiplied by three equals six,' that 'her Majesty Queen Anne has ceased to exist,' is to advance what is perfectly . . . reasonable; but other thinkers have attained the same knowledge of facts and history, and coinciding perfectly with every one of these propositions, may not care to have them discussed in print. . . ."

He continued in this vein:

"There are words—such a cornucopia of them as the world has few examples of; but the thoughts are scarce in the midst of this plentifulness, the opinions for the most part perfectly irreproachable, and the *ennui* caused by their utterance profound.

"The 'Spirit of the Age' [sic] gives us pictures of a considerable number of the foremost literary characters of the day. It is to be followed, should the design of the projectors be fully carried out, 'by the political spirit of the age, the scientific spirit of the age, the artistical spirit of the age, and the historical, biographical, and critical spirit of the age,' nay, an infantine spirit of the age is also hinted at as a dreadful possibility. The matter is serious, as it will be seen. Only give Mr. Horne encouragement to the task, and he will go and do it. He never doubts about anything. He would write the dancing spirit of the age, or the haberdashing spirit of the age, with as little hesitation; and give you a dissertation upon bombasines, or a disquisition on the true principles of the fandango. In the interest of the nation, people ought to speak, and beg him to be quiet. Now is the time to entreat him to hold his hand; otherwise, all ranks and classes in the empire, . . . may find themselves caught, their bodies and souls turned inside out, so to speak, by this frightful observer, and consigned to posterity in red calico. For the sake of the public, we say, stop; we go down on our knees, . . . and say so."

Clearly, Thackeray had polished off R.H. Horne, and when that writer discovered the identity of the author of the unsigned review, he became his bitter enemy. Long after most people had forgotten *A New Spirit of the Age*, Horne finally completed an impassioned defense of his work, accusing Thackeray of, among other things, writing his review in a "half-cynical, half-rollicking, Royster-Doyster mood."

But Thackeray did not desist from such attacks. In the 1840's, while he was working on the novel by which, as he wrote his mother, he expected to "make a great deal of money," he proceeded to launch, in the humor magazine *Punch*, a series of parodies of the most popular novelists of the times. Though he judiciously omitted Charles Dickens—the great writer whose talent he actually admired, even if he was destined to quarrel with him more than a decade later—he managed to demolish a total of seven victims in the complete series; and of these none was more harshly treated than Edward Bulwer-Lytton.

It was almost always the custom of Bulwer-Lytton, the author of *The Last Days of Pompeii*, to capitalize such words as Life, Death, the True, the Beautiful, and Fate, an easy habit for Thackeray to satirize with his own liberal sprinkling of capital letters. Thus, Thackeray now wrote of the Labyrinth of Life, Smile, Gold, Love, the Truthful, and, with proper reverence, the Bank. In his parody, the reader was led slowly toward the central figure, who bore the name of George de Barnwell and who was employed as a shop clerk because, though a nobleman, he was impoverished. The shop in which the hero worked handled exotic goods brought from strange cities in the distant corners of the world. ". . . in a word," as Thackeray revealed in a crashing anticlimax, "a Grocer's." Once inside the store, Thackeray records a conversation between the clerk and an attractive customer who was examining the Figs. The passionate De Barnwell and the overwrought customer are soon involved in a dramatic exchange, with De Barnwell exclaiming to her: "Figs pall; but oh! the Beautiful never does. Figs rot; but oh! the Truthful is eternal. I was born, lady, to grapple with the Lofty and the Ideal . . ."

In later parodies, Thackeray discovered another way to irritate Bulwer-Lytton, who sometimes signed himself as "Edward Lytton Bulwer Lytton, Baron Lytton." At first he had referred to the self-satisfied author as "Bullwig" or "Sir Bulmer," but soon he moved in another direction, signing one of his parodies: "Sir E.L.B.L.BB.LL.BBB.LLL., Bart."

Soon after Thackeray's burlesque appeared in *Punch*, the now self-conscious Bulwer-Lytton began removing from a few of his works some of the stylistic horrors mocked by Thackeray, as he prepared them for permanent collected editions. Yet, though he exhibited this much agreement with some of his critic's harsher comments, Bulwer-Lytton continued, even late in life, to accuse the irreverent Thackeray of assailing him with "a kind of ribald impertinence offered, as far as I can remember, to no other author of my time."

This lament would undoubtedly have been disputed by Benjamin Disraeli. For when Disraeli's *Coningsby* was published in 1844, Thackeray called it "the fashionable novel, pushed, we do really believe, to its extremest verge, beyond which all is naught. It is a glorification of dandyism, far beyond all other glories which dandyism has attained."

About Disraeli himself, Thackeray said: ". . . he fancies himself young. . . . his soul wears a jacket and a turned-down collar; it eats lollypops at school, . . ." He also stated that the social-climbing Disraeli "out-duked all the dukes in the land . . ."

All this appeared only as a review. Thackeray's real attack on the novel did not come until 1847, when *Punch* published *Codlingsby* by D. Shrewsberry, Esq., in which Thackeray made much of Disraeli's preoccupation with luxury and extravagant decoration. In one scene, for example, he wrote, in imitation of Disraeli:

"They entered a moderate-sized apartment—indeed, Holywell Street is not above a hundred yards long, and this chamber was not more than half that length—and fitted up with the simple taste of its owner."

Then he described the furnishings in elaborate—and impossible—detail:

"The carpet was of white velvet . . . painted with flowers, arabesques, and classic figures, . . . The edges were wrought with seed-pearls, and fringed with Valenciennes lace and bullion. The walls were hung with cloth of silver, embroidered with gold figures, . . . The drops of dew which the artificer had sprinkled on the flowers were diamonds. . . . Divans of carved amber covered with ermine went round the room, and in the midst was a fountain, pattering and babbling with jets of double-distilled otto of roses."

For thirty-three years, Disraeli nourished his grudge. His own career in politics flourished and waned; Thackeray grew famous, then wearied and died, and some of the reforms introduced by Disraeli as Prime Minister changed England forever. But through all these decades, the great political leader remembered and resented *Codlingsby*.

Finally, at seventy-five, freed from the daily demands of political office, Benjamin Disraeli got his revenge. He published a novel entitled *Endymion*, and, in a character named St. Barbe, many readers were quick to recognize Thackeray.

"This is Mr. St. Barbe," wrote Disraeli, "who, when the public taste has improved, will be the most popular author of the day. In the meantime, he will give you a copy of his novel, which has not sold as well as it ought to have done . . ."

Wherever St. Barbe appears in the pages of *Endymion*, he invariably talks about money, titles, fame, or ill treatment. He meets a rich man and immediately says to Endymion: "If I had only known him a year ago! I would have dedicated my novel to him. He is the sort of man who would have given you a cheque immediately. He would not have read it, to be sure, but what of that?" In other scenes, St. Barbe complains that while others receive social invitations, he is overlooked. "No lord ever asked me to dinner . . ." he says. "The aristocracy of this country are doomed." And he complains about the success of other novelists—in this case Dickens, with whom Thackeray had by that time actually had his greatest feud. "[Gushy writes] like a penny-a-liner drunk with ginger beer . . ." Disraeli quotes St. Barbe as remarking. ". . . I am as much robbed by that fellow Gushy as men are on the highway."

At one point, St. Barbe calls Endymion's attention to a man named Trenchard, and tells him that only Trenchard's brother stands between him and an income of four thousand pounds a year. Later, he enviously reports that the brother, whose death would bring Trenchard the inheritance, is seriously ill, and, speculating about his chances of recovery, he wonders just what he should say to Trenchard if the brother dies. St. Barbe-Thackeray, according to Disraeli, seriously ponders this question: ". . . I could not go and congratulate Trenchard on his brother's death . . . though he had been lying awake all night chuckling over the event."

Long before Disraeli published *Endymion*, however, those who knew Thackeray well had made a revealing discovery. This discovery was that the same Thackeray who was ready to slash out at the untalented but inoffensive Horne and to mock the popular but absurd Bulwer-Lytton could not abide any public criticism of himself!

In his early days, the future novelist's limited reputation had usually protected him from attack. Only once had he been chided, and that time he had struck back with every weapon at his command.

One day in 1843, he had opened his copy of *Fraser's Magazine* and noticed this passage in a gossipy article by Deady Keane:

"The first person we met in the coffee-room was Bill Crackaway, one whom we have always looked upon as a bird of ill omen. His long ungainly person is crowned with a face which Dame Nature must have fashioned just after making a bad debt, and, therefore, in the worst of tempers. A countenance of preternatural longitude is imperfectly relieved by a nose on which the partial hand of Nature has lavished every bounty—length, breadth, thickness, all but a—bridge; a mouth that seemed suddenly arrested in the act of whistling, and, from its confirmation, could only eliminate a sinister sneer, but was incapable of the candour of an honest laugh . . .

"The first question this worthy lispingly asked of us was, 'Have you heard the news?' To which, answering in the negative, he proceeded to inform us that Lord Edward Softhead had, to use our informant's expression, 'cut his stick and bolted.'

" 'On what account?'

" 'Oh, the bums [police], are making some kind inquiries after him.'

" 'And how much does he owe?' we asked.

" 'Only 300,000£,' was the answer, 'but then, it is to the discounters, and I suppose, as he is rather green, he will not have touched more than 30 or 40,000£.'

"Now, as Crackaway added to the occupation of editor of a pseudophilosophical magazine the business of a bill-broker in the City, we take it for granted he knew something about these matters."

Thackeray had been outraged. Not only was he offended by the references to his nose, which had been broken twice, but he was also acutely annoyed by Keane's all too realistic reference to his brief but far from glorious career in London's financial world. With the rather awesome anger that he was later to direct at the most famous of his fellow novelists, he wrote at great length to the editor of *Fraser's*.

"I was at no loss" he wrote, "in reading the amusing 'Illustrations of Discount' in the Magazine to discover the name of the author. Mr. Deady Keane shook me by the hand only a fortnight since and at the very same time no doubt was writing the libel on me which appeared to my no small surprize [sic] in that very article.

"I have advisedly let a week pass without deciding upon the course I ought to pursue. Few people (none that I have seen) know that the attack in question is levelled at myself, nor indeed have I any desire to make the public acquainted with that fact. But—as in a private house or an inn, if any person with no other provocation but that of drunkenness or natural malice, should take a fancy to call me by foul names, I should have a right to appeal to the host, and request him to have the individual so offending put out of doors—I may similarly complain to you that I have been grossly insulted in your Magazine.

"Having written long in it; being known to you (please God) as an honest man and not an ungenerous one; I have a right to complain that a shameful and unprovoked attack has been made upon me in the Magazine, and as an act of justice to demand that the writer should no longer be permitted to contribute to *Fraser*.

"If Mr. Deady Keane continues his contributions in any shape, mine must cease. I am one of the oldest and I believe one of the best of your contributors . . . I have been grossly abused in the magazine, and must perforce withdraw from it unless I have your word that this act of justice shall be done me.

"I make this demand not in the least as an act of retaliation against Mr. Keane . . . it cannot be said that . . . his attack has rendered me particularly vindictive. It would be easy to fight him with the same weapons which he uses, could I condescend to employ them: but I feel myself, and I hope one day he will discover, that they are unworthy of an honest man. If he only take care to let it be publicly known that it is his intention to abuse in the public prints any private individuals, whose personal appearance or qualities may be disagreeable to him, it is surprising how popular he will become, how his society will be courted, and his interests · in life advanced . . ."

This extraordinarily exaggerated reaction to a minor and foolish attack by an unimportant journalist revealed a characteristic of the seemingly self-assured Thackeray which was to become even more apparent after the publication of *Vanity*

Fair. He was, as he himself later admitted, "thin-skinned." And he had also developed a rather austere public personality. Many people who met him briefly came away with an impression of rather chilly dignity and deep reserve. As one acquaintance said, his speech was "as polished as a steel mirror and as cold."

Yet there was another Thackeray who was seen by a few close friends and by children. When the talk around a table or in a formal sitting room became too solemn, this Thackeray would break into an imitation of a music-hall dance or sing a comic song. He also enjoyed casually improvising light verse while helping his daughters entertain their friends, who included the daughters of Charles Dickens. While carving a turkey at a party for children, he once sang out:

> Any little child that wants a little fowl
> Must raise its little hand and give a little howl!

And he had once turned to a little girl who was sitting uncomfortably, surrounded by adults, at a dinner table and asked:

> Little maid with sparkling eye,
> Will you have some mutton pie?
> Little maid with tender heart,
> Will you have some apple tart?

It was, however, the frosty, thin-skinned public figure, not the kind and rarely seen Thackeray, who became involved in perhaps the greatest of the Victorian literary feuds with his fellow novelist Charles Dickens.

On the surface, the relationship between the two giants of nineteenth-century English fiction had always seemed amicable enough. But beneath the surface, things had seldom been serene. Very early in his career Thackeray, hoping to make a living not from his writings but from his satiric drawings, had offered to illustrate Dickens' *The Pickwick Papers* and the offer had been rejected.

Understandably, Thackeray was rankled as *The Pickwick Papers* gained an enormous reputation for both Dickens and the illustrator he had finally chosen. And then Thackeray had watched enviously as Dickens' fame spread around the world, while his own reputation remained disappointingly slight. He had also watched as Dickens became one of the wealthiest writers who had ever lived, while his own irregular income was barely sufficient to cover his expenses.

Later, too, as his own books began to sell reasonably well, Thackeray still felt some chagrin over the far greater popularity of Dickens. He once recorded that one of his Christmas books, *Mrs. Perkins's Ball*, was finding many readers and that it was "a great success—the greatest I ever had." Then he added, with chagrin: ". . . very nearly as great as Dickens. That is, Perkins 500, Dickens 25,000—only that difference."

The extremely successful Dickens, on the other hand, after dominating the English literary scene for many years, now heard the voices of those who hailed Thackeray's *Vanity Fair*, and he realized that he had a rival. In addition, many of his friends resented the attention paid the relative newcomer and were even more acutely conscious of Thackeray's sudden rise. It was these fervid Dickensians—a group to whom Thomas Carlyle referred as the "squad"—who now began criticizing Thackeray both publicly and privately, reporting quickly to the sensitive Dickens any comment by Thackeray or his coterie that seemed insufficiently respectful to his genius.

To Thackeray, it was clear that Dickens and his friends found it difficult to "forgive" him his success with *Vanity Fair*. They behaved, Thackeray told a friend, "as if there was not room in the world for both of us!" In an atmosphere of such rivalry, only a spark was needed to set things off; and that spark was struck in May, 1858, while Thackeray was attending the derby at Epsom. For it was there that he met a friend who told him that Dickens was involved with a young actress named Ellen Ternan.

The origin of that report could be traced back to April, 1857, when the middle-aged and restless Dickens had gone backstage at a London theater to meet the members of the cast of the play *Atalanta*.

As he passed one dressing room, he heard a young actress sobbing. The solicitous Dickens asked what was troubling her, and Ellen Ternan told him that she was disturbed by the immodesty of the costume she had been given. Later, Dickens recorded, specifically if somewhat inelegantly, that her unhappiness was the result of her having "to show so much leg."

Dickens' second meeting with the small, fair-haired, rather pretty actress occurred in Manchester in August of the same year. He had agreed to produce and act in a melodrama, *The Frozen Deep*, at the Free Trade Hall in that city on the twenty-first and twenty-second of the month, and, perhaps by coincidence, Ellen, her mother, and her sister, were engaged to take the women's parts in the play.

The novelist had once considered a career for himself in the theater and he had a natural instinct for the stage. Now, coaching Ellen in her lines, he found her an apt pupil who tried to capture the exact inflection of his voice, and faithfully to duplicate the gestures he demonstrated. When each day's rehearsals ended, she sat at his feet and listened as he talked of the famous people he knew: fellow novelists, painters, political figures, and lords and ladies. Ellen, whose own life had been relatively limited despite her theatrical background, was fascinated, and, for his part, Dickens was at first flattered and then captivated by the attention of the simple, uncomplicated girl.

One day, he slipped away from the rehearsal hall and found his way to a jeweler's. There, he selected a bracelet for Ellen and asked that it be suitably engraved with her name. He then gave the jeweler his own name and address.

By mistake the gift was delivered to Mrs. Dickens in London, and this rather melodramatic incident, which Dickens might have used in one of his own novels, was the first hint Catherine Dickens had that her troubled marriage, which had somehow survived at least two previous infatuations on the part of Dickens, was once again in danger.

For many years, as Catherine Dickens was aware, Dickens had felt a growing disenchantment with his phlegmatic, perhaps not very intelligent, wife. "I seem always to be looking for something I have never found in life," he once wrote to a friend, and after his meeting with Ellen Ternan, he rightly or wrongly began to blame Catherine for whatever it was that was missing. "Poor Catherine and I are not made for each other, and there is no help for it," he confided to his biographer, John Forster, in September, 1857. "It is not only that she makes me uneasy and unhappy, but that I make her so too—and much more so. She is exactly what you know, in the way of being amiable and complying; but we are strangely ill-assorted for the bond there is between us. God knows she would have been a thousand times happier if she had married another kind of man, and that her avoidance of this destiny would have been at least equally good for us both. I am often cut to the heart by thinking what a pity it is, for her own sake, that I ever fell in her way . . ."

Then he added: ". . . reasons have been growing . . . which

make it all but hopeless that we should even try to struggle on. . . ."

To Victorians, such a situation was scandalous. Even the worldly Thackeray was appalled by the rumor of Dickens' domestic difficulties, for, among other things, he liked Catherine Dickens and considered her ill-used. After he returned to London, Thackeray was doubly shocked to hear an even more disturbing report. As he entered the Garrick Club one evening, a friend asked him if he had heard that Dickens was leaving Catherine because she was outraged by his disgraceful *affaire* with her own younger sister, Georgina Hogarth.

"No . . . such thing," Thackeray immediately replied, "It's with an actress."

Later, he talked about his reason for making this unfortunate remark. He would have said nothing at all about Dickens' personal problems under ordinary circumstances, he explained, but he "heard the other much worse story, whereupon I told mine to counteract it."

It was perhaps the greatest misjudgment of Thackeray's life, for, instead of counteracting the more vicious rumor, the remark simply added fuel to the fire. Already, Dickens was classifying everyone he knew into two groups: the "true friends," who assumed that he was absolutely right and that the luckless Catherine was absolutely wrong, and the "enemies," who either favored Catherine or felt that her side of the story deserved a hearing before a decision was reached. His followers immediately reported to him what his antagonist had said, and Dickens, his earlier suspicions of his rival's hostility apparently confirmed, put Thackeray's name near the top of the list of his "enemies."

Soon all literary England was divided between the two camps, and soon, too, this division was made irrevocable by the action of a completely unknown young journalist named

Edmund Yates. It was Yates—a "true friend" of Dickens who considered Thackeray a snob—who was to turn this deepening alienation into an open quarrel.

The twenty-seven-year-old Yates was a writer and editor of a small, unimportant penny paper called *Town Talk*. One of his responsibilities was the job of dropping in at the printer's just before press time each week to make certain that enough copy was available to fill the skimpy pages of his gossipy publication. And when he made his weekly visit to the shop early in June, 1858, he was told by the printer that a column was needed to fill the remaining space in the issue that was about to go to press.

Years later, still somewhat amazed by it all, Yates recalled that evening when he unwittingly brought on the battle of the giants. "I took off my coat, mounted a high stool at a high desk, and commenced to cudget my brains," he wrote. "It happened that in the previous week's number I had written a pen-and-pencil sketch of Dickens, which had given satisfaction and I felt I could not do better than follow on with a pen-portrait of his great rival."

Then, as the printer looked in impatiently from time to time, Yates scribbled an exceedingly gossipy—and very unflattering—word portrait of Thackeray, in the usual style of his publication. "His face is bloodless," Yates wrote, "and not particularly expressive, but remarkable for the fracture of the nose, the result of an accident in youth . . ."

He added a few details about other aspects of Thackeray's physical appearance, and then turned to the man's general deportment.

"No one meeting him could fail to recognise in him a gentleman," he wrote sneeringly, "his bearing is cold and uninviting, his style of conversation either openly cynical or affectedly goodnatured and benevolent; his bonhomie is forced, his wit biting, his pride easily touched . . ."

Then he focused on another aspect of his subject. Thackeray had lectured in the United States, and some Englishmen felt that he had pandered to the anti-British prejudices of the Americans. Now Yates wrote:

"No one succeeds better than Mr. Thackeray in cutting his coat according to his cloth. Here he flattered the aristocracy, but when he crossed the Atlantic, George Washington became the object of his worship, the 'Four Georges' the objects of his bitterest attacks. . . ."

The ambitious young journalist concluded the portrait with a conjecture regarding Thackeray's future career.

"Our own opinion," he wrote, "is that his success is on the wane; his writings never were understood or appreciated even by the middle classes; the aristocracy have been alienated by his American onslaught on their body; and the educated and refined are not sufficiently numerous to constitute an audience; moreover, there is a want of heart in all he writes, which is [not] to be balanced by the most brilliant sarcasm and the most perfect knowledge of the workings of the human heart."

Ordinarily, such an attack in so unimportant a journal as *Town Talk* would have received little notice and been soon forgotten. But now, one of Thackeray's friends, recalling that there had been another brief but vitriolic mention of Thackeray in an earlier issue of *Town Talk*, looked up the original item, and sent both old and new issues to Thackeray.

At once, Thackeray sat down to squash the offensive scribbler.

His letter began calmly:

"I have received two numbers of a little paper called 'Town Talk' containing notices respecting myself, of which, as I learn from the best authority, you are the writer."

He disposed of the first brief item in a single sentence:

"In the first article of 'Literary Talk,' " he wrote, "you think fit to publish an incorrect account of my private dealings with my publishers."

Then he gave an indignant summary of the second article.

"In this week's number appears a so-called 'Sketch' containing a description of my manners, person, and conversation, and an account of my literary works, which of course you are at liberty to praise or condemn as a literary critic. But you state, with regard to my conversation, that it is either 'frankly [sic] cynical or affectedly benevolent and goodnatured;' and of my lectures that in some I showed 'an extravagant adulation of rank and position . . .'

"As I understand your phrases, you impute insincerity to me when I speak good-naturedly in private; assign dishonorable motives to me for sentiments w^h I have delivered in public, and charge me with advancing statements w^h I have never delivered at all."

The letter grew increasingly angry as Thackeray's pen raced over the pages.

"Had your remarks been written by a person unknown to me, I should have noticed them no more than other calumnies," Thackeray wrote, "but as we have shaken hands more than once, and met hitherto on friendly terms, (You may write to one of your employers, Mr Carruthers of Edinburgh, & ask whether very lately I did not speak of you in the most friendly manner) I am obliged to take notice of articles w^h I consider to be, not offensive & unfriendly merely, but slanderous and untrue.

"We meet at a Club [the Garrick] where, before you were born I believe, I & other gentlemen have been in the habit of talking, without any idea that our conversation would supply paragraphs for professional vendors of 'Literary Talk,' and I don't remember that out of that Club I ever exchanged 6 words with you. Allow me to inform you that the talk w^h you may have heard there is not intended for newspaper remark; & to beg, as I have a right to do, that you will refrain from printing comments upon my private conversation; that you will forego discussions however blundering, on my private affairs; & that you will henceforth please to consider any question of my personal truth & sincerity as quite out of the province of your criticism."

To be so castigated by one of the "enemy" was a jarring experience for the youthful Yates. He was first astonished by this letter, then angered. His articles about Thackeray were no more malicious than many of the sketches he was accustomed to write about other public figures, and he soon convinced himself he had been very badly used.

"I think it must be admitted by the most impartial reader that this letter is severe to the point of cruelty," he later recorded in his memoirs. "Whatever the silliness and impertinence of the article, it was scarcely calculated to have provoked so curiously bitter an outburst of personal feeling against the writer; that in comparison with the offence committed by me, the censure administered by Mr. Thackeray is almost ludicrously exaggerated."

Yates also convinced himself—and with some justification—that Thackeray had less claim to immunity from such a public attack than anyone else in London, since Thackeray had, after all, a long history of publishing his own parodies on fellow novelists. And this conviction spurred Yates to his own defense. In an angry reply to Thackeray's letter he reviewed past offenses by Thackeray against the dignity and privacy of prominent people.

With more caution than he usually displayed, Yates then decided to show Thackeray's letter and his own reply to a fellow member of the Garrick Club—someone who would know them both. Unfortunately, the first member he planned to consult was not at home. Then, of all people, Yates turned to Charles Dickens.

Dickens was dressing to go to dinner when Yates dropped by. But when he was told that the matter involved Thackeray, he decided to take a few minutes to counsel his young friend. He told Yates frankly that the second article in *Town Talk* was "in bad taste" and "would have been infinitely better left alone." But he demonstrated his partisanship for Yates by being indignant about Thackeray's letter.

Encouraged, Yates now showed Dickens the reply he had written. No, Dickens said, it would not do. It was "too flippant and violent." Dickens would show the young man how this kind of thing should be handled. A new reply was drafted, in Yates's handwriting, but the words were dictated by Dickens. It read:

"I have to acknowledge receipt of your letter. You will excuse my pointing out to you that it is absurd to suppose me bound to accept your angry 'understanding' of my 'phrases.' I do not accept it in the least: I altogether reject it."

With the cold and formal tone firmly set, the brief Dickens-Yates letter continued:

"I cannot characterise your letter in any other terms than those in which you characterise the article which has given you so much offence. If your letter to me were not both 'slanderous and untrue,' I should readily have discussed its subject with you and avowed my earnest and frank desire to set right anything I may have left wrong. Your letter being what it is, I have nothing to add to my present reply."

When he received this note, Thackeray decided to take further action. And as a Clubman, he decided that the appropriate action was to bundle up Yates's articles, a copy of his

own letter, and a copy of Yates's reply, and submit these to the
governing committee of the Garrick Club.

In a formal petition, he asked the committee "to decide
whether the complaints I have against Mr. Yates are not well
founded, and whether the practice of publishing such articles
. . . will not be fatal to the comfort of the Club, and is not
intolerable in a Society of Gentlemen."

After some discussion, members of the committee informed
both parties that they hoped a quiet solution could be achieved
in the unfortunate situation. Perhaps, they suggested judiciously, Yates could clear up the entire matter by apologizing to
Mr. Thackeray.

It seemed to him, Yates replied, that the Garrick Club
should not involve itself in this private quarrel. He reminded
the committee that he had not mentioned the Garrick Club
in his *Town Talk* columns.

The committee was, however, controlled by Thackeray's
friends, not those of Dickens, and its members refused to be
moved. Soon a demand "to make an ample apology to Mr.
Thackeray, or to retire from the Club" was received by the
recalcitrant Mr. Yates.

Now Yates shifted his ground. He was willing to apologize
to the Club (which he had not mentioned in his articles)
but he would, he said, never apologize to Thackeray (whom
he had attacked by name).

Again the committee called a meeting, this time of the
entire membership of the Club, so that the subject might be
considered thoroughly. This meeting was to take place on
July sixth.

Suddenly, in the midst of all this maneuvering, Dickens
made a sweeping personal decision. He owed it to his faithful
readers, he decided, to take them into his confidence about

his marital problems. He had already moved Mrs. Dickens out of his house and had settled six hundred pounds a year upon her, and since reports of the separation were now heard everywhere in London, he felt it only proper that he should prepare statements to be published in *The Times*, in *Punch*, in his own magazine, *Household Words*, and perhaps in a few other magazines and newspapers!

A horrified friend talked him out of offering a "personal statement" to *The Times*, and his old friend Mark Lemon argued that such a document would look rather out of place in a humor magazine like *Punch*. But on June 12, 1858, Dickens succeeded in printing a rather vague and mystifying statement on the front page of his *Household Words*. After referring to certain rumors, he announced that they were "abominably false" and he added that "whosoever repeats one of them after this denial, will lie as wilfully and as foully as it is possible for any false witness to lie before Heaven and earth."

He had already prepared a more detailed statement which he sent to Arthur Smith, who served as manager for Dickens' public readings.

"You have not only my full permission to show this," an accompanying letter said, "but I beg you to show [it], to any one who wishes to do me right, or to any one who may have been misled into doing me wrong."

Smith let a reporter read the extraordinary document, and it soon appeared in the New York *Tribune*.

"Mrs. Dickens and I have lived unhappily together for many years," the statement began. "Hardly any one who has known us intimately can fail to have known that we are, in all respects of character and temperament, wonderfully unsuited to each other. I suppose that no two people, not vicious in themselves, ever were joined together, who had a greater difficulty in understanding one another, or who had less in common. . . ."

After crediting Georgina Hogarth, Mrs. Dickens' younger sister, with keeping the family together and being "playmate, nurse, instructress, friend, protectress, adviser and companion" to the Dickens children, he added what he evidently considered a kind estimate of his wife's failure as a mother:

"In the manly consideration toward Mrs. Dickens which I owe to my wife, I will merely remark of her that the peculiarity of her character has thrown all the children on some one else." His wife recognized her own shortcomings, he continued, and had often said "it would be better for her to go away and live apart." He referred to "a mental disorder under which she sometimes labors" that made her "unfit for the life she had to lead as my wife . . ."

His financial settlement on Mrs. Dickens, he said, had been "as generous as if Mrs. Dickens were a lady of distinction and I a man of fortune."

Then he concluded with his own vague comment on his affair with Ellen Ternan:

"Two wicked persons," he wrote, "who should have spoken very differently of me, in consideration of earned respect and gratitude, have . . . coupled with this separation the name of a young lady for whom I have a great attachment and regard. I will not repeat her name—I honor it too much. Upon my soul and honor, there is not on this earth a more virtuous and spotless creature than that young lady. I know her to be innocent and pure, and as good as my own dear daughters. . . ."

There is still some uncertainty whether he and Ellen Ternan were actually living together at the time he issued this statement. In fact, some Dickens enthusiasts still deny that he ever had an "affair" with the young actress. But letters and documents have since supplied convincing evidence that they soon did live together under the assumed names of "Mr.

and Mrs. Charles Tringham," and that neighbors were told that Mr. Tringham was writing a mystery story.

On July sixth, the members of the Garrick Club held their general meeting to consider the dispute between Yates and Thackeray. The incident had now produced a "frightful mess, muddle, complication, and botheration," as Dickens later wrote.

On Yates's side were Dickens, Wilkie Collins, and a group of writers who were considered wild young Bohemians. But Thackeray had the support of those Club members who were active on *Punch*—and of most of the members who considered themselves true-born gentlemen, including Sir Charles Taylor, who was a famous sportsman, and such well-known figures as Anthony Trollope and John Blackwood.

That the gentlemen outnumbered the Bohemians was clearly indicated by the final vote of seventy for Thackeray and forty-six for Yates. The result: a resolution was adopted requiring Yates to apologize to Thackeray or to retire from the Garrick Club.

Dickens was furious. He said the members who had chastised Yates had "gone perfectly mad," and he denounced the group as acting with "preposterous imbecility." Then Yates, still urged on by Dickens, considered the possibility of bringing a lawsuit against the Club to force it to readmit him. And, when someone told him that he would have no cause to sue unless he were physically ejected from the Garrick, Yates explained this legal problem to the Club secretary, who obligingly co-operated in taking him lightly by one arm and gently ejecting him. Yates even discussed his proposed suit with one of the most prominent—and most highly paid—members of the bar. But he lost interest when this barrister, having some idea of the limited amount of money an obscure gossip writer might be able to borrow, told him that the suit could drag on for years and drain away hundreds of pounds.

It was Dickens who now managed to fan the flames of the feud. He made the unfortunate mistake of writing to Thackeray personally to propose a conference "between me, as representing Mr. Yates, and an appointed friend of yours, as representing you, with the hope and purpose of some quiet accommodation of this deplorable matter, which will satisfy the feelings of all concerned." Realizing that Thackeray, encouraged by his victory at the general meeting, might be less than enthusiastic about such a conference, Dickens also added a note to the letter, in which he asked Thackeray to burn the message if the proposal did not appeal to him.

Thackeray replied curtly.

"I grieve to gather from your letter," he wrote Dickens, "that you were Mr. Yates's adviser in the dispute between him and me." In fact, he had made up his mind to this effect months before, so that when a friend had chastised him for getting involved in a public dispute with someone as "young and unimportant" as Yates, Thackeray had replied that his quarrel was not really with Yates. "I am hitting the man behind him," he said.

More than two years after writing this letter to Dickens, Thackeray was seated in the Drury Lane theater one evening when Dickens and Wilkie Collins entered the adjoining stall. After the first shock, the two rivals shook hands, but they exchanged not a single word.

". . . if he read my feelings on my face as such a clever fellow would," Thackeray wrote a friend, "he knows that I have found him out."

In January, 1859, the defeated Yates published a scurrilous poem in the *Illustrated Times*, and signed it, "By W.M. T--CK---Y." It read:

I show the vices which besmirch you,
    The slime with which you're covered o'er,
Strip off each rag from female virtue,
    And drag to light each festering sore.

All men alive are rogues and villains,
    All women drabs, all children cursed;
I tell them this, and draw their shillin's,
    They highest pay when treated worst.

I sneer at every human feeling,
    Which truth suggests, or good men praise;
Then, tongue within my cheek concealing,
    Write myself "Cynic"—for it pays!

But when six members of the *Illustrated Times* staff threatened to quit in disgust if such attacks continued, Yates finally subsided. Though he later became an editor, a minor novelist (vaguely in the style of Dickens), and an indefatigable writer of memoirs, his life from that moment on was really a literary anti-climax.

The ending for the Thackeray and Dickens feud was appropriately Victorian. It might have been written by either writer for one of his own novels. There was still one strong tie between the two men. During Thackeray's years of obscurity, the daughters of both men had become close friends, and Thackeray himself had developed a particularly strong affection for Dickens' daughter, Kate.

As the years passed, Thackeray often dropped by to talk with Kate. Sometimes he spent hours with her, even discussing her father's writing habits, his books, and his daily life. Clearly, the feud continued to bother him, for, despite everything, he had always admired Dickens' work. And in this frame of mind, one day he suddenly said to Kate: "It is ridiculous that your father and I should be placed in a position of enmity towards one another."

Kate agreed.

So he quickly added: "You know he is more in the wrong than I am."

Nor did Kate dispute this point. She did say, however, that it would be necessary for Thackeray to make the first move in any reconciliation. Dickens, she explained, was "more shy of speaking."

It was a few weeks later that Thackeray was in the lobby of another of his clubs, the Athenaeum, when Dickens walked by without nodding or offering a greeting.

Thackeray took a few steps toward Dickens, reached for his hand, and said: "We [have] been foolish long enough . . ."

He said later that he saw tears in Dickens' eyes.

At his next meeting with Kate, Thackeray mentioned the reconciliation.

"How did it happen?" she asked.

"Oh, your father knew he was wrong and was full of apologies, . . ." said Thackeray.

"You know you are not telling me the truth," Kate said. ". . . what really did happen?"

Then Thackeray described the actual scene. He told her that he had held out his hand.

"Your father grasped it very cordially," he said, "—and—and we are friends again, thank God!"

A few days after that reconciliation, Thackeray suffered a "cerebral effusion," following an attack of indigestion, and died. At his funeral, the sentimental Dickens was among the mourners, and in September, 1870, an anonymous writer in *Harper's* Magazine described the scene which took place:

"I remember Dickens at the grave of Thackeray . . . ," he wrote. "When all others had turned aside from the grave, he still stood there, as if rooted to the spot, watching with almost haggard eyes every spadeful of dust that was thrown upon it. Walking away with some friends, he began to talk, but presently . . . his voice quavered a little, and shaking hands all round rapidly, he went off alone."

MR. WELLS

& MR. HENRY JAMES

Reach a polite but

Hopeless impasse.

ON THE evening of January 5, 1895, *Guy Domville*, a drama by the American-born expatriate novelist, Henry James, was presented in London at the St. James Theater. The result was one of the most disastrous opening nights in the long history of the English stage and, for its author, one of the most painful experiences of his life.

James was a great novelist, but he was also a ponderous, pompous, somewhat absurd public figure; an Anglophile; a sometimes brilliant but often wearying conversationalist who frequently got lost in the maze of his own sentences; and a writer who, though greatly respected, was little read. He himself sometimes felt, he said, that his readers were preceding him to the grave, since the sales of his books declined with each passing year.

Thus, although he detested and denounced the money-grubbing of his fellow Americans, Henry James had decided, by 1895, that it would be very nice to increase his comparatively moderate income.

He had, however, found it impossible to write acceptably for the newspapers, after an abortive experience with the New York *Tribune*. The editor of that paper, Whitelaw Reid, had told him that his letters from Europe were really "too good" for a newspaper and had asked him to try writing in a less literary style; to which the usually stuffy James had replied, with some humor: "If my letters have been 'too good' I am honestly afraid that they are the poorest I can do, especially for the money!" He was also convinced that his short stories and novels could not be made more palatable to the masses. But he felt that he had learned a thing or two about writing plays that should earn him a fortune in the theater, and, with money coming in from two or three successful dramas, he hoped to live as comfortably as the English aristocrats whose homes he loved to visit.

And, of course, being Henry James, he also felt he could at the same time raise the deplorably low tone of the London theater.

James did not witness the opening performance of his *Guy Domville*. After some hesitation, he had decided instead to look in on the work of his fellow playwright, Oscar Wilde, whose *An Ideal Husband* had opened only two nights previously to enthusiastic reviews. Now, watching Wilde's production, James was appalled by what he saw.

To him, *An Ideal Husband* seemed ". . . so helpless, so crude, so bad, so clumsy, feeble and vulgar," as he later wrote, that he was completely baffled. Yet the play was, unquestionably, a success. The audience laughed at all the obvious jokes, listened appreciatively to the epigrams, and then applauded stormily at the end of the tiresome farce.

". . . *that* gave me the most fearful apprehension," James also wrote. If this was the kind of thing audiences liked, his hopes for *Guy Domville* might, James feared, be unwarranted.

Emerging from the Haymarket, which was playing the Wilde piece, James started across St. James square to the theater which was offering *Guy Domville*. Still puzzled by the reaction of the audience to *An Ideal Husband*, he paused. He was, as he later admitted, ". . . paralysed by . . . terror . . . afraid to go on and learn more" about the fate of his own play.

Actually, *Guy Domville* had gotten off to a promising start. The dialogue was rather more involved and convoluted than theater audiences generally expected, but, after all, this was the work of the great Henry James and no one expected it to be easy to follow. Yet, after giving respectful attention to the first act, the members of the audience found themselves bored by the tedious second act. Especially in the cheaper seats —in the gallery and the pit—there were unmistakable signs of growing restlessness.

And then, unfortunately, as one observer later recalled, an elderly actress "entered in a costume which struck them [the audience] as grotesque." ". . . at the unexpected laughter," as the observer recorded, "the actress took fright, she became timid, apologetic, she tried to efface herself. Now the spectacle of a stately dame whose balloon-like skirts half filled the stage and whose plumes smote the heavens trying to efface herself was genuinely ludicrous, and the laugh became a roar. After this the audience got out of hand; they grew silly and cruel and ready to jeer at everything."

It was no wonder, then, that when the noted actor George Alexander, who played Guy Domville, announced dramatically: "I'm the *last*, my lord, of the Domvilles," the inevitable occurred.

"It's a damn good thing you are!" shouted a patron in the gallery, in response to the line.

All this had happened, however, while James was at the nearby Haymarket Theater trying to understand what the people around him saw in Wilde's artificial lines.

Now, as James entered the playhouse just as his play ended he heard only the feeble applause following his final curtain. But he did not realize that few in the galleries or the pit were joining in even this perfunctory gesture, nor that the disenchanted playgoers in these sections were sitting in silence, hostile in their boredom and uncertain how best to express their true opinion of the drama.

It was even more unfortunate for James that a few of his devoted fans sitting in the stalls now called out: "Author! Author!"

George Alexander, who was still on stage, could have ignored the polite call, but as the observer later recalled, "Disaster was too much for Alexander that night. A spasm of hate for the writer of . . . [the fatal lines he had been forced to utter as an actor] surely must have seized him. With incredible cruelty he led the doomed James, still not understanding clearly how things were with him, to the middle of the stage, and there the pit and gallery had him."

The always-correct James bowed modestly to the audience. Apparently, he had rehearsed a little speech for this occasion. But the words were never uttered.

"I have never heard any sound more devastating than the crescendo of booing" that met the startled James, the observer later reported. "The gentle applause of the stalls was altogether overwhelmed. For a moment or so James faced the storm, his round face white, his mouth opening and shutting, and then Alexander, I hope in a contrite mood, snatched him back into the wings. . . ."

The observer who was later to record George Alexander's cruelty and Henry James's confusion in such vivid detail was an ambitious young reporter on the *Pall Mall Gazette,* who was destined to achieve his own international fame in a different literary milieu. His name was H.G. Wells.

Just a week or so before the opening of *Guy Domville,* the editor of the *Gazette* had called in the then-inexperienced Wells and asked him whether he would like to write dramatic criticism for the journal.

"I'm willing to have a shot at it, . . ." said the twenty-nine-year-old Wells in his unmistakably Cockney twang. Then he confessed to the editor that he had been to the theater only twice in his life.

"Exactly what I want," the editor replied. And he explained why: "You won't be in the gang."

For the brash and self-confident Wells, the assignment was a welcome opportunity. It would enable him to gain a close look at those who were running England and the British Empire—a group he had already classified as nincompoops and fools. He felt sure that such people would gather for the opening of a new play by Henry James or Oscar Wilde, and he considered it important to meet them—not because he expected to learn anything from them, but because he was certain he could sooner or later teach them how wrong and misguided they were. His own days as a writer-for-hire were now drawing to a close, since a publisher had already accepted the manuscript of his *Time Machine,* the first of the books of science fiction that were to make him both famous and wealthy.

Wells's first assignment as a theater critic was to review the fabulously successful *An Ideal Husband.* Then, two evenings later, he attended the far more memorable first night of *Guy*

Domville and recorded the agony of Henry James. It was his initial contact with the aging writer who was soon to adopt him as something of a protégé, who was to offer him advice that other young novelists would have considered invaluable, and who was finally to renounce him as a writer who, in James's words, had "cut loose from literature."

And yet, in keeping with the character of Henry James, few feuds in the history of literature were to be so high-minded, so polite—and so irreconcilable.

The differences between the youthful H.G. Wells and the mature Henry James were so basic and numerous that it seems almost miraculous that they ever knew each other well enough to have started a feud. James was fastidious and was preoccupied in many of his works with matters of taste and high society. Wells could be slovenly, considered James's taste artificial, and found any young scientist far more interesting than a room full of dukes and duchesses. James was an artist who seemed to feel the chief value of life was to give him subjects for his novels. Wells wanted to have a hand in reshaping life and constructing a new world, and considered his books merely useful tools toward these ends. James would agonize for hours over a single sentence, refining and refining it until sometimes only his most devoted readers cared to thread their way through the innumerable clauses he found necessary for communication of his exact meaning. Wells scoffed as such painstaking craftsmanship, and preferred to state his ideas so that even the slowest reader could follow him without difficulty. James was an artist, however tortured his sentences finally became. Wells was a propagandist, however skillfully he stated his sometimes complex ideas.

Long after their friendship had ended, Wells tried to sum up the basic differences in their ways of looking at life, and in trying to express the essence of these differences he ended by discussing James's hats, caps, and canes. "On the table [of

James's house] . . . at Rye," Wells recalled in his autobiography, "lay a number of caps and hats, each with its
appropriate gloves and sticks, a tweed cap and a stout stick
for the Marsh, a soft comfortable deerstalker if he were to
turn aside to the Golf Club, a light-brown felt hat and a cane
for a morning walk down to the Harbour, a grey felt with a
black band and a gold-headed cane of greater importance, if
afternoon calling in the town was afoot." James, he said, was
not only certain that one particular correct costume should
be worn for each particular occasion, but he also felt that
"correct behavior" could be equally well defined.

To Wells, of course, all this was preposterous.

Yet something drew these two ill-matched men together,
and the mutual attraction was strong enough to sustain their
friendship for sixteen years. It seems likely that the fundamental differences were in themselves part of the attraction.
James, who always knew his own secure place in society, was
fascinated by the cheeky Wells, who was the son of a gardener
and a lady's maid and who had broken into English drawing
rooms through the force of his talent. Wells, even when bored
by James's endlessly modified sentences and his exhausting
search for the precise word, enjoyed studying this representative of the world of fashion and culture, which both intrigued
and repelled him. And both were able to talk about books
with unflagging interest, even though they viewed them in
almost opposite ways. To James, furthermore, Wells was a
devoted if sometimes critical reader of his books at a time
when they were attracting fewer and fewer readers. And to
Wells, James was the enormously intelligent old master who
took Well's work seriously at a time when most critics still
treated his novels as curiosities or trifles.

Yet, though the great Henry James was not only willing
but eager to come down from his pedestal into the rough and
brawling world of H.G. Wells, the fundamental differences
between the two were certain, sooner or later, to lead to a

clash—however polite and restrained it might be. For Wells was a crude and careless writer and James could not compromise for long with his standards. Even in his own milieu, James's inability to give full praise to anything he considered even slightly blemished had often led to some delicate but embarrassing confrontations of other writers. He had a polite habit of almost always praising the work of others in sometimes extravagant terms at the beginning. But then, his stubborn perfectionism compelled him to introduce one of his famous "howevers," which was a signal that he was about to whittle away at the compliment until nothing was left.

The American novelist Edith Wharton, who, like James, preferred to live in Europe, once wrote of such an occasion. One of her short stories had been published in *Scribner's* magazine, and Mrs. Wharton's husband asked James whether he had seen it.

"Oh, yes, my dear Edward," James replied, "I've read the little work—of course I've read it." He paused, and then offered his generous compliment: "Admirable, admirable; a masterly little achievement."

But he couldn't leave the matter there. Instead, he turned to Edith Wharton herself, who had overheard the remark.

"Full of a terrifying benevolence," as Mrs. Wharton later recalled, he said to her, "Of course so accomplished a mistress of the art would not, without deliberate intention, have given the tale so curiously conventional a treatment."

He paused again.

"Though indeed, in the given case," he continued, "no treatment *but* the conventional was possible; which might conceivably, my dear lady, on further consideration, have led you to reject your subject as—er—in itself a totally unsuitable one."

In James's defense, Mrs. Wharton also recorded her explanation of this roundabout criticism from her colleague.

"Yet it would be a mistake to imagine that he deliberately

started out to destroy my wretched tale," she has written. "He had begun, I am sure, with the sincere intention of praising it; but no sooner had he opened his lips than he was over-mastered by the need to speak the truth, and the whole truth, about anything connected with the art which was sacred to him. . . . On all subjects but that of letters his sincerity was tempered by an almost exaggerated tenderness; but when *le métier* was in question no gentler emotion prevailed."

It was this James, always kindly but frequently inept, who was now to bumble so badly in his earliest meeting with Wells. The two first actually met about three years after the *Guy Domville* disaster, at a time when James found it increasingly comforting to his own ego to take an interest in promising younger writers.

During this period, Wells had been trying to prove he could make his living as a writer without depending upon journalism for his regular income. It had been a long struggle, and sometimes a discouraging one. Much earlier, he had kept a careful accounting of his efforts and his extremely small reward for a year's work. It had read:

1 short story	Sold	£1
1 novel	Burnt	—
1 novel unfinished	Burnt	—
Much Comic Poetry	Lost	—
Some Comic Prose	Sent away never returned	—
Humorous essay	Globe did not return	—
Sundry Stories	Burnt	—
1 story	Wandering	—
Poem	Burnt	—
		£1

In 1896, too busy to keep careful records, he had simply summed up his income from his writings as £1,056, 7s. 9d. Yet, there were still to be a few uncertain years ahead before Wells became a commercially valuable property to book, magazine, and newspaper publishers. And, in 1898, his prosperity was briefly threatened by a recurrence of a kidney ailment that left him depressed about unpaid medical bills and uncompleted books.

It was during this stage of his career that, as he was recuperating at a seaside cottage, he was one day startled to look up and recognize two unannounced and unexpected callers: Henry James and the writer Edmund Gosse.

James and Gosse were both patrons of the Royal Literary Fund, established to aid writers during periods of adversity, and they had come to Wells's cottage on a mission of mercy: to see if he needed assistance in meeting his bills.

But the visit got off to an uncomfortable start. Wells did not realize what their real mission was and so was frankly baffled about why they had come. He had seen James only a time or two since that disastrous evening in the St. James's Theater three years earlier, and he had not thought of Gosse as a close friend either.

As the afternoon wore on, the almost comically correct James asked a few questions that were personal and prying.

Wells became still more puzzled. But, always ready to talk, he spoke freely about his work, his health, his plans, and even his finances.

After a while, the two older writers gravely shook his hand, wished him luck, and went on their way.

For years Wells puzzled over that strange afternoon, until he finally realized why he'd had the unexpected visit: his two callers, recognizing that he did not need money as desperately as they had supposed, had not wanted to offend the young writer by telling him the real reason for their visit. Thus they had departed as mysteriously as they had arrived.

But the Henry James who needed the comfort of helping younger writers had nevertheless been impressed by Wells. And soon after that mysterious visit, when Wells recovered his health and was successfully launched on his career, the great James virtually adopted the younger writer as one of his protégés.

In fact, the kindly James seemed ready to find enormous merit in every one of Wells's works. He took pains to call Wells's science-fiction story, *When the Sleeper Awakes,* a "magnificent romance," when it was published, and he wrote the young author that his *Tales of Space and Time* "fill me with wonder and admiration." He called Wells's *Anticipations* "brilliant," found *The First Men in the Moon* "stupendous," and said that *Mankind in the Making* "thrills and transports me." While he also expressed an occasional reservation about some of Wells's novels, James's early letters were filled with such extravagant praise. After reading *A Modern Utopia* and *Kipps,* he wrote to Wells:

"Let me tell you, . . . simply, that they have left me prostrate with admiration, and that you are, for me, more than ever, the most interesting 'literary man' of your generation—in fact, the only interesting one." He added: "I am lost in amazement at the diversity of your genius."

Clearly, this unquestioning—and largely undeserved—praise could not continue indefinitely, the more so since, along with an occasional work of some value, the hasty and impatient Wells was also churning out one crude, undistinguished novel after another. Sooner or later, the honest Henry James would be forced to recognize that his young "genius" was capable of producing trash.

Thus, as Wells's books began to occupy more and more

space on James's bookshelves, the old master's uncontrollable need to speak the truth brought a gradual change in the tone of his letters to his young protégé. And, in 1909, Wells discovered that the master could offer well-mannered complaints as well as compliments, after sending James a copy of his newest novel, *Ann Veronica.*

This time, James, as was his custom, began with extravagant praise:

"I took down *Ann Veronica* in deep rich draughts during the two days following your magnanimous 'donation' of her," he wrote to Wells. ". . . you stand out intensely vivid and alone, making nobody else signify at all. And this has never been more the case than in A.V., where your force and life and ferocious sensibility and heroic cheek all take effect in an extraordinary wealth and truth and beauty and *fury* of impressionism."

Then, for the first time in his correspondence with Wells, the famous pause, the dangerous moment that always preceded James's "howevers," became almost visible on the notepaper. For now James abruptly shifted course.

"I don't think the girl herself—her projected Ego—the best thing in the book . . . ," he began. Then, having hinted that the very Ann Veronica about whom the book *Ann Veronica* had been written might have deserved a more expert presentation, he finally came out flatly and said so. "I think it [the portrait of the character Ann] rather wants clearness and *nuances,*" he wrote.

It was all very polite. But it was also very clear that James was at last unable to conceal the fact that he and Wells were at opposite ends of the literary pole.

When *The New Machiavelli* reached him in 1911, James again spoke of Wells's "great gift" and his "big feeling for life," and said that the first half of the book was "alive and kicking and sprawling! . . . vivid and rich and strong."

Then came the customary pause, and there followed:

". . . I make my remonstrance—for I do remonstrate—bear upon the bad service you have done your cause by riding so hard again that accurst autobiographic form which puts a premium on the loose, the improvised, the cheap and the easy. Save in the fantastic and the romantic . . . it has no authority, no persuasive or convincing force—its grasp of reality and truth isn't strong and disinterested. . . . There is, to my vision, no authentic, and no really interesting and no *beautiful*, report of things on the novelist's . . . part unless a particular detachment has operated, unless the great stewpot or crucible of the imagination, of the observant and recording and interpreting mind in short, has intervened and played its part . . ."

More than a month later, Wells, having assimilated his critic's sweeping letter, wrote James: ". . . I think I wholly agree and kiss the rod. . . . But oh! some day when I'm settled-er if ever, I will do better. . . ."

The hopeless exchange might have continued in this general vein indefinitely, except for one development: *The Times Literary Supplement* three years later asked James to give his evaluation of "The Younger Generation" of novelists, and, after much hesitation, James agreed.

It was, James was fully aware, a difficult assignment, for many of the writers he would be discussing were the young men he considered his friends, and he was torn between his desire to be kind and his absolute compulsion to speak the truth about the art to which he had dedicated his life.

He undertook the task in his usual manner, but this time he was not as successful as usual. Early in the essay he made one comment about hastily written and hastily published novels that undoubtedly troubled two of his young friends and protégés, Hugh Walpole and H.G. Wells.

"Never was the reservoir so bubblingly and noisily full [of novels], . . . and this tide, swollen by extravagant cheap contribution, the increase of affluents turbid and unstrained, shows us the number of ways in which the democratic example, once gathering momentum, sets its mark on societies and seasons that stand in its course. . . ."

Wells was never quite sure just what James meant to say about him in this essay, but, after rereading several ambiguous comments, he did decide that he disliked James's estimate of his importance.

Wells's confusion arose quite naturally from the perennial Jamesian custom of first giving praise and then taking it away. One comment in "The Younger Generation" seemed extremely generous: H.G. Wells "affects us as taking all knowledge for his province and as inspiring in us to the very highest degree the confidence enjoyed by himself . . . enjoyed, we feel, with a breadth with which it has been given no one of his fellow-craftsmen to enjoy anything."

But then James said:

"Such things as 'The New Machiavelli,' 'Marriage,' 'The Passionate Friends,' are so very much more attestations of the presence of material than of an interest in the use of it that we ask ourselves again and again why so fondly neglected a state of leakage comes not to be fatal . . . we wince at a certain quite peculiarly gratuitous sacrifice to the casual in 'Marriage' very much as at seeing some fine and indispensable little part of a mechanism slip through profane fingers and lose itself."

Now the correspondence had, in effect, been placed on the public record, and Wells was able to convince himself that he was fully justified in following the old master's example. He had rarely accepted even the most restrained criticism from anyone except James without striking back. One observer had already noted that when Wells reacted to even the gentlest remonstrances he "wounded and injured often beyond cure. . . ." Unwittingly, he was about to do that again, and his victim was now to be the kindly and honest James.

The wound was inflicted by a curious book, bearing the lengthy title of *Boon, the Mind of the Race, the Wild Asses of the Devil, and the Last Trump*. This hastily assembled volume, which was to become commonly known simply as *Boon*, included some sketches Wells had written years earlier, but the section that readers turned to first was the most recently composed one. The section was entitled "Of Art, of Literature, of Mr. Henry James."

Perhaps with more malice than he could ever acknowledge, Wells wrote:

". . . James's denatured people are only the equivalent in fiction of those egg-faced, black-haired ladies, who sit and sit, in the Japanese colour-prints, the unresisting stuff for an arrangement of blacks. . . ."

After assembling a few such "eviscerated people," Wells said, James then began to make up stories. "What stories they are!" he now wrote. "Concentrated on suspicion, on a gift, on possessing a 'piece' of old furniture, on what a little girl may or may not have noted in an emotional situation. These people cleared for artistic treatment never make lusty love, never go to angry war, never shout at an election or perspire at poker . . ."

According to Wells, James's characters spent endless days nosing out suspicions, "hint by hint, link by link." And he asked: "Have you ever known living human beings [to] do that?" He went on to complain: "The thing his novel is *about* is always there. It is like a church lit but without a congregation to distract you, with every light and line focused on the high altar. And on the altar, very reverently placed, intensely there, is a dead kitten, an egg-shell, a bit of string. . . ."

In writing these novels, Wells continued, James "brings up

every device of language to state and define. Bare verbs he rarely tolerates. He splits his infinitives and fills them up with adverbial stuffing. . . . His vast paragraphs sweat and struggle . . . And all for tales of nothingness. . . . It is leviathan retrieving pebbles. It is a magnificent but painful hippopotamus resolved at any cost, even at the cost of its dignity, upon picking up a pea . . ."

In accordance with past custom, Wells sent one of the first copies of *Boon* to one of James's London clubs, expecting once again to receive one of those famous, friendly, self-conscious letters. After some weeks, on July 6, 1915, the aging and weary James explained why his acknowledgment of Wells's newest work had been so long delayed:

"I was given yesterday at a club your volume *Boon, etc.* . . . which . . . you kindly sent . . . me and which . . . appears to have lurked there for a considerable time undelivered. I have just been reading, to acknowledge it intelligently, a considerable number of its pages . . ."

But even James, though still polite, was unable to devise an opening compliment to precede his "however." He plunged in at once with an evaluation.

". . . to be perfectly frank," he wrote, "I have been . . . beaten for the first time—or rather for the first time but one —by a book of yours: I haven't found the current of it draw me on and on this time—as unfailingly and irresistibly [as] before (which I have repeatedly let you know)."

He had, he said, however, ". . . more or less mastered your appreciation of H.J., which I have found very curious and interesting, after a fashion—though it has naturally not filled me with a fond elation. It is difficult of course for a writer to put himself *fully* in the place of another writer who finds him extraordinarily futile and void, and who is moved to publish that to the world . . ."

Still, he had to make the effort to see himself as Wells saw him. He wrote: ". . . the fact that a mind as brilliant as yours *can* resolve me into such an unmitigated mistake, can't enjoy me in anything like the degree in which I like to think I may be enjoyed, makes me greatly want to fix myself, for as long as my nerves will stand it, with such a pair of eyes. . . ."

Clearly, however, his sensitive nerves could not stand it very long. ". . . one *has* to fall back on one's sense of one's good parts—one's own sense," he admitted, "and I at least should have to do that, I think, even if your picture were painted with a more searching brush." Then, after an explanation of his own purpose in writing a novel, James concluded with uncharacteristic abruptness. "However, there are too many things to say," he wrote, "and I don't think your chapter is really inquiring enough to entitle you to expect all of them. . . ."

Two days later, the abashed and apologetic Wells responded.

"You write me so kind and frank a letter after my offences that I find it an immense embarrassment to reply to you," he began.

Then he explained why he had attacked his old friend:

". . . I have a natural horror of dignity, finish and perfection, . . . You may take it that my sparring and punching at you is very much due to the feeling that you were 'coming over' me, and that if I was not very careful I should find myself giving way altogether to respect."

Of course, there was a more basic motive, too, Wells realized. He noted that there was "a real and very fundamental difference in our innate and developed attitudes towards life and literature. To you literature like painting is an end, to me literature like architecture is a means, it has a use.

Your view was, I felt, altogether too dominant in the world of criticism, and I assailed it in tones of harsh antagonism."

Floundering, looking for some satisfactory further reason for having published his comments, Wells now offered a strange excuse.

". . . writing that stuff about you was the first escape I had from the obsession of this war," he found himself writing in the second year of World War I. "*Boon* is just a waste-paper basket. . . . But since it was printed I have regretted a hundred times that I did not express our profound and incurable difference and contrast with a better grace. . . ."

He finished his letter with an embarrassingly elaborate tribute. "And believe me, my dear James," he wrote, "your very keenly appreciative reader, your warm if rebellious and resentful admirer, and for countless causes yours most gratefully and affectionately . . ."

But James was not appeased. On July 10, 1915, he wrote his final letter to the man he had once considered the "most interesting" of younger novelists—and his friend. Aristocratically, he deigned to point out Wells's lack of manners, but still very politely.

"I am bound to tell you," he began, "that I don't think your letter makes out any sort of case for the bad manners of *Boon*, so far as your indulgence in them at the expense of your poor old H.J. is concerned—I say 'your' simply because he has *been* yours, in the most liberal, continual, sacrificial, the most admiring and abounding critical way, ever since he began to know your writings: as to which you have had copious testimony. . . ."

Carefully and precisely, in his elegant style, he defined the function of waste-paper baskets.

"Your comparison of the book to a waste-basket strikes me as the reverse of felicitous," he explained, "for what one throws into that receptacle is exactly what one *doesn't* commit to publicity and make the affirmation of one's estimate of one's contemporaries by. I should liken it much rather to the preservative portfolio or drawer in which what is withheld from the basket is savingly laid away. Nor do I feel it anywhere evident that my 'view of life and literature,' or what you impute to me as such, is carrying everything before it and becoming a public menace . . ."

His conclusion was elevated—and blistering.

"Meanwhile," he wrote, "I absolutely dissent from the claim that there are any differences whatever in the amenability to art of forms of literature aesthetically determined, and hold your distinction between a form that is (like) painting and a form that is (like) architecture . . . wholly null and void. There is no sense in which architecture is aesthetically 'for use' that doesn't leave any other art whatever exactly as much so . . . It is art that *makes* life, makes interest, makes importance, for our consideration and application of these things, and I know of no substitute whatever for the force and beauty of its process. If I were Boon I should say that any pretence of such a substitute is helpless and hopeless humbug; but I wouldn't be Boon for the world, and am only yours faithfully

Henry James"

Wells wrote a half-hearted reply, but James did not acknowledge it, and a few months after the final exchange, James died.

In 1934, looking back on his friendship with James and their later estrangement, Wells, in his *Experiment in Autobiography*, summed up the famous writer who had offered him so much help and encouragement:

". . . James was a strange unnatural human being," he explained, "a sensitive man lost in an immensely abundant brain, which had had neither a scientific nor a philosophical training, but which was by education and natural aptitude alike, formal, formally aesthetic, conscientiously fastidious and delicate. Wrapped about in elaborations of gesture and speech, James regarded his fellow creatures with a face of distress and a remote effort at intercourse, . . . [He was] the most consciously and elaborately artistic and refined human being I ever encountered, and I swam in the common thought and feeling of my period, with an irregular abundance of rude knowledge, aggressive judgments and a disposition to get to close quarters with Madame Fact even if it meant a scuffle with her. James never scuffled with Fact . . .

"We were," H.G. Wells observed, "by nature and training profoundly unsympathetic."

7

The patriotic MR. JONES protects The British Empire From The irreverent MR. SHAW.

IN THE mid-1880's, the youthful, red-bearded George Bernard Shaw and his friend, William Archer, decided to collaborate on a play. Shaw agreed to write the dialogue, and Archer, who later became famous as a critic, felt that he knew enough about play structure to contribute the plot.

As a beginning, Archer borrowed some ideas from a comedy by the French playwright, Emile Augier. He added some new characters and developments, and discussed the resulting concoction with Shaw, who seemed to like it.

Six weeks later, Shaw startled Archer by saying: "Look here, I've knocked off the first act of that play of ours and

130

haven't come to the plot yet. In fact, I've forgotten the plot. You might tell me the story again."

Archer, who at first thought this might be a bit of Shavian humor, read Shaw's enormously long first act and realized that his energetic collaborator was simply telling him the truth. With his faith in the project somewhat shaken, Archer nevertheless decided to try again. He sat down with Shaw and reviewed the rather elaborate plot he had previously worked out. Shaw expressed his appreciation and left.

Three days later, Shaw again visited Archer.

"I've written three pages of the second act and have used up all your plot," Shaw said in a matter-of-fact manner. "Can you let me have some more to go on with?"

Archer recalled later becoming rather stern at this point. He explained that a plot was not ordered like yards of cotton in a draper's shop.

But Shaw was not discouraged, and he wrote on and on until he had finished the second act.

One afternoon he came by to read it to his collaborator, and Archer, who listened testily to the reading of the first act, fell asleep before the end of the second. Seeking a more appreciative listener, Shaw asked a new acquaintance, the extraordinarily prolific, popular—and hollow—playwright Henry Arthur Jones, to give him an expert opinion on the play. Jones agreed, and even stayed awake.

But at the end of the reading, he asked one question:
"Where's your murder?"

The reaction was discouraging enough to cause Shaw to set the script aside for seven years. When he dug it out in 1892 and finished it, the play became one of the most famous of all his early works: *Widowers' Houses.*

Although he is now considered a minor playwright, Henry Arthur Jones was a major figure during the last two decades of the nineteenth century. Today, the titles of his plays sound incredibly quaint and abominably saccharine. The list includes: *Hearts of Oak, Honour Bright, Home Again, A Bed of Roses, Welcome Little Stranger, A Noble Vagabond,* and *Heart of Hearts;* some of these offerings were almost as bad as the titles. After seeing a few of them, Oscar Wilde said there were only three rules a young playwright should be required to follow: "The first rule," Wilde observed, "is not to write like Henry Arthur Jones . . ." He added that ". . . the second and third rules are the same!"

Yet, Mr. Jones was not always as poor a playwright as Wilde implied, and he sometimes surprised his Victorian audiences by a tendency to stray along forbidden paths. Once, he astonished his fans by implying in one of his dramas that an unfaithful husband could not expect his wife to remain faithful. When he offered this play—under the title of *The Case of Rebellious Susan*—to his old friend, the actor Sir Charles Wyndham, that worthy fellow, after reading the script with steadily increasing indignation, finally wrote Jones in great concern:

"I stand as bewildered to-day as ever," said Sir Charles, "at finding an author, a clean living, clear-minded man, hoping to extract laughter from an audience on the score of a woman's [Susan's] impurity. I can realise the picture of a bad woman and her natural and desirable end being portrayed, but that amusement pure and simple should be expected from the sacrifice of that one indispensable quality in respect for womanhood astounds me."

He then delivered a Victorian opinion regarding the probable financial fate of such an offering, even if it were to be produced.

"I am equally astounded," he wrote, "at a practical long-experienced dramatic author believing that he will induce married men to bring their wives to a theatre to learn the lesson that their wives can descend to such nastiness, as giving themselves up for one evening of adulterous pleasure and then return safely to their husband's arms, provided they are clever enough, low enough, and dishonest enough to avoid being found out. . . . "I am puzzled to wonderment as to the source from which he [the author] expects to draw his audience, since it is evident to me that married men will not bring their wives and mothers will not bring their daughters. . . .

"No man, to my mind, who has daughters of his own can advance such a theory as you wish in this piece—that a weak woman often goes to these extremes and then when there is no other refuge left, sneaks back to her husband's bed. I am not speaking as a moralist, I am simply voicing the public instinct. . . ."

Solemnly, Wyndham concluded:

"Finally—I want to warn you. Whether the Box Office supports or contradicts my views . . . people will wonder why instead of taking pains to construct a piece, you should rely on a gross and unnecessary piece of impropriety to give strength to a comedy which, coming from the hands of so successful a man, ought to have been above any such necessity. . . .

"The tendency of the drama should always, if possible, be elevating. . . ."

Wyndham had a ready solution which might have appealed to Solomon, if not to Queen Victoria. He proposed that the whole question of Susan's infidelity be handled so delicately and in such vague terms that the pure-minded would be comforted by the suspicion that her "mind has strayed, but not her soul." At the same time, he implied, the more worldly theater-goers could be equally sure that she had sinned abominably—and, if they so wished to interpret things, that she had enjoyed it.

But Henry Arthur Jones was no fool. Though he listened to Sir Charles's advice, he chose to ignore what he had heard, for he fully realized that such a "solution" would serve only to ruin his play. When *The Case of Rebellious Susan* was produced, he managed to make it unmistakably clear to even the most pure-minded members of his audience that Susan's soul had strayed right along with her mind.

Soon Henry Arthur Jones discovered that he had written one of the greatest hits of his long career.

Jones could be forthwright in expressing his opinions, whether he was denouncing woman's suffrage, berating social reformers for introducing general public education, defending the British Empire from all its critics (and forever capitalizing such words as "Patriot" and "Patriotism"), or, for that matter, fighting alongside far more radical writers against the censorship of plays.

He had been characteristically forthright the evening he first met George Bernard Shaw in 1885. On that evening he had attended a meeting of the Shelley Society, and, after the preliminary business had been accomplished, he had watched and listened as the red-bearded man with flashing eyes rose to speak.

"Ladies and gentlemen," Shaw had begun, "I am an atheist, a vegetarian, and a Socialist . . ."

At this point Henry Arthur Jones nudged a fellow member and commented: "Three damned good reasons why he ought to be chucked out."

This comment revealed the basic differences in the two men's views of the world. And they were differences which were eventually to make Jones Shaw's most vociferous critic. Yet, for two decades the two managed to be exceptionally close friends, despite their occasional disagreements about political questions and the future of the theater—and even after their feud erupted, the usually ferocious George Shaw managed a surprising display of kindness toward the aroused Henry Arthur Jones. For, unlike Wilde, Shaw respected Jones as a craftsman and considered him "first, eminently first, among the surviving fittest of his own generation of playwrights." However, Shaw was equally certain that the stage was about to undergo a profound revolution, and he knew that he would be the leader in that revolt.

Since Jones had listened courteously to the first reading of the script that was later called *Widowers' Houses,* Shaw now bundled up several of his unproduced plays and asked his new-found mentor to give him a frank opinion of them. Jones obliged.

"I have read the plays," he responded, quite characteristically, "with varied feelings—at times interested, here and there exhilarated, sometimes bored . . . , oftentimes provoked, but always with respectful attention. Much of them is not dramatic and would never be interesting in any circumstances to any possible audience, but there is a good deal that is very dramatic and would fail on our English stage because of the defective machinery now in use for conveying the author's meaning and design to our not over-intellectual audiences—by defective machinery, I mean those people from whose mouths our words issue . . ."

The negative aspect of these comments did not disturb Shaw. Nor did they deter Jones. Even though he retained his reservations about Shaw's talent as a playwright, he was always ready, during the 1890's and early 1900's, to interrupt his own work in order to read and criticize the younger writer's newly completed manuscripts.

Furthermore, he took the trouble to offer Shaw detailed and useful advice about the business side of the theater. When, for example, a producer offered Shaw a contract for the American rights to *Arms and the Man,* Shaw asked Jones, who had so much experience, for advice.

"Can I do better?" he wrote. "Am I being had? I have to ask you because you are the only person I know whose business faculty inspires me with the smallest confidence."

The flattered Henry Arthur Jones responded promptly, suggesting some modification of the terms.

Soon Shaw wrote again. "I enclose a duplicate of the draft agreement for America," he explained, "from which you will see that I did exactly what you told me. . . ."

The relationship was so intimate that Shaw even consulted Jones on a highly important personal matter. In 1898, at the conclusion of a letter complimenting Jones on the play *Grace Mary,* the now rather widely known Shaw inquired:

"By the way, would you advise me to get married?"

Jones's reply was both affirmative and instructive.

"Yes," he wrote, "I would get married if I were you. But read the chapters in Rabelais and the advice that was given to Panurge on the subject. . . ."

A few weeks later, the newly wed Shaw found time to drop another note to his old friend.

"We are having such a honeymoon of it," he wrote. "A couple of days ago I fell downstairs and broke my left arm; so here I am disabled hand and foot, helpless as a baby, I am only able to scrawl postcards. . . ."

And Jones was properly sympathetic.

There were, of course, during these years, small signs of the basic differences in the two writers. For instance, whenever Jones ventured beyond the bounds of the Victorian theater, Shaw was almost too quick to applaud him and to urge him forward. And, although Jones made complimentary remarks from time to time about one or another of Shaw's plays, he also revealed his real feelings in a comment to his daughter, Doris.

"Shaw isn't a dramatist," he told Doris, "he is a journalist with a sense of the theatre."

Nor was Jones favorably impressed by Shaw's admiration for Henrik Ibsen. From his point of view, the protagonist, Nora, of Ibsen's *The Doll's House* was a "tiresome hussy." It was Jones's opinion that after Nora had walked out on her husband, the final scene should have portrayed the relieved husband helping himself to a whisky and soda and saying: "Thank God, she's gone."

In fact, as the techniques of Ibsen and Shaw and their allies and followers began to dominate the theater, Jones grew increasingly critical of these new ideas and experiments. And yet, as late as 1913, he could still discuss his young rivals with wry humor.

"I have a young friend —a very young friend—," he wrote to Shaw in 1913, "who hails your recent enlargement of the bounds of morality. He had written a play which seems to me likely to advance your views—if we can only get it produced. Its *dramatis personae* are five Hottentots, eleven monkeys, and thirteen goats. They are all quite naked, and delightfully un-ashamed."

He continued, slyly:

"There is no coherent story, no vestige of a plot, and no discoverable purpose. The characters simply come on, and talk, talk, talk, talk, in the frankest way—I am sure it will please you. The dialogue is not so witty as your own, but it is far more fearless. My own criticism of the piece is that the eleven monkeys seem to me superfluous; our simian gibberings and antics being already sufficiently reproduced in our musical comedies and reviews. However, my young friend's monkeys have the advantage of being naked, while their congeners in revues and musical comedies are partially dressed.

"And now, how can we get our young friend's play pro-duced? I have sent him on to you, as being the very man to see it through. You may object that if this play is done, you may find it difficult to go one better. . . ."

It was not until a year later, in 1914, that the real split came between the two writers, and, even then, George Bernard Shaw did not lose his sense of humor.

Now, with the beginning of World War I, Jones's habit of capitalizing such words as "Patriot" and "Patriotism" suddenly took on fresh meaning; he became absolutely convinced that the future of civilization depended upon Great Britain's victory and Germany's defeat. Such an attitude was in direct opposition to that of the internationalist Shaw, who opposed wars in wartime as well as during periods of peace. It was also Shaw's conviction that neither England nor Germany could be considered blameless. The war, he felt, would settle nothing.

Naturally, the outspoken Shaw proclaimed these views aloud, and it was his insistence on doing so that soon touched off the feud.

"I never felt more angry with any man," the patriotic Jones wrote his daughter, after what he regarded as a particularly reprehensible pronouncement on the part of the Irish-born Shaw regarding the relationship between England and Ireland. "He is trying to keep up the strife between England and Ireland. I do not think I can meet him in the future."

It happened that Shaw and Jones were members of both the Shelley Society and the Dramatists' Club as well; now, as the Irish pacifist voiced his criticism of British politicians and British policies, it became clear to Jones, among others, that several playwrights had stopped attending meetings of the latter Club in order to avoid "contamination" by Shaw. In fact, there were several members of the organization who felt that Shaw should be asked to stop using the Club as a forum for his unpopular opinions, and, at Jones's and other members' request, the secretary soon wrote Shaw a letter informing him of the situation. The secretary asked if Shaw would like to be dropped from the list of those receiving notices of Club meetings. Shaw scrawled across the bottom of the letter, which he sent on to Jones:

"My dear H.A.J.,

"I hope you are not one of the 'several members,' though in these raving mad times it is hard to know.

"Cheerful sort of Club, isn't it?"

Three days later, he had Jones's reply:

"My dear Shaw," wrote Jones. "In reply to yours, I was present at last Wednesday's lunch, and I strongly supported the proposal that Paull [the club secretary] should write to you in the terms of the letter you enclose.

"I believe that England's cause is a most righteous one. I am sure that England did not provoke this war. I am sure that Germany did. These are, to me, not matters of opinion, but clearly established facts.

"Your writings on the War have done great harm to our cause in America and neutral countries. Germany is everywhere making use of your utterances to justify her own actions and to befoul and slander England. Whether you know it or not, and whether you care or not, you are one of our country's worst enemies. And you are an enemy within our walls. . . .

"Even if what you said was true, it was yet a foolish, mad, and mischievous thing to say at that moment.

". . . If you do not allow that our cause is just, do you wonder that every Englishman is against you? Do you wonder that you are regarded as a man who, for the sake of showing his agility, kicked and defamed his mother when she was on a sick-bed? You will say that England is not your mother—well then put it that Englishmen regard you as a man who kicked and defamed *their* mother when she was on a sick-bed.

"This is not intolerance; it is mere natural human feeling
—always so hard for you to understand. But it is the primal
instincts and emotions that govern men in days like these.
. . ."

It was a severe scolding. But George Bernard Shaw was
never at a loss for wit. He began his reply the very next day
in almost the singsong rhythm of a nursery rhyme:

"Henry Arthur, Henry Arthur; what is your opinion of the
war?" he asked.

"If you think you are going to put ME off with a sheet of
notepaper containing extracts from the *Daily Express* copied
with your own fair hand, you have mistaken your man.

"Come! give me a solid Buckinghamshire opinion: I know
the German-American-would-be-British-Patriotic opinion;
what's yours?

"England's cause is righteous," Shaw continued. "Good;
but what is its cause? Besides, it isn't fighting for its own
cause, but for [Czarist] Russia's. Are you a sound Russian
patriot too? And a true blue Serbian? And do you fill the air
with shouts of 'Banzai!'? I take it for granted that you will
shed the last drop of your blood for *Liberté, Egalité, Frater-
nité*. And we all love Italy. But what is the cause (since you
mention it solemnly): WHAT is the cause? What IS the Cause?
What is the CAUSE? . . . Oh, Henry Arthur, Henry Arthur,
author of *Saints and Sinners, The Crusaders,* and *The Philis-
tines,* do you believe that the editor of the *Daily Express* IS
England? . . ."

It is quite possible that aside from matters of "Patriotism,"
Jones's attitude toward Shaw at this time may have been
shaped partly by his slow realization that his own day in the
British theater was ending, and that the day of the irreverent
"journalist" Shaw was beginning. In her biography of her
father, Jones's daughter lists the astonishing total of seventy-

seven plays which were written by Jones between 1878 and
1915. Her list ends with five titles: *The Right Man for Sophie*
(1916), *The Pacifists* (1917), *Finding Themselves* (1917),
The Lifted Veil (1919), and *The Woman I Loved* (1922).
Four of these titles are followed by an asterisk referring to an
ominous footnote, which reads: "*Never produced."

It may well have been for this reason, as well as that of
politics, that Jones now began to refer to Shaw as an "irrespon-
sible braggart," a "blaring self-trumpeteer," and "the pope of
chaos." So intense did his indictment of his former colleague
become that he was once moved to cry out: ". . . you,
George Bernard Shaw, face me and answer me. We breed a
rare progeny of native traitors, but none of them equal to
you . . ."

For a brief period following the end of the war in 1918,
Jones's patriotic efforts were diverted from his increasingly
violent attacks on Shaw. The reason: he had found another
target in the person of the novelist H.G. Wells.

Wells, who had traveled in Russia shortly after the revolu-
tion, had sent back reports to British newspapers which struck
Jones as unduly favorable to Lenin and the Communists.
Soon, although he himself had never been to Russia either be-
fore or after the revolution, Jones began offering rebuttals to
Wells's reports.

"So you are back in England," he wrote, after reading the
published versions of several of Wells's reports. "I thought it
possible that you might be offered some high advisory post in
Russia, which your love of Bolshevist Government would
constrain you to accept . . ."

And, when Wells refused to be drawn into a public argument, Jones chided him: "Let it not distress you that you
find it impossible to argue with me. I will continue the con-

troversy all alone, and will furnish the necessary arguments for us both . . ."

Wells then responded by indicating that he found Jones's "dreary hostility" tiresome rather than provocative. He compared Jones with a foghorn. "You never know when the damned thing won't be hooting again," he wrote.

But as Jones published attack after attack, Wells finally lost his temper. He called Jones a "liar," a "silly ranter," "an excited imbecile," "an out-and-out liar," and a "damned thing."

Pleased by the attention, Jones, who confessed that he had become obsessed with this quarrel, responded by hailing Wells's "magnificent performances in vituperation" and said that he treasured Wells's epithets "as examples of your method in controversy and as a measure of your prowess in argument." Then he decided to gather all his letters attacking the writer into a volume to be entitled *My Dear Wells.* As a precaution, however, he had his secretary write to Wells to ascertain his reaction—and probably to discover whether the book would provoke Wells into bringing a charge of libel, although Wells had previously said he "would as soon think of bringing a legal action against a barking cur."

Now Wells responded:

"I have no objection to Mr. Jones publishing any stuff about me that he likes," he wrote, "provided he does not tell lies about me. I am afraid it is too much to ask him to verify his quotations, and to footnote anything he puts with inverted commas, with a reference."

Then he delivered his final word on the matter.

Jones, he said, "is altogether too silly and incoherent for controversy . . ."

Yet, even in *My Dear Wells,* Jones found ample space for side attacks on his old friend, Shaw.

"The Nag Sedition was your mother," he wrote of Shaw, "and Perversity begot you; Mischief was your midwife, and

Misrule your nurse, and Unreason brought you up at her feet—no other ancestry and rearing had you."

Invited to review *My Dear Wells*, the unshakable Shaw wrote: ". . . dear Jones knows that he is welcome to abuse me until he is black in the face without estranging me in the least." And he invited readers of his review to share his own enjoyment of Jones's invective. "Read the eighteen pages he has consecrated to me in this book," Shaw suggested. "Read the sentence beginning with 'Know that this is your appointed lot' . . . It contains more than 800 words, and stops then only because the printer, in desperation, has bunged in a full-point. I read that sentence to my wife, and at the end we found ourselves cheering with excitement . . ."

He referred to Jones's description of Shaw as "a freakish homunculus germinated outside lawful procreation."

"I protest," said Shaw. "I am the unquestioned lawful heir of my mother's property and my father's debts . . . extraordinary as I am, I am none the less unmistakeably the son of my reputed father." Still refusing to express an enmity he did not feel, he observed correctly: "I flatter myself that his [Jones's] publishers would never have ventured on such a roaring libel if he [Jones] has not given them his guarantee that my friendship could be depended on."

"And," Shaw concluded, "he was quite right."

Soon Wells became a minor figure in Jones's demonology. Shaw was the real devil, and Jones became almost obsessed with the need to exorcise him. He confessed that during these years of incessant controversy his last thought before going to bed at night and his first thought upon getting up in the morning was devoted to devising new means of smiting the men he saw as England's enemies. The furious energy that had once gone into writing an astonishingly large number of lengthy plays was now spent in composing angry denunciations. His daughter remembers that almost all of his conversation at breakfast, lunch, and dinner was devoted to an endless tirade against traitors—and the chief traitor was George Bernard Shaw.

Shaw, however, displayed a little-known side of his own complex personality during this period. The usually contentious man, who was ready to argue heatedly with any stranger at a street-corner meeting and who was always eager to denounce super-patriots as fools or rogues, held his tongue when Jones launched public attack after public attack. He simply looked on with good-natured tolerance. He might have been a supremely wise and self-confident parent watching a favorite child who was unaccountably throwing a tantrum.

Jones's temper reached boiling point in 1925, when Shaw was chosen to offer the official toast to Shakespeare at the annual Shakespeare festival in Stratford. To the patriot-dramatist Jones, the invitation seemed a supreme calamity. Feverishly, he wrote to the newspapers, reminding millions of British readers that Shaw had often slandered Shakespeare —and referring particularly to an article Shaw had once published in *The Saturday Review* of England.

". . . There are moments when one asks despairingly why our stage should ever have been cursed with this 'immortal' pilferer of other men's stories and ideas," Shaw had written in 1896. With more than his usual bombast he had denounced the bard's "monstrous rhetorical fustian, his unbearable platitudes, his pretentious reduction of the subtlest problems of life to commonplaces against which a Polytechnic debating society would revolt, his incredible unsuggestiveness, his sententious combination of ready reflection with complete intellectual sterility, and his consequent incapacity for getting out of the depth of even the most ignorant audience, except where he solemnly says something so transcendently plati-

tudinous that his more humble-minded hearers cannot bring
themselves to believe that so great a man really meant to talk
like their grandmothers.

"With the single exception of Homer," Shaw had continued, "there is no eminent writer, not even Sir Walter Scott,
whom I can despise so entirely as I despise Shakespeare when
I measure my mind against his. The intensity of my impatience with him occasionally reaches such a pitch, that it
would positively be a relief to me to dig him up and throw
stones at him, knowing as I do how incapable he and his wor-
shippers are of understanding any less obvious form of indignity . . ."

As Archibald Henderson has pointed out, Shaw had enjoyed making such an assault upon Shakespeare chiefly because he relished the "convulsive start of the British public,
like that of the 'edgy' patient when the dentist strikes at a
nerve." And Shaw himself once said, "If you do not say a
thing in an irritating way, you may just as well not say it at
all."

But now, to Jones, the article became simply one more clear
proof of Shaw's eagerness to subvert British culture and the
British Empire.

Once again he decided to gather his vituperation into a
book in order that it might be preserved for future generations.
He planned to address the volume to the Mayor of Stratford-
on-Avon, and therefore chose as his title: *Mr. Mayor of
Shakespeare's Town.*

Soon the publisher, Eveleigh Nash, accepted the book, and
Jones blithely signed the contract for its publication—a contract which contained the usual clause warranting that the
author had not included any libelous material. But when the
directors of Nash's firm read portions of the manuscript, they
decided that Jones had interpreted the libel laws rather more
liberally than would a court of law, and they convinced Nash
that he should not publish the book. As a result, Jones was

forced to offer *Mr. Mayor* to publisher after publisher, both in England and the United States.

One editor—acting without Jones's permission or knowledge —asked Shaw to promise not to sue for libel if the book were to be published.

But Shaw now declined. He was not, he said, concerned about the possible effects of the book on his own reputation. He was, he said, disturbed simply by Jones's continued waste of his talent on political invective, and hoped that his refusal to co-operate would force Jones to give up his tiresome campaign and return to his real work of writing plays.

The truth was that Shaw had remained genuinely fond of his old friend and that he was making every effort to effect a reconciliation. In 1926, he wrote to Jones, who had become ill.

"I meant to congratulate you," he began genially, "on my seventieth birthday (the 26th July, 1926), but was afraid of sending your temperature up 10 degrees at a critical moment. I am assured now by Max Beerbohm that you are well enough to stand anything; so I insist on affirming that the news of your illness gave me as much concern, and of your safe deliverance as much relief, as if we were still the best of friends. Our quarrel has always been a hopelessly one-sided affair; and I have rejoiced in your vigorous invective far too much to feel any malice at the back of it. . . .

"People who obviously pity my dotage have a well-meant but disagreeable habit of reminding me that Sophocles wrote his best plays at 80. I suppose they say the same to you. They know nothing about it; but you seem to me to have more drive and style than ever. I wish I could say the same for myself; but at present I feel that my bolt will be shot when I have got through the final struggle to finish my book on Socialism, with every word of which you will agree. The truth is, I am for the moment so completely done up by work on top of illness (the result of an accident) that the writing

of this letter would tire me for the rest of the day if the feeling it expresses were not so nourishing. So you really are
doing me good.

"Do not bother to reply—though I warn you I shall put the
friendliest interpretation on silence. This birthday business,
involving as many congratulations (on being 70! Good God!!)
as your recovery is bringing you, has shown me how easy it
is to kill a strong man by a full broadside from the post office.
Just note that I am not to be shaken off, and turn over for
another nap with a groan of resignation."

Jones showed the letter to a few close friends, but as the
leader of a holy crusade, he felt he could not exchange
pleasantries with the chief demon. His campaign had now
attracted devoted followers, and one of these wrote him:

"May I say how passionately I admire your championing
of the *things that matter?* Shakespeare and Patriotism. (The
two are synonymous.)"

Two-and-a-half years later, however, just a few hours before his death, Jones finally changed his mind about replying
to the man he had first met more than four decades before.

"I have somewhere," Shaw once wrote Hesketh Pearson, "a
pathetic little scrap of paper on which he tried to scrawl when
he was dying that he had no personal feeling against me."

And, after Jones's death, Shaw sent a letter to the daughter
of his most virulent critic.

". . . I never had the slightest doubt," wrote Shaw calmly,
kindly, and thoughtfully, "that the real old friendly relations
between your father and myself were there all the time under-
neath the top dressing of denunciatory rhetoric which
amused us both. After the War, which doesn't count, as everyone was mad then, it was a queer sort of play which perhaps
only a fellow-playwright would have understood. . . .

"Wells and I were only part of a world that was too foolish
and cruel for him [Jones] to suffer gladly. . . ."

8

As a would-be Messiah, MR. D.H. LAWRENCE endures his sad lot among a host of friends.

IN THE spring of 1912, David Herbert Lawrence, who was to become one of the most widely praised and most widely banned of twentieth-century novelists, was suffering from the lung congestion that was destined to kill him. Blaming his illness on the chill damp English climate, and convinced that he could recover his health in Germany, he sought a post as lecturer at a German university.

In pursuit of this goal, Lawrence went to Nottingham to see a Professor named Ernest Weekley, who had once shown some interest in him, and, while waiting for Weekley to return home from his classes, spent half an hour talking with the

Professor's wife, Frieda von Richthofen Weekley. The two sat in her room, as Frieda later wrote, with the "French windows open, curtains fluttering in the spring wind," while her children played on the lawn. The pale, intense young man told her during this first meeting that "he had finished with his attempts at knowing women." She was "amazed at the way he fiercely denounced them," she later recalled. "I had never before heard anything like it. I laughed, yet I could tell he had tried very hard [with women], and had cared. We talked about Oedipus and understanding leaped through our words."

The ensuing lunch with Professor Weekley brought Lawrence no closer to a job, but he soon returned to the house in Nottingham for another talk with the Professor's wife.

"You are quite unaware of your husband," he told her this time, "you take no notice of him."

Frieda later recalled that she "disliked the directness of this criticism." But when Lawrence suggested that she meet him a few days later at a railroad station in Derbyshire, she agreed without hesitation. On the appointed day, Frieda brought her two small girls with her, and Lawrence took all three of them for a long walk.

"We came to a small brook, a little stone bridge crossed it," Frieda wrote of that afternoon. "Lawrence made the children some paper boats and put matches in them and let them float downstream . . . Crouched by the brook, playing there with the children, Lawrence forgot about me completely. Suddenly I knew I loved him . . .

"After that, things happened quickly. He came to see me one Sunday. My husband was away and I said: 'Stay the night with me.' 'No [Lawrence replied], I will not stay in your husband's house while he is away, but you must tell him the truth and we will go away together, because I love you.' "

Soon they were actually making their plans to go away, but the first attempt was ludicrously unsuccessful, and Lawrence found himself offering an absurd explanation as to why the bold plan had to be postponed: "I couldn't come today because I was waiting for the laundry . . ." he wrote. "I am sorry if it makes things tiresome."

It was not until May third that they met at Kings Cross station in London.

Wrote Frieda, subsequently: "This young man of twenty-six had taken all my fate, all my destiny, into his hands. And we had known each other barely for six weeks."

During the early months of this same year, a similar upheaval was occurring in the already confused lives of two other people with whom the Lawrences were shortly to come into intimate contact. These were the writers Katherine Mansfield and John Middleton Murry, neither of whom suspected that they were shortly to fall under the influence of a man like Lawrence.

The very independent Katherine Mansfield had previously married a singing teacher named George Bowden on March 2, 1909, and had then left him the following morning. A few weeks later, she had had an affair with another man, and, upon discovering that she was pregnant, had then gone to Germany to await the arrival of the baby, which was still-born.

Returning to London, she had tried to straighten out the tangled web of her life. She again lived with Bowden for a few weeks, but, as he later wrote, "a great change came over all her affairs" after the literary magazine *New Age* accepted some of her stories. "Since the independence she yearned for was on the horizon," Bowden has explained, "our relationship lapsed into the episode which it essentially was . . ."

Thus, in 1912, Katherine, freed of her occasional husband, met the handsome twenty-two-year-old John Middleton Murry, a writer and editor who recognized her talent and encouraged her to continue her experiments with the short story. And one day in April of that year—the same month in which Lawrence was convincing Frieda that she was "unaware" of her husband—Murry mentioned to Katherine he was looking for a place to live in London. What he needed, he said, was a room that would cost only a few shillings a week.

"I have a suggestion to make . . . ," Katherine said. He could have one room of her large London apartment, and the rent would be only seven shillings, six pence a week.

". . . in those days things simply happened to me," Murry has written. "I was completely passive. The only form of activity I knew was gliding out of situations that promised to throttle me." Some of these previous "situations" had involved women—or men—who were also attracted by the basically passionless Murry. Now, he accepted Katherine's suggestion passively.

Whatever the neighbors thought of his moving in with the slightly older and highly unorthodox woman writer, the living arrangements were at first simply a convenience for Murry. In their memoirs, both he and Katherine have recalled the many evenings during which they stayed up late to discuss literature in the sitting room of the large apartment. When the talk died down, one or the other would rise, and they would solemnly shake hands.

"Good night, Murry," Katherine would say.

"Good night, Mansfield," he would reply.

Then they would go to separate bedrooms.

Late one evening, after many nights had passed in exactly this manner, there was a lull in the literary conversation. Katherine glanced at Murry and asked:

"Why don't you make me your mistress?"

Murry, who at the moment was lying on the floor with his feet in the air, considered the question, then replied:

"I feel it would spoil . . . everything."

Yet the question remained in his mind, and a few evenings later, when the conversation ended, they did not shake hands and part.

In 1912, the little magazine *Rhythm*, which was now edited by Murry with Katherine's help, accepted one of Lawrence's early stories. And, as a result, in 1913 the Lawrences met these two unorthodox lovers. It was to be the first of many meetings.

"I think theirs was the only spontaneous and jolly friendship we had," Frieda, who did not like some of Lawrence's admirers, was later to write.

The fact is, however, that the friendship was a much more complicated affair than Frieda realized. For Lawrence, who desperately needed a coterie of followers all his life, had clearly been flattered by Murry's apparently instantaneous hero-worship for him. The Murrys were immediately invited for a weekend at a cottage the Lawrences had rented some distance from London, and thus began a series of invitations and refusals which were to characterize the Lawrence-Murry-Mansfield relationship for as long as it lasted.

This first weekend, however, the Murrys, despite their acceptance of Lawrence's invitation, simply failed to show up. The reason: they did not have enough money to pay the necessary rail fare. Understandably, Lawrence was annoyed by this failure on the part of his new friends. Then Edward Marsh, a writer who knew both Lawrence and Murry, explained to Lawrence that Murry was practically penniless; and, his vanity restored, Lawrence immediately wrote a friendly but brutally direct letter to both Katherine and John.

"Oh," he scolded them, "but why didn't you come and let us lend you a pound. I think that when times have been so rough, you *shouldn't* bring about a disappointment on yourselves, just for the money. That seems to me wrong. We

could just as well lend you five pounds as have it in the bank
—if you want it. I consider now that your not coming on
Sunday was a piece of obtuseness on your part. You are one
of the people who *should* have a sense of proportionate values;
you ought to know when it's worth while to let yourself
borrow money, and when it isn't. . . .

"When Marsh said on Sunday, because we couldn't understand why you hadn't come: 'I suppose they hadn't the money
for the railway tickets,' I thought it was stupid, because you
seemed so rich . . . I had no idea."

Typically, the man who so desperately needed disciples
proceeded to take matters into his own hands.

"So now I think you'd better come down for the week-end,"
he wrote. "Come on Saturday and stay till Monday morning.
We can put you up. Don't on any account bring chickens or
any such-like rubbish. We can get them down here."

In the end, however, having reflected a moment about the
cost of chickens, he added:

". . . perhaps they are cheaper in town. Bring one if you
like."

This time the Murrys arrived (with Katherine's allowance
providing money for the tickets), and the two couples "bathed
naked in the half-light," and then feasted sumptuously on
fried steak and tomatoes.

Of their second meeting, Murry later wrote:

"Lawrence was a really new experience. I was quite un-
prepared for such an immediacy of contact. In an astonishingly short time he knew all about me: all, at any rate, that I
could tell him, and no doubt a good deal more."

Yet, even this early Murry recognized the trait in Lawrence
which was to persist throughout their relationship. It was this
characteristic which was to bring about the feud between the
two that lasted until Lawrence's death. For Murry wrote:

"He [Lawrence] seemed straightway to be taking charge of my affairs . . . he was very insistent that we should seize the opportunity of breaking away from England and coming to live beside him at Lerici in Italy . . . we were in danger of being swept clean off our feet by the intensity of his concern for us."

Aldous Huxley, who knew both Lawrence and Murry intimately, has explained the attraction between the two:

"Murry's was an acute & subtle mind," Mr. Huxley has written, "and there was something curiously fascinating about his conversation. Moreover he would radiate a kind of religious enthusiasm—about Dostoevsky & his ideas, about 'metabiology', about Lawrence as 'The Son of Man', The 20th Century Messiah. . . . Lawrence, like most other people, was fascinated by Murry at first, was convinced by his show of passionate enthusiasm—and also flattered, I'm afraid, by the ascription to himself of messianic qualities." Lawrence did not realize that all this was "only a stage effect" and that "Murry . . . had a strange way of churning . . . [himself] violently & indefatigably, in the hope of transforming a native inability to feel very strongly or continuously into a butter-pat of genuine emotion, true passion, unquestioning faith."

Naturally, Katherine, who had spent most of her life rejecting discipline, was disturbed by Lawrence's readiness to take charge of their lives. Yet, for the time being, she remained silent.

Murry, on the other hand, began to seek Lawrence's advice even on problems many people would normally have kept to themselves. There was, for example, the question of money. As the daughter of a banker, Katherine received a small but regular allowance from her father, and this worried Murry because he felt he should not be living off her income. He asked Lawrence's counsel on this matter, and, typically, the master replied with a complete philosophy of behavior in such financial situations.

"When you say you won't take Katherine's money," Lawrence wrote, with abundant confidence, "it means you don't trust her love for you. When you say she needs little luxuries, and you couldn't bear to deprive her of them, it means you don't respect either yourself or her sufficiently to do it."

From this premise, Lawrence bravely launched into a generalization which might have made Katherine speak up, if she had seen the letter. He wrote:

"It looks to me as if you two, far from growing nearer, are snapping the bonds that hold you together, one after another. I suppose you must both of you consult your own hearts, honestly. She must see if she really *wants* you, wants to keep you and to have no other man all her life. It means forfeiting something. But the only principle I can see in this life, is that one *must* forfeit the less for the greater. Only one must be thoroughly honest about it."

He proceeded, almost insufferably, to dictate the future romantic, as well as financial course, to be taken by both Katherine and Murry.

"She must say," Lawrence wrote, " 'Could I live in a little place in Italy, with Jack, and be lonely, have rather a bare life, but be happy?' If she could, then take her money. If she doesn't want to, don't try. But don't beat about the bush. In the way you go on, you are inevitably coming apart. She is perhaps beginning to be unsatisfied with you. And you can't make her more satisfied by being unselfish. You must say, 'How can I make myself most healthy, strong, and satisfactory to myself and to her?' If by being lazy for six months, then be lazy, and take her money. It doesn't matter if she misses her luxuries: she won't die of it. What luxuries do you mean? . . ."

He summarized his recipe for the Murry-Mansfield affair:

"If you work yourself sterile to get her chocolates, she will most justly detest you—she is *perfectly* right. She doesn't want you to sacrifice yourself to her, you fool. Be more natural, and positive, and stick to your own guts. You spread them on a tray for her to throw to the cats.

"If you want things to come right—if you are ill and exhausted, then take her money to the last penny, and let her do her own housework. Then she'll know you love her. . . ."

This was a philosophy which appealed greatly to the worshipful Murry. As a result, he was no longer disturbed by the prospect of living off Katherine's money.

Nor was Murry disturbed by Lawrence's proposal that the little magazine be abandoned and that they all go off to live in Italy together. In fact, he was strongly attracted to the idea. Yet something still held him back, and, fortunately for himself as well as for Katherine, the Lawrences traveled to Italy alone.

Soon, however, the restless travelers were back in England, and Lawrence, still undaunted, was making elaborate plans for founding another colony of faithful followers. No number of delays and disappointments would ever convince him that the idea itself was unsound.

Thus, in December, 1915, the would-be Master made another appeal—this time to Katherine.

"There remain only you and Murry in our lives," he wrote. "We look at the others as across the grave. . . . I want you and Murry to live with us, or near us, in unanimity; not these separations. Let us all live together and create a new world. If it is too difficult in England, because here all is destruction and dying and corruption, let us go away to Florida: soon. But let us go *together*, and keep together, several of us, as being of one spirit. Let it be a union of the unconsciousness, not in the consciousness . . . let us all try to be happy *together*, in unanimity, not in hostility, creating, not destroying."

For a while, Florida continued to be Lawrence's dream of

Utopia, but with the beginning of World War I he and Frieda were not allowed to leave England. Yet he became more determined than ever to withdraw from the world. On February 7, 1916, he wrote to Lady Ottoline Morrell, his patron: "As far as I possibly can, I will stand outside this time. I will live my life and, if possible, be happy, though the whole world slides in horror down into the bottomless pit. There is a greater truth than the truth of the present, there is a God beyond these gods of today."

In this same year, paradoxically, Lawrence finally discovered a haven. It was right in England, five miles from St. Ives in Cornwall where he found a "tiny granite village nestling under high, shaggy moorhills" with a "big sweep of lovely sea beyond, such a lovely sea, lovelier even than the Mediterranean."

"I feel we ought to live here," he wrote to both Murry and Katherine, "[we could] pitch our camp and unite our forces, and become an active power here, together."

Close by the cottage which he and Frieda had rented near St. Ives were four other structures, including a tower house, and, typically, Lawrence decided that Murry and Katherine— as well as some other friends—should take over these places.

Of course, he reserved the largest structure for the Murrys. ". . . we [will] all eat together in the dining-room of your house," he wrote.

In case such a plan might seem presumptuous to Katherine, he did his best to explain: "This . . . is the best place to live . . . which we shall find in England, I firmly believe."

He was very certain of his plan. They could live, he said, as though they were in "a little monastery."

Three days later, he again described the tower house he had chosen for the Murrys. "Really, you must have [it] . . . ," he wrote. "I keep looking at it. I call it already Katherine's house,

Katherine's tower. There is something *very* attractive about it. It is very old, native to the earth, like rock, yet dry and all in the light of the hills and the sea. It is only twelve strides from our house to yours: we can talk from the windows . . .

"You must come, and we will live there a long, long time, very cheaply."

Naturally, Katherine hesitated.

But Murry was attracted by the invitation, and, finally, after some delay, both he and Katherine arrived on a chilly April day at St. Ives, "sitting," as Frieda has described it, "on a cart, high up on all the goods and chattels . . ."

Now, Lawrence and Frieda, too, felt that their Utopian experiment was off to a really encouraging start. ". . . we all enjoy ourselves," Lawrence wrote to Lady Morrell on April 7, 1916, only a few days after the Murrys had arrived. Then, with some smugness, he added: "The Murrys are happy with each other now."

Yet nine days later, even he was sounding a somber note:

"It is queer," he wrote, "how almost everything has gone out of me, all the world I have known, and the people, gone out like candles. When I think of . . . [the guests] who are here, it is with a kind of weariness, as of trying to remember a light which is blown out. Somehow, it is all gone . . ."

One reason for this sudden change in Lawrence undoubtedly lay in Katherine's disenchantment with the supposed Utopia. "I am very much alone here," she wrote to a friend. "It is not a really nice place. It is so full of huge stones. . . . It is so very temporary. It may all be over next month; in fact, it will be. I don't belong to anybody here."

But the chief reason for the change lay in Lawrence's own behavior, which, now that they were all living in such close proximity, Katherine could no longer ignore. ". . . I cannot describe the frenzy that comes over him [Lawrence]," she wrote in wonderment. "He simply *raves*, roars, beats the table, abuses everybody. But that's not such great matter. What makes these attacks insupportable is the feeling one has at the back of one's mind that he is completely out of control, swallowed up in an acute, *insane* irritation. After one of these attacks he's ill with fever, haggard and broken."

And to this account, even the seemingly willing disciple Murry was later to add:

"[Lawrence] talked of the blood-brotherhood between us and hinted at the need of some inviolable sacrament between us—some pre-Christian blood-rite in keeping with the primeval rocks about us. Timidly, I withdrew only the more. And his exasperation increased.

"The clashes between him and Frieda became more frequent, and to me more desperate and frightening. One evening . . . Frieda burst in at the door crying, 'He'll kill me!' Lawrence followed, white as a ghost, but in a frenzy of fury . . . crying, 'I'll *kill* her, I'll *kill* her!' The chairs were scattered; I just managed to save the lamp. Katherine sat still in a corner, indifferent, inexpressibly weary . . .

"Quite suddenly, Lawrence collapsed into a chair by the fire. The frenzy had left him, bleached, blanched and inert. And there was a great silence, which no one dared to break."

To those who knew Lawrence well, such scenes were familiar. For, since the blissful days of his first meetings with Frieda, there had been numerous instances of his unrestrained violence toward her. He often cursed her, sometimes threw dishes at her, and at least once tried to hit her over the head with a chair. She returned his curses, skillfully dodged the dishes, and wrenched the chair out of his hands. She seemed to expect his occasional outbursts, and some friends felt that

she enjoyed them. Since her calm strength during these periods increased Lawrence's respect for her, they were in a
strange way an ideally matched couple.

But to the Murrys, all this was new and, though they could
not afford another move, they felt they had no choice. They
found a cottage at Mylor and hired a man to cart their furniture to the new place.

Sadly, even Lawrence was forced to recognize that his experiment was a failure, though he characteristically neglected
to consider his own part in it. Instead, he blamed a combination of the location and the weather. "Unfortunately," he
wrote to Lady Morrell, "the Murrys do not like the country—
it is too rocky and bleak for them. They should have a soft
valley, with leaves and the ring-dove cooing. And this is a hill-
side of rocks and magpies and foxes. The walls of their house
too are wet from the rain: though this could be put right. . . ."

Lawrence helped the Murrys load their possessions into the
cart, but he was deeply hurt. Only Frieda remained unconcerned.

"When the last rope was tied," Murry has written, "I said
goodbye and hoped they would come over to see us. Frieda,
who took such incidents lightly, said they would; but Lawrence did not answer. I wheeled my bicycle to the road and
pedalled off, with the feeling that I had said goodbye to him
for ever."

There were to be more quarrels, partings, and reconcilia-
tions before the climax of the Lawrence-Murry relationship
eight years later.

After the experiment in the "little monastery," Katherine
and Murry were caught up in their own problems, and during
a good part of World War I the Lawrences were cut off from
everyone, because Frieda was considered an enemy alien by
the British War Office. Thus the close relationship between

the Murrys and the Lawrences was not resumed until 1919, when Murry, who had become the editor of the *Athenaeum*, asked Lawrence to write for the magazine.

It was a request which was made by Murry not without some qualms. "I was rather nervous," he later admitted, "because I knew he [Lawrence] was in a condition of rebellion against England and all its works [because of his experience with the War Office]; if he gave full vent to his resentment [in the *Athenaeum*], it would shock the remnant of respectable readers of that ancient organ out of their skins."

In addition, Murry felt none too secure in his own new position.

Fortunately, however, Lawrence seemed to understand the situation, and in deference to the magazine's readers, as well as to Murry, he promised to "try to be pleasant and a bit old-fashioned." And his first article was indeed a harmless contribution, a "subdued hymn of praise to the coming of spring," suitably entitled "Whistling of Birds"!

But the second offering was another matter. It was, in fact, both Murry and Katherine agreed, so "embittered and angry" that they decided not to publish it, thus annoying Lawrence so greatly that he contributed nothing more to the *Athenaeum*. Even a full year later, Lawrence, still stung by this rejection, struck out at Katherine in a letter of such bitterness that she apparently destroyed it.

"Lawrence," she wrote Murry, "sent me a letter today. He spat in my face and threw filth at me and said: 'I loathe you. You revolt me stewing in your consumption . . . The Italians were quite right to have nothing to do with you' and a great deal more.

"Now I do beseech you," she pleaded, "if you are my man, to stop defending him after that and never to crack him up in the paper. *Be proud!*"

And to spur on the male in Murry, she added:

"In the same letter he said his final opinion of you was that you were 'a dirty little worm.' Well, *be proud.* Don't forgive him for that please."

Murry's immediate reaction was to offer to punch Lawrence in the nose for Katherine. Characteristically, however, he finally expressed his hostility not by using physical violence but by publishing almost hysterically unfavorable reviews of two of Lawrence's latest novels. In *The Lost Girl,* he found an example of "a general and progressive deterioration" in the work of the writer he had once acclaimed. Lawrence, said Murry in this attack, "writes of his characters as though they were animals circling round each other; and on this sub-human plane no human destinies can be decided. [The protagonists] become for us like grotesque beasts in an acquarium, shut off from our apprehension by the misted glass . . . Life, as Mr. Lawrence shows it to us, is not worth living; it is mysteriously degraded by a corrupt mysticism. Mr. Lawrence would have us back to the slime from which we rose . . . Mr. Lawrence's decline is in himself . . ." Of *Women in Love,* which contained some scenes that had already caused one popular magazine to scream, "A Book the Police Should Ban," Murry wrote: "[Lawrence is] deliberately, incessantly, and passionately obscene in the exact sense of that word."

The criticism was particularly hard on a man who, hounded by the self-appointed defenders of public morals all his life, was always baffled when anyone expressed shock at his treatment of sex. Lawrence considered himself the first novelist to give serious, thoughtful attention to a subject that had previously been avoided entirely or treated only in a leering or dishonest way. He was deeply offended when anyone told an off-color story in his presence, since he saw his own mission as a celebrator of life and a defender of the dignity of sex.

Then, quite suddenly after his attacks on Lawrence, Murry became contrite. Once again the disciple, he wrote Lawrence a personal letter which the American poet, Witter Bynner, has described as "highly overwrought—several closely written pages of adulation and of contrition concerning something he had done to alienate Lawrence. He begged at eloquent length for reconciliation. . . . the letter, addressing Lawrence as Master, declared that, if only signal were given, the disciple would on his knees follow his master to the ends of the earth."

And, shortly after that, even Katherine softened. In August, 1922, fearing the approach of death as the result of an illness she had been suffering for years, she made out a new will. She had little property of her own left, after her life with Murry, but she asked him to send one of her books as a memento to each of her close friends. The last name on her list was D.H. Lawrence. She thus made her peace with Lawrence. She died a few months later.

The climax of the Murry-Lawrence relationship was now approaching.

After he received the news of Katherine's death in January, 1923, Lawrence was kind enough to write a thoughtful letter to Murry. But his increasing impatience with his unfaithful disciple was becoming obvious. One day he said to Witter Bynner: "Katherine Mansfield was worth a thousand Murrys! But he drove her sick, neglected her, wandered away from her till she died, and then he prowled back like a hyena to make a meal of her!" In complete disenchantment, he darkly predicted: "He'll do the same to me!"

Fortunately or unfortunately for Murry, however, this remark did not reach his ears, and a short time later he was writing to urge his Master to return to England. He also sent Lawrence some copies of *Adelphi*, the new magazine he had started, and, after repeated invitations, Lawrence had a change of heart. On October 25, 1923, he wrote Murry:

"Yes, I think I shall come back now. I think I shall be back by the beginning of December. Work awhile with you on the *Adelphi*. Then perhaps we'll set off to India. *Quien sabe?"* It was the beginning of the end.

When Lawrence's boat train reached London one day in December, 1923, Murry was waiting on the station platform, with Frieda and the translator, S.S. Koteliansky. To Murry, Lawrence looked weary and sick. Otherwise, however, he considered him unchanged. Of England, the Master said, "I can't bear it." Of the new magazine, he advised: "[It should] attack everything, everything; and explode in one blaze of denunciation."

Almost immediately, he began making plans for an elaborate dinner. It was destined to be an evening of appeal, betrayal, and renunciation without parallel in literary history.

Several of those who were present left some account of that melodramatic evening, and the accounts differ in some details. But the most vivid—and most widely accepted—narrative was written by Catherine Carswell, a perceptive observer who neither then nor later was considered a friend of one of the chief actors, John Middleton Murry.

The site Lawrence selected for his gathering of the faithful was the well-known Café Royal. There, he engaged a special private room, ordered supper for ten, and scowled when the manager insisted upon an advance cash payment. The guests were to be Frieda, Murry, and Koteliansky; Mark Gertler, a painter; Mary Cannan, an actress once married to James M. Barrie; the Honorable Dorothy Brett, a painter and daughter of a viscount; and Catherine Carswell and her husband Donald, who was a barrister and journalist.

Lawrence was sometimes ill at ease in large social gatherings, even after he had become a famous man, but on the evening of the great dinner, he was unusually warm and relaxed, as he greeted his friends and admirers. As Mrs. Carswell later described the scene, he seemed to be saying to his guests: "You'll see I'm quite up to this . . . Mind you play up to me, so that nobody will have the slightest idea that we don't dine in marble halls all the year round."

He had indeed ordered an excellent dinner, and it was served with a flourish, while he beamed at the faithful, and made a special effort to charm the Honorable Dorothy Brett, whom he had heard about but had not met before this evening.

Yet, there was an ominous undertone at the feast, for the truth was that the guests were united only in their feeling for Lawrence. The translator, Koteliansky, detested the barrister, Donald Carswell, who was seated next to him at the table, and pointedly ignored him. The painter, Mark Gertler, regarded the other diners with obvious contempt, and did not bother to join in the desultory conversation. Catherine Carswell and Mary Cannan, uncertain about Lawrence's reasons for inviting them, sat puzzled and silent. Lawrence himself, soon troubled by his guests' restraint, urged them to drink their claret, and, when they had taken a few sips, he immediately refilled their glasses.

Then someone suggested that port should be drunk with the dessert.

Lawrence protested. He sometimes had problems with port.

But one of the men said loudly: "Port is a man's drink." And Lawrence, still determined to make the evening a success, accepted a glass of it.

Koteliansky, who had given in easily to Lawrence's calls for everyone to drink up, had grown increasingly enthusiastic with each glass. Now, as the port was served, he decided to make a speech.

At last, the Master was to be recognized!

"Lawrence is a great man," Koteliansky shouted, and he smashed his wine glass on the table.

Someone handed the speaker another glass, and he continued:

"Nobody here realizes how great he is."

He demolished the second glass.

"Especially no woman here or anywhere can possibly realize the greatness of Lawrence," he proclaimed, making it a man's affair.

Then he crashed another glass on the splinter-covered table.

"Frieda does not count," he suddenly added, in deference to her long life with Lawrence. "Frieda is different. I understand and don't include her. But no other woman here or anywhere can understand anything about Lawrence or what kind of being he is."

Catherine Carswell has recalled the reaction to Koteliansky's passionate words. "We women were silent," she has said. "We felt, I think, very sympathetic to Kot. Anyhow I did. Sympathetic to his jealous, dark and overpowering affection— even inclined to agree with what he said.

"Lawrence looked pale and frightfully ill, but his eyes were starry to an extraordinary degree."

Looking at Lawrence and the broken wine glasses and the faces of the "disciples," Mrs. Carswell was suddenly reminded of the Last Supper.

The faithful were awaiting Lawrence's reply to Koteliansky's extraordinary speech.

Now the Master rose. He spoke quietly. He could not remain in England, he said. England was dying; he must return to the New World, to Mexico or New Mexico. Would they —any of them—go with him?

He looked at each of them in turn, waiting for their answers. Then, as suddenly as it had come, the enchantment of the occasion evaporated.

Mary Cannan was the first to reply. "No," she said, bluntly. "I like you, Lawrence, but not so much as all that . . . I think you are asking what no human being has a right to ask of another."

Lawrence waited for the rest to comment.

One by one, the others responded with vague half-promises, which Lawrence recognized as rejections. Only two seemed ready to follow him: the Honorable Dorothy Brett, who had been completely charmed by Lawrence within ten minutes of this first meeting, and John Middleton Murry.

It was at this moment that the essentially passionless Murry, carried away by the drama of the evening and perhaps by the claret and port, went up to Lawrence and kissed him in a gesture so effusive that Catherine Carswell felt "afflicted" by it.

Seeming to feel her reaction, Murry turned to her:

"Women can't understand this," he told her, echoing Koteliansky's toast. "This is an affair between men. Women can have no part or place in it."

"Maybe," Mrs. Carswell replied, dubiously. Then she added, caustically: ". . . anyhow, it wasn't a woman who betrayed Jesus with a kiss."

But Murry simply embraced Lawrence again.

According to Mrs. Carswell, the Master "sat perfectly still and unresponsive, with a dead-white face in which the eyes alone were alive."

"I *have* betrayed you, old chap, I confess it," Murry said to the silent Lawrence. "In the past I *have* betrayed you. But never again. I call you all to witness, never again."

All eyes were on Lawrence, but the Master now said nothing. Then, as they watched, he, "without uttering a sound," as

Mrs. Carswell has reported, "fell forward with his head on the table, was deadly sick, and became at once unconscious."

Next morning, about nine-thirty, Catherine Carswell found Lawrence looking "fresh and serene."

"Well, Catherine," he said, "I made a fool of myself last night. We must all of us fall at times. It does no harm so long as we first admit and then forget it."

Yet, the Master was never to forget what Murry had said at the Café Royal. And when Murry failed to show any further interest in dropping everything to follow him to a new world, Lawrence felt completely betrayed.

In February, 1924, he wrote defensively to Murry from Paris:

"I don't know if you really want to go to Taos. . . . You seemed to me really very unsure. . . . decide for yourself, . . . Don't think you are doing something for me. I don't want that. Move for yourself alone. Decide for yourself, in your backbone. I don't really want any allegiance or anything of that sort. I don't want any pact. I won't have anything of that sort. If you want to go to America, *bien*. Go without making me responsible."

The bitterness of his disappointment became even clearer as he continued:

". . . a man like you, if he does anything in the name of, or for the sake of, or because of somebody else, is bound to turn like a crazy snake and bite himself and everybody, on account of it.

"Let us clear away all nonsense. I don't *need* you. . . . I need nobody. Neither do you need me. If you pretend to need me, you will hate me for it."

He then broadened his attack:

"Your articles in the *Adelphi* always annoy me. Why care so much about your own fishiness or fleshiness? Why make it so important? Can't you focus yourself outside yourself? Not for ever focused on yourself, *ad nauseam?*"

With each succeeding paragraph, in fact, the spurned Master's denunciation grew wilder:

"You know I don't care a single straw what you think of me. Realize that, once and for all. But when you get to twisting, I dislike you. And I very much dislike any attempt at an intimacy like the one you had with ———— ———— and others. When you start that, I only feel: For God's sake, let me get clear of him.

"I don't care what you think of me, I don't care what you say of me, I don't even care what you do against me, as a writer. . . . Leave off being emotional. Leave off twisting. Leave off having any emotion at all. You haven't any genuine ones, except a certain anger. . . .

"I tell you, if you want to go to America as an unemotional man making an adventure, *bien, allons!* If you want to twist yourself into more knots, don't go with me. That's all. I never had much patience, and I've none now."

The alienation seemed final on March 5, 1924, when Lawrence, Frieda, and the faithful but somewhat tiresome Dorothy Brett sailed on the *Aquitania*. Murry, whose doubts about the venture had grown stronger with each passing week, drove to the railroad station with Dorothy. But, according to her, he was "cold, unelated and silent."

At the station, Lawrence and Frieda had already arrived and found places in a second-class carriage. And there, as Lawrence arranged the baggage and tipped the porters, Murry leaned through the window to say that he would soon be following them to America!

At this point, Lawrence reached his final conclusion about Murry. His lips twisted "into a grim smile." He had, according to Aldous Huxley, at last discovered that Murry's "flame was only a stage effect." The real truth, he decided, was "that the enthusiasm and the earnestness were not spontaneous . . ." He had been "taken in by the hypocrisy—& the . . . charm, . . ." Now, "he was appalled & indignant, all the more indignant for having been taken in."

On May 16, 1924, the now-distant Lawrence wrote a laconic note to Murry:

"We learn from Brett that you are marrying a girl called Violet le Maistre on the 20th of this month . . . If you can settle down with her and be happy I am sure it is the best for you. Better, as you say, than wild-goose-chasing in other continents. I hope you will have a nice place in Dorset, and make friends with your own destiny. I'm sure you can, if you will, take the rest of your life peacefully, with a wife, a home, and probably children. Anyhow, that's what I wish you—an acquiescent, peaceful happiness."

Two days later, the same Lawrence confided to Catherine Carswell his own despondency and dark memories:

"At present I don't write—don't want to—don't care. . . . The world is as it is. I am as I am. We don't fit very well.—I never forget that fatal evening at the Café Royal. That is what coming home means to me. Never again, pray the Lord."

He added:

"One doesn't talk any more about being happy—that is child's talk."

For a few months, he continued to write to Murry with a kind of weary tolerance, but on November 17, 1924, he again struck out at his false disciple by accusing him of "going softer and softer inside . . ."

Finally, his irritation grew too strong for him to control. Wildly, he said that Murry was involved in "an absolutely prize sewer-mess," and then returned again to his own interpretation of the inglorious evening he could not forget:

"You remember that charming dinner at the Café Royal that night? You remember saying: I love you, Lorenzo, but I won't promise not to betray you? Well, you CAN'T betray me, and that's all there is to that. Ergo, just leave off loving me. Let's wipe off all that Judas-Jesus slime.

"Remember, you have betrayed everything and everybody up to now. It may have been your destiny. . . .

"One day, perhaps, you and I may meet as men. Up to now, it has been all slush. Best drop that Christ stuff: it's putrescence."

The Master-Messiah had spoken. The whole world now seemed stale to Lawrence. Nowhere could he find his Utopia. To him, London had become "like some hoary massive underworld, a hoary ponderous inferno [where] the traffic flows through the rigid grey streets like the rivers of hell through their banks of dry, rocky ash." The French were "really *foul*" and Italy was "a ridiculous kingdom." Malta was "a horrible island" and Capri "a stewpot of semi-literary cats." Of literary people in general, he now said:

"Curse the idiotic editors and the more idiotic people who read: shall I pander to their maudlin taste? They bore me."

During the year 1925, Murry and Lawrence exchanged casual letters, but on January 4, 1926, the Master's deep repugnance of his false disciple was once again crystallized.

"My dear Jack," he now agonized in writing, "*it's no good!* All you can do now, sanely, is to leave off. . . .

"In short, shut up. Throw the *Adelphi* to the devil, throw your own say after it, say good-bye to J.M.M. . . .

"My dear chap, people don't want the one-man show of you alone, nor the Punch and Judy show of you and me. Why, oh why, try to ram yourself down people's throats? Offer them a tasty tit-bit, and if they give you five quid, have a drink on it."

This letter was followed by three years of silence, at the end of which Murry, trying once again to stir up some warmth in the ashes, received an aloof reply from the Master: "I didn't know your handwriting any more," Lawrence wrote, "it seems to have gone so small and sort of invisible."

In May, 1929, Murry, having heard reports that the Master was ill, suggested a final meeting, and Lawrence at last wrote finis to the strange seventeen-year relationship.

"I don't understand you, your workings are beyond me," Lawrence began. "And you don't get me. . . . Believe me, we belong to different worlds, different ways of consciousness, you and I, and the best we can do is to let one another alone, for ever and ever. We are a dissonance.

"My health is a great nuisance, but by no means as bad as all that, and I have no idea of passing out. . . . So don't think of coming to Mallorca. It is no good our meeting . . ."

Then he penned the final epitaph:

". . . even when we are immortal spirits," he declared, "we shall dwell in different Hades."

Nine and a half months later, David Herbert Lawrence died. But John Middleton Murry spent the rest of his life tracing and retracing the course of the troubled friendship he could neither sustain nor surrender.

The "Ridiculous"

MR. WALPOLE Endures Agonies at the Hands of MR. MAUGHAM.

9

LATE one evening in September, 1930, the English novelist Hugh Walpole returned home from the theater. Before retiring to his room, he tucked under his arm a set of printer's proofs for a new novel, *Cakes and Ale*. The novel had been written by his old friend, W. Somerset Maugham, and, as a member of the selection committee of the English Book Society, the illustrious Mr. Walpole hoped he would be able to recommend it to the Society's members.

More than one important critic had begun to refer to Mr. Walpole as "a great novelist," "a genius," and even "the twentieth-century Dickens." He saw no reason to dispute them. Pleased with the deference shown to him as a public figure this evening at the theater, he didn't suspect that these proofs which he carried so casually into his cluttered bedroom were about to make him a public laughingstock. Nor had he any suspicion that this was to be the beginning of one of the most intriguing literary mysteries of the twentieth century.

Nineteen years earlier, the sometimes sardonic and un-obliging Mr. Maugham had given advice and encouragement to the then youthful Walpole, who had decided to abandon an unpromising career as a teacher with the hope of becoming a rich and famous novelist. In those days, Mr. Walpole had thoroughly enjoyed the company of his quiet little friend. True, Maugham had now and then revealed a penchant for suddenly stammering forth malicious comments about some of the most eminent literary figures of the times—about the pomposity of the great Henry James, or the vastly inflated reputations of George Meredith and Thomas Hardy, or the inability of one or another noted critic to distinguish between good books and pretentious frauds. But the friendship of the two young writers had gone along quite pleasantly for nearly two decades, and the period had proved exceedingly profitable for them both.

Every twelve months the industrious Walpole had pro-duced at least one fat volume, and in his best year he had turned out four. His shelves were now weighed down by thirty-one published books, with each new book giving evi-dence of a livelier sale than the one before.

Yet, with all his success, Hugh Walpole was an unhappy man. He suffered from an overwhelming sense of insecurity which, in moments of self-examination, he was able to trace back to the wounds and fears of his childhood. Of these early years he sometimes observed, "No one liked me—not masters, boys, friends of the family, nor relations. . ." His teachers remembered him as a sad and easily terrified little boy who, unable to learn spelling or arithmetic, frequently retreated into daydreams. His schoolmates had sometimes forced him to stand naked, while they jeered at him and stuck pins into his skin; but more often they had ignored him. Even his father and mother had hurt him. One night, as he lay in bed worrying about the approach of another school term, he overheard them discussing his faults and voicing complete despair for his future.

Despite these dark memories, however, the now-famous Walpole seemed outwardly hearty, self-confident, and contented. A friend who had been taken in by his apparent happiness and boisterous laugh had even said of him, "Life is good to Hugh Walpole, everything is wonderful, everybody is interesting." The tortured man revealed his thoughts only in his diaries and private journals. Sometimes, too, he awoke, screaming, in the middle of the night.

It was this troubled man who, after hanging up his hat and jacket and taking off his shoes, sat on the edge of his bed and began to read *Cakes and Ale*. At first, as he records it, he read "idly." But his attitude soon changed. To his diary he confided the next day, "[I] read on with increasing horror. Unmistakable portrait of myself." And it did indeed seem to be an "unmistakable portrait" that began to take shape at the beginning of *Cakes and Ale*, for within the first few pages, Maugham introduced into his narrative a supposedly fictional novelist named Alroy Kear.

". . . no one," wrote Maugham of this Alroy Kear, "could show a more genuine cordiality to a fellow novelist whose name was on everybody's lips, but no one could more genially turn a cold shoulder on him when idleness, failure, or someone else's success had cast a shade on his notoriety. . . ."

Here was the charge of opportunism that had frequently been leveled against Walpole himself, and no one was more aware of it than he. Charles Marriott, who had been one of the first writers to encourage the ingratiating youth, was to write of Walpole, "Not long after we settled in London Hugh had engaged to dine with us but threw us over for an invitation from old Lady Lovelace, explaining quite frankly that she would be of more use to him in that stage of his career as a writer. Personally I was not scandalized; given Hugh's temperament, his determination to get on, and his uncertain position at the time, his desertion seemed to me at least logical, and what interested me most was Hugh's candour and his apparent inability to see why it should have given offence; but it upset the feminine part of my family a good deal."

Yet the same accusation might be made against many another ambitious young writer, and thus Walpole could by no means be certain that Maugham thought of him as the model for Alroy Kear. He read on:

"I had watched with admiration his [Alroy Kear's] rise in the world of letters. His career might well have served as a model for any young man entering upon the pursuit of literature. I could think of no one among my contemporaries who had achieved so considerable a position on so little talent. . . ."

The mark hit home. Nervously, Walpole continued reading:

"He [Alroy Kear] was perfectly aware of it [this fact], and it must have seemed to him sometimes little short of a miracle that he had been able . . . to compose already some thirty books. I cannot but think that he saw the white light of revelation when first he read that Charles Dickens . . . stated that genius was an infinite capacity for taking pains. He pondered the saying. If that was all, he must have told himself, he could be a genius like the rest . . ."

This figure of "some thirty books" was dangerously close to Walpole's own thirty-one. A few pages later, another passage seemed aimed even more directly at him:

"Roy was very modest about his first novel. It was short,

neatly written, and, as is everything he has produced since, in perfect taste. He sent it with a pleasant letter to all the leading writers of the day, and in this he told each one how greatly he admired his works, how much he had learned from his study of them, and how ardently he aspired to follow, albeit at a humble distance, the trail his correspondent had blazed. He laid his book at the feet of a great artist as the tribute of a young man entering upon the profession of letters to one whom he would always look up to as his master. Deprecatingly, fully conscious of his audacity in asking so busy a man to waste his time on a neophyte's puny effort, he begged for criticism and guidance. Few of the replies were perfunctory. The authors he wrote to, flattered by his praise, answered at length. . . . Here, they felt, was someone worth taking a little trouble over."

Poor Walpole! Now he found it disturbingly easy to substitute "Hugh" for "Alroy" on every page. Before submitting the manuscript of his first novel to a publisher, he had sent it not only to Charles Marriott but also to the novelists Ethel Colburn Mayne and E. M. Forster, and in each case he had prepared the way of offering lavish praise for the work of the older writer. Furthermore, all three had "answered at length" —Marriott with detailed suggestions, Forster with a five-page epistle, and Miss Mayne with a twelve-page treatise. And this was not all. Other flattering letters, sometimes accompanied by manuscripts, had helped him gain the attention and, later, the friendship of a host of useful celebrities, including Arnold Bennett, Henry James, Thomas Hardy, Rudyard Kipling, Virginia Woolf, H. G. Wells—and W. Somerset Maugham. Some of these notable people had even returned the favor by sending their own manuscripts for criticism to him, and Walpole, like Alroy Kear, "could never find a thing amiss." The invariable result of his dependably enthusiastic reaction to their work had been that, as Maugham said of Alroy Kear,

"They thought him not only a good sort, but a sound judge."
The struggling Walpole had also developed a shrewd
method of dealing with hostile critics. And, to his horror, he
came across a description of Kear's method, so similar to his
own, of handling such matters:

". . . when someone has written a stinging criticism and
Roy, especially since his reputation became so great, has had
to put up with some very virulent abuse, he does not, like
most of us, shrug his shoulders, fling a mental insult at the
ruffian who does not like our work, and then forget about it;
he writes a long letter to his critic, telling him that he is very
sorry he thought his book bad, but his review was so interesting in itself, and if he might venture to say so, showed so
much critical sense and so much feeling for words, that he felt
bound to write to him. No one is more anxious to improve
himself than he and he hopes he is still capable of learning.
He does not want to be a bore, but if the critic has nothing
to do on Wednesday or Friday will he come and lunch at the
Savoy and tell him why exactly he thought his book so bad?
No one can order a lunch better than Roy, and generally by
the time the critic has eaten half a dozen oysters and a cut
from a saddle of baby lamb, he has eaten his words too. It is
only poetic justice that when Roy's next novel comes out the
critic should see in the new work a very great advance."

Walpole's own practice of writing to critics to invite them
to lunch had, in fact, long ago become his almost automatic
response either to praise or to attack. Once, he had been so
disturbed by a reviewer's "virulent abuse" that he had indeed gone so far as to write an angry instead of a humble
letter, but he still recoiled from his mistake. The critic he
had thus openly challenged was Rebecca West, and his resentment had arisen not only as a result of Miss West's
published comments about his books, but also because he had
been told—as it so happens, quite falsely—that Miss West had

once described him as "by far the most brilliant and beautiful of the Bishop of Edinburgh's daughters."

All his life Walpole was to keep Miss West's waspish reply to his own letter:

"What is this about 'girding at you for a lot of years'?" Miss West had countered with asperity. "So far as I can remember I have made but two references to you in my six years of journalism—one this allusion to *The Dark Forest* [Walpole's seventh novel]. The other a review of *The Golden Scarecrow* [his first collection of short stories]. . . ."

Then Miss West had grown more scathing:

"I suggest that this talk about my 'continuing for ever and ever this public scalping' is literary gossip without any basis in fact. I do not conceal my feelings when I think people are talking nonsense . . . I also do not conceal my feelings when I think people are talking sensibly and beautifully . . . If people choose to remember the far less frequent occasions of my dislike rather than the quite numerous occasions of my appreciation it is hardly my fault! . . . It's certainly true that I don't like your work; I think it facile and without artistic impulse. This is a sincere judgment on purely literary grounds; for I have never met you but once, at a tea-party of Mrs. Belloc Lowndes' some months ago . . . I have never made any attempt to get your books to review . . . When one is sent to me I review it without, so far as I can remember, any remarkable paroxysm of dislike. I then never mention you again for . . . years . . . You then write to me and accuse me of having girded at you for years. And make the startling suggestion that 'if you think me no good at all then leave me altogether alone'—as if it might not be the duty of a critic to point out the fallaciousness of the method and vision of a writer who was being swallowed whole by the British public, as you are! Really, Mr. Walpole! I probably shall leave you alone as I am less keen than ever on reviewing novels now—but I am appalled by the theoretical aspects of your demand. Really, Mr. Walpole! . . ."

What a slip this had been! And it had convinced him that reviewers were a dangerous lot, to be approached with a respect bordering on reverence. So he had been extremely careful in addressing Katherine Mansfield when she had written in the *Athenæum*, ". . . we think the critic, after an examination of *The Captives*, would find it hard to state with any conviction that Mr. Walpole is a creative artist."

He had asked her most contritely *why* she detested his book. And the soft approach had brought a soft answer. The flattered Miss Mansfield had replied, very sweetly, that she "*far* from detested" *The Captives*. She even went so far as to call the book "almost a spiritual exercise in . . . courage." She still had her reservations about it, she admitted, but she added, ". . . I feel that Hugh Walpole's next novel will be the one to look for." Soon, in her correspondence with Mr. Walpole, Miss Mansfield was signing herself, "Your from-this-time-forth '*constant reader*.' "

As he continued his reading of *Cakes and Ale*, the unhappy Walpole found other passages that seemed to caricature him. In one section, he noticed a paragraph that apparently mocked his custom of announcing to the newspapers his opinion on every issue of the moment. Wrote Maugham:

"He [Alroy] was never impatient with the persons who call up the celebrated on the telephone at inconvenient moments to ask them for the information of newspaper readers whether they believe in God or what they eat for breakfast. . . . the public knew what he thought of prohibition, vegetarianism, jazz, garlic, exercise . . ."

Even his method of ordering a lunch or a dinner for the guests he invited to his club seemed to be mimicked in

Maugham's gleeful parody. The pretentious Alroy Kear escorts his guest to the dining room of *his* club:
"'I can recommend the veal-and-ham pie,' said Roy.
"'All right.'
"'I'll mix the salad myself,' he told the waiter in an off-hand and yet commanding way, and then, casting his eye once more on the bill of fare, generously: 'And what about some asparagus to follow?'
"'That would be very nice.'
"His manner grew a trifle grander.
"'Asparagus for two and tell the chef to choose them himself. Now what would you like to drink? What do you say to a bottle of hock? We rather fancy our hock here.'
"When I had agreed to this he told the waiter to call the wine steward. I could not but admire the authoritative and yet perfectly polite manner in which he gave his orders. You felt that thus would a well-bred king send for one of his field marshals. . . .
"'Hulloa, Armstrong, we want some of the Liebfraumilch, the '21.'
"'Very good, sir.'
"'How's it holding up? Pretty well? We shan't be able to get any more of it, you know.'
"'I'm afraid not, sir.'
"'Well, it's no good meeting trouble halfway, is it, Armstrong?'
"Roy smiled at the steward with breezy cordiality. . . ."

It was late, and Walpole was weary, but he found it impossible to stop reading. When he finally finished the book, he was so distraught that he could not possibly go to sleep. Had his old friend Maugham used him as a model for the fatuous Alroy Kear? Or were his fears unfounded? True, there were parts of the description which did not quite fit Walpole. For example, Kear had come from a civil service family, while Walpole's father was a bishop. Then, too, Kear was "six feet high in his stockinged feet," while Walpole was about an inch and a half shorter. Kear was a golfer, a fox hunter, and a man who enjoyed the company of women; Walpole took little exercise, did not like to hunt, and was a lifelong bachelor who had intense friendships with a small number of men but felt an obvious fear of his female contemporaries. Yet these discrepancies were minor, and, he realized with a shudder, the similarities between himself and Kear far outnumbered any trivial differences. Both shared the most ordinary physical characteristics: they had, in common, "broad shoulders," light-brown hair, a rather short, broad nose, and a square chin. Both, Walpole had to admit, were "not handsome, but in a manly way agreeable to look at."

It was a puzzled as well as frightened Walpole who telephoned the writer J. B. Priestley early the next morning. Priestley was also a member of the English Book Society selection committee, and he, too, had received a set of printer's proofs of *Cakes and Ale*.

For the moment, Priestley proved of some comfort to his badly shaken caller. He told Walpole that he had already asked Maugham on whom the character of Alroy Kear was based. Somewhat relieved after their talk, Walpole was able to record in his diary: ". . . he [Priestley] says that Maugham absolutely denies that it is me." Still suspicious, however, he added, in a cry so plaintive that one could almost hear it, "But how can he, when there are in one conversation the very accents of my voice?" A few days later, he expressed continued worry in his diary: "Still fussed over the book . . . I think the thing will be a scandal, and I cannot imagine what Maugham was about in publishing it." With his occasional ability to see himself as others saw him, he also admitted, rue-fully, "It will amuse my enemies though."

As more and more people in London's literary world heard about *Cakes and Ale*, the scandal predicted by Walpole was quick to develop. Yet, perversely, the public's attention first focussed not on Alroy Kear, but on a second character in the book, one Edward Driffield. To many early readers, Driffield clearly seemed to be based on the late, great novelist, Thomas Hardy. Both Driffield and Hardy had come from peasant stock. Both had written about the lives of simple people who lived in rural areas. Both had married twice, had gained their fame late in life, and had been decorated with the Order of Merit. Hardy had died only two years previously, and now the most vocal of the literary critics were censuring Maugham for "trampling on the grave" of a distinguished man, since Driffield had been portrayed as a somewhat simple-minded fellow who sang ribald comic songs, who was partial to dropping in at the neighboring pub, and who once hastily left town late at night to avoid paying his accumulated bills.

To Walpole, this public fickleness was the final blow. Hardy was dead, and a little mockery could not hurt him. But he, Walpole, was alive and suffering! "It is the stab in the back that hurts me so," he complained in his diary. "He [Maugham] has used so many little friendly things and twisted them round. Anyway it's a caddish book."

There was only one thing to do. After days of hesitation, he decided to clear up the entire mystery by writing directly to the author.

Bracing himself, he wrote a letter accusing his old friend of drawing "a cruel portrait." Carefully, he indicated the passages which seemed to identify Kear as a lightly disguised

Walpole. Indignantly, he pointed out the very words of a conversation he remembered once having had with Maugham during a chance meeting in California. The book, Walpole said, reproduced this exchange exactly.

To his great relief, he received a soothing reply:

"I am really very unlucky," Maugham responded, in seemingly injured tones. "As you may have seen I have been attacked in the papers because they think my old man [Edward Driffield] is intended to be a portrait of Hardy. It is absurd. The only grounds are that both died old, received the O.M. [Order of Merit] and were married twice. You know that for my story I needed this and that there is nothing of Hardy in my character. Now I have your letter. I cannot say I was surprised to receive it because I had heard from Charlie Evans that Priestley and Clemence Dane had talked to him about it. He told them that it had never occurred to him that there was any resemblance between the Alroy Kear of my novel and you; and when he spoke to me about it I was able very honestly to assure him that nothing had been further from my thoughts than to describe you. . . ."

Maugham took pains to emphasize the most obvious differences between the fictional Kear and the real Walpole.

"I do not see any likeness," he wrote. "My man is an athlete and a sportsman, who tries to be as little like a man of letters as he can. Can you really recognize yourself in this? Surely no one is more the complete man of letters than you are and really you cannot think of yourself as a famous golfer and a fervid fox-hunter. Nor is the appearance described anything like yours. Nor so far as I have ever seen do you frequent smart society. . . . The only thing that you can go on is the fact that you also are a lecturer. I admit that if I had thought twice of it I would have omitted this. But after all you are not the only English man of letters who lectures, but only the best known . . ."

He dismissed, somewhat airily, two of Walpole's basic griev-
ances.

"The loud laugh is nothing," he wrote. "All big men with
the sort of heartiness I have described have a loud laugh. The
conversation you mention in California has entirely slipped my
memory and I cannot place it in the book. I certainly was not
conscious of repeating it. Really I should not have been such
a fool. I certainly never intended Alroy Kear to be a portrait of
you. He is made up of a dozen people and the greater part of
him is myself. There is more of me in him than of any writer
I know. I suggest that if there is anything in him that you recognize it is because to a greater or less extent we are all the
same. Certain characteristics we all have and I gave them to
Alroy Kear because I found them in myself. They do not seem
to me less absurd because I have them.

"I do not think for an instant that there will be any reference to this business in the papers, but if there is I promise
you that I will immediately write, protest and vehemently
deny that there has ever been in my mind any thought of
portraying you."

At first, Walpole was mollified by this lengthy and con-
crete denial. He succeeded in *almost* convincing himself that
his earlier suspicions of his old friend had been unwarranted.
". . . I've no doubt that the picture was composite," he wrote
jubilantly in his journal a few weeks later. And again, cling-
ing to every thread that offered support, "He [Maugham] said
himself that he had taken much of the figure from himself,
and I think that is true." He was overjoyed at being able to
blame the flaws in Kear's character on the very man who had
conceived him.

Yet nagging doubts persisted in his mind. Perhaps these
resulted from his unhappy childhood, which had taught him
to expect betrayals, or perhaps he knew the sometimes malicious Maugham too well. At any rate, his joy was short-lived,

for he was soon wondering miserably whether it was possible that the *least* attractive traits of the supposedly Maugham-like Kear had been taken not from Maugham but from himself. No, he tried to tell himself, this could not be true. Surely he could acquit himself "on most of the criticism." Actually, he decided, he was a pretty fine fellow. Then, forlornly, but with startling clarity, he admitted, ". . . I can quite clearly see that I might appear just such a figure to a cynic and an uneasy unhappy man like Willie. It is his nature to be deeply sentimental and to be revolted by his sentimentality, so that he turns on anyone he thinks sentimental. . . ."

In the closing days of the year, he was still worrying whether or not he possessed the worst characteristics of Alroy Kear. If he did, he wrote disconsolately, ". . . then the sooner I pass out the better."

A year later, none other than W. Somerset Maugham was experiencing some sleepless nights. And, ironically enough, it was Hugh Walpole who offered him comfort and help. The public watched and was delighted.

American friends had sent to Maugham in England the page proofs of a new novel entitled *Gin and Bitters,* a book described by its publishers as "a novel about a novelist who writes novels about other novelists." It had been published in the United States under the pseudonym of "A. Riposte."

Obviously, Walpole had the strongest justification for publishing a *riposte* to Maugham, and English readers of the proofs were quick to whisper that here was revenge for *Cakes and Ale.* With a friend named Gerald Haxton, if biographer Karl G. Pfeiffer is to be believed, Maugham ". . . sat up all one night feverishly reading it . . ." but decided he would not sue the publisher for libel, for if he did, he would only puff a mediocre work into a *succès de scandale.* The novel was published in England under the title *Full Circle*, but, according to Rupert Hart-Davis, "Maugham either brought an injunction or got it stopped in some other way, and it was quickly withdrawn from sale." Pfeiffer also asserts that Maugham "took steps to suppress the novel in England," but Maugham has denied this in a letter to the author, with the comment: "I never met the author of *Gin and Bitters* and I would never have dreamt of trying to suppress it."

One reviewer called *Gin and Bitters* "a wittily competent novel devoted to stripping the flesh off the trivial bones of [a fictional character named] Leverson Hurle, successful English novelist." He added, "But the technique of this merciless literary attack is not so much that of fencing as of consecrated butchery."

The butchery begins in chapter one, when the ambitious young writer, Hurle, is shown in bed with Mrs. Cynthia Stoddard, the thirty-five-year-old wife of his employer. But his mind isn't on Mrs. Stoddard. ". . . young as he was, he felt himself old, bored and disgusted: not so much with Mrs. Stoddard as with life itself: the small amount of notice it had, up to now, taken of him . . ."

Before going downstairs to begin his day's work as Stoddard's secretary, Hurle puts a dab of perfume on his handkerchief, which he then applies to his forehead. He half-wishes that Mr. Stoddard would come storming into the bedroom and make a scene, so that he would then have "something really worth writing about."

When Hurle reports for work, Mr. Stoddard notices the aroma from his handkerchief and comments calmly on the smell of Hurle's cigarettes, which he has noticed in his wife's bedroom. "People who are out of—shall we say the top-drawer? —are so careful about things of that sort," Stoddard explains.

Hurle is dismissed, and much of the rest of *Gin and Bitters* is devoted to his travels in remote parts of the world, where he searches for material for his stories and uses people "without any sort of scruple . . ." After accepting hospitality, he puts his hosts "bodily—their most private affairs, their loves and hates and sorrows—into his books. For though he was acclaimed as a great writer he was quite unable to work without someone actual to work upon." And later, "he took to lambasting his fellow writers, alive and dead . . . One living writer in particular . . ."

As rumors spread that Walpole had written this thinly veiled attack upon Maugham, English literary figures could offer some convincing reasons why the speculation might be right. The fact that the book had appeared so soon after *Cakes and Ale* could serve as evidence since Walpole was in the habit of churning out a book every few months. And some readers felt that the Machiavellian Walpole had cleverly inserted a false trail to conceal his responsibility for the book. A minor—and unimpressive—character in *Gin and Bitters* was named Mr. Polehue, and he was a novelist. It was clear that the name was formed by combining the second syllable of Walpole with a misspelling of Hugh. To add to the suspicions, Walpole reacted like a frightened child found with sticky fingers after a piece of candy had been stolen. Terrified by the thought that his old friend might hear the rumors and believe them, he wrote to Maugham immediately:

"I do hope you won't think me impertinent in writing you this line," he pleaded, ever humble in his letters. "I've just read *Gin and Bitters* and I do most earnestly beg you to injunct its publication in England. It is a *foul book* (I have no idea who wrote it save that it's a woman). If there were any doubt for whom it is intended that would be different, but already there have been paragraphs in the press here making it quite clear. It will undoubtedly make a sensation and although you may not care what anyone says, it is a disgrace that people who don't know you should have that impression of you. Heinemann (even if they publish it, which I hope they won't) can't prevent the general odiousness that will follow the publication. I am sure you can obtain an injunction. I'm willing to give evidence on your behalf to any extent and I'm sure many others would. The book is *foul* and you ought to stop it. I'm not writing this from hysteria or any motive but one of real and true affection for yourself. I do beg you to stop the thing as I'm *sure* you can."

The public was wrong. After intensive sleuthing, reviewers were able to identify the actual author of *Gin and Bitters*. The book was not Walpole's at all. It was the work of one Elinor Mordaunt, a facile and prolific writer of novels, of stories for the women's magazines, and of travel books. According to one biographer, she had "followed in Maugham's footsteps in Tahiti and other South Sea islands, and collected everything unpleasant about him that she could."

But the identification of Elinor Mordaunt did not mean that the Maugham-Walpole mystery had ended. Many readers were certain that Maugham *had* lampooned Walpole in *Cakes and Ale*. They also delighted in the sting of Walpole's comments on *Gin and Bitters*. For even if Walpole hadn't actually written the book, he had positively identified the monster Hurle in this "foul" book as his old friend Maugham. Even close acquaintances of the two writers now made a game of watching for a cooling in the friendship between them. When Walpole accepted an invitation to a large dinner party given by his supposed mocker, his presence was recorded as arousing "much mirth among the literati . . ."

Yet, poor Walpole wanted desperately to believe that Maugham was still his friend. As edition after edition of *Cakes and Ale* was published, he accepted the book's continuing popularity without any outward sign of pain. In 1937, he did, rather weakly, introduce into the narrative of his novel,

The Life and Adventures of John Cornelius, a cynical novelist named Archie Bertrand, who was probably intended to represent Maugham. But the caricature was so pale and the novel itself so insipid that few readers even noticed the attempt. So, with only a show of revenge, Hugh Walpole died, in 1941, with the mystery of Alroy Kear's true counterpart still unsolved.

It was said that *Cakes and Ale* had not only ruined the last eleven years of Walpole's life, but also his reputation as a writer.

In 1950, nine years after Walpole's death, the American publishers of the popular Modern Library editions decided to issue *Cakes and Ale*. They commissioned the author to write a special introduction, and thus, suddenly, the entire mystery of Alroy Kear's identity was solved.

"It was true," Maugham announced, after years of denying it, "that I had had Hugh Walpole in mind when I devised the character to whom I gave the name of Alroy Kear." His excuse: "No author can create a character out of nothing. He must have a model to give him a starting point; but then his imagination goes to work, he builds him up, adding a trait here, a trait there, which his model did not possess . . . It is only thus that a novelist can give his characters the intensity, the reality which makes them not only plausible, but convincing. . . ."

But, Maugham wrote, his intention had not been vicious.

"I had no wish to hurt Hugh Walpole's feelings," he said. "He was a genial creature and he had friends who, though they were apt to laugh at him, were genuinely attached to him. He was easy to like, but difficult to respect. When I devised the character of Alroy Kear I did all I could to cover my tracks; I made him a sportsman who rode to hounds, played tennis and golf much better than most, and an amorist who skillfully avoided the entanglement of marriage. None of this could be said of Hugh Walpole. When I replied to his letter I told him this, and I added that I had taken one characteristic from an author we both knew and another from another, and moreover that above all I had put in Alroy Kear a great deal of myself. . . . But the fact remained that I had given Alroy Kear certain traits, certain discreditable foibles which Hugh Walpole too notoriously had, so that few people in the literary world of London failed to see that he had been my model."

Somewhat more gently Maugham concluded:

"If his [Hugh's] ghost wanders uneasily in the book shops to see that his works are properly displayed and he remembers how I mocked at his ambition one day to be the grand old man of English literature, he must chuckle with malicious glee when he sees that I, even I, who laughed at him, seem to be on the verge of reaching that sad, absurd and transitory eminence."

Had, then, the aging Mr. Maugham softened somewhat with the passage of time toward the man who had earlier in the century cut such a pompous—yet pathetic—figure in the world of English letters? The answer is no.

"Walpole's reputation was never very great," he wrote in the fall of 1961. Nor did he see any reason whatsoever to change his opinion of Mr. Walpole as a man. In fact, wrote Mr. Maugham, still very much in the spirit of *Cakes and Ale,* and quite unrelentingly, "Hugh was a ridiculous creature."

10

Mr. Hemingway proves a good sport~~ But only to himself.

ONE evening in the winter of 1920–1921, Sherwood Anderson, who was already famous as the author of *Winesburg, Ohio,* visited an old friend named Y.K. Smith, who had a large apartment at 100 East Chicago Avenue in Chicago. Smith was at that time working for an advertising agency, but he hoped some day to support himself as a writer, and he rented rooms in his apartment to several young men with similar ambitions.

Most of Smith's tenants spent more time in talking about writing than in actually writing, but there was one notable exception among the group. This was a boyish veteran of twenty-two who had already gained some experience as a newspaper reporter and who reacted impatiently when his fellow roomers talked effetely about symbols, form, and experimentation in writing.

The young roomer's name was Ernest Hemingway.

"Artist, art, artistic!" Hemingway shouted after one such discussion. "Can't we ever hear the last of that stuff!" And he returned to his room and his battered typewriter, leaving the others to continue their literary discussion in more subdued voices.

Yet even Hemingway was interested in meeting Sherwood Anderson, who was, after all, a major literary figure. And he was soon fascinated by Anderson's talk of his travels, of the eminent people he had met, of his past writings and his ideas for future stories.

In turn, after that first meeting, Sherwood Anderson also expressed to Smith an interest in Hemingway.

"Thanks for introducing me to that young fellow," he said. "I think he's going to go some place."

Anderson did not realize that he was to be among the first of many talented people who would help the ambitious Hemingway on his way—nor that the consequence of this aid would be eventual alienation. This was a lesson in the fine art of literary mayhem that many of the youthful Hemingway's friends were only later to learn.

After that first meeting, Anderson returned frequently to the Smith apartment, and the husky, fresh-faced Hemingway was always there. Sometimes Anderson brought along a story he had just finished, and, if Smith and the others insisted, he would consent to read it to them. Usually, they did insist, and on such occasions Hemingway was the most eager of listeners.

As a rule, a group discussion followed each reading, and, as long as Anderson was still present, the comments were almost always enthusiastic. After all, editors were begging for Anderson's stories and critics were devoting long and respectful essays to his experiments in fiction. Only after Anderson had left the apartment was doubt expressed. And the one who expressed this doubt was none other than Ernest Hemingway. One comment by the young writer is still remembered. Of a line in one of Anderson's stories, Hemingway is reported to have said that a writer shouldn't "let a sentence like that go."

But such criticism came always after Anderson had left. The younger man did not trouble Anderson himself with it. Instead, he spent many evenings questioning the older man about Paris, where an entire generation of young Americans seemed to be developing their talents, freed of the necessity of working at the kind of dull job Hemingway was at the time burdened with in Chicago.

Then, approximately a year after he had first met Anderson, Hemingway made up his mind to go to Paris himself. And on December 3, 1921, Anderson, in an effort to help him, sat down to dash off a seventy-seven-word letter introducing the "young fellow" to the Buddha-like figure around whom the many American writers in Paris seemed to gather.

"Dear Miss Stein," Anderson wrote, "I am writing this note to make you acquainted with my friend Ernest Hemingway, who with Mrs. Hemingway is going to Paris to live, and will ask him to drop it in the mails when he arrives there.

"Mr. Hemingway is an American writer instinctively in touch with everything worth-while going on here, and I know you will find Mr. and Mrs. Hemingway delightful people to know.

"They will be temporarily at the Hotel Jacob, rue Jacob.

                              "Sincerely
                                   "Sherwood Anderson"

Thus it was to Sherwood Anderson that Hemingway owed the introduction which was to prove of such inestimable help to him in his career as a writer, and, for the time being, at least, he seemed grateful for it. Just before leaving Chicago for Paris, Hemingway and his first wife, Hadley, discovered that they had some canned food left over. They gathered up the cans and dropped them into a knapsack. Tossing the knapsack over his shoulder, Hemingway made his way to Anderson's apartment.

". . . I remember his coming up the stairs, a magnificent broad-shouldered man, shouting as he came," Anderson wrote later. "That was a nice idea, bringing thus to a fellow scribbler the food he had to abandon . . ."

Soon after he and his wife had reached Paris, Hemingway found his way to the comfortable, art-crammed apartment at 27 rue de Fleurus, which had already become a shrine for would-be writers.

"I remember very well the impression I had of Hemingway that first afternoon," Gertrude Stein later recalled in *The Autobiography of Alice B. Toklas,* a book she wrote in the person of her own companion. "He was an extraordinarily good-looking young man, . . . rather foreign looking, with passionately interested, rather than interesting eyes. He sat in front of Gertrude Stein [wrote Gertrude Stein] and listened and looked.

"They talked then, and more and more, a great deal together," she continued. "He asked her to come and spend an evening in their [his and Hadley's] apartment and look at his work. Hemingway had then and has always a very good instinct for finding apartments in strange but pleasing localities and good femmes de ménage and good food. . . ."

She continued in this third-person-first-person account:

"We spent the evening there and he and Gertrude Stein went over all the writing he had done up to that time. He had begun the novel that it was inevitable he would begin and there were the little poems afterwards printed . . . in the Contact Edition. Gertrude Stein rather liked the poems, they were direct, Kiplingesque, but the novel she found wanting. There is a good deal of description in this, she said, and not particularly good description. Begin over again and concentrate, she said."

And Hemingway listened closely. Sometimes, during these apprentice years, he seemed, in fact, to listen too closely.

". . . he comes and sits at my feet and praises me," Ford Madox Ford was shortly to remark to Gertrude Stein. "It makes me nervous."

The Gertrude Stein to whom Hemingway paid such worshipful attention in the 1920's was not yet really famous, despite her circle of admirers. Though she had been writing for fifteen years and though her work was beginning to appear in many of the little magazines, she was still receiving—and saving—puzzled rejections from the editors of the better-known magazines, as well as from book publishers.

"Dear Madam," the editor of *The English Review* wrote to her when she submitted some short pieces to his magazine, "I really cannot publish these curious Studies." And Frank Palmer, a British book publisher, was equally unsympathetic. "I have read through a portion of the MS which you gave me on Friday," he wrote to her, "but I regret that I cannot make you any proposition concerning the same. I say I have only read a portion of it, because I found it perfectly useless to read further, as I did not understand any of it. . . ."

Another British book publisher wrote a cheerful letter of rejection, in which he burlesqued the "rose-is-a-rose-is-a-rose" style that was to be so often satirized by the millions who never actually got around to reading Gertrude Stein's books. "Dear Madam," he wrote, "I am only one, only one, only one. Only one being, one at the same time. Not two, not three, only one. Only one life to live, only sixty minutes in one hour. Only one pair of eyes. Only one brain. Only one being. Being only one, having only one pair of eyes, having only one time, having only one life, I cannot read your M.S. three or four times. Not even one time. Only one look, only one look is enough. Hardly one copy would sell here. Hardly one. Hardly one.

"Many thanks. I am returning the M.S. by registered post. Only one M.S. by one post. Sincerely yours, A.C. Fifield."

Ellery Sedgwick, the editor of *The Atlantic Monthly*, also returned one of her submissions with a brief note, which read:

"Your poems, I am sorry to say, would be a puzzle picture to our readers. All who have not the key must find them baffling, and—alack! that key is known to very, very few."

But while others remained skeptical, Gertrude Stein never doubted. She had made up her mind early in her life that she was a genius. Undismayed by rejections, she proceeded to gather up another sheaf of pages from her ever-growing stacks of sketches, poems, and novels, and to ship this collection off to *The Atlantic* with a suggestion that Sedgwick take another look while he could still redeem himself as the editor of a magazine intended for the literati.

Again, Sedgwick declined her work.

". . . you misjudge our public," he wrote this time. "Here there is no group of *literati* or *illuminati* or *cognoscenti* or *illustrissimi* of any kind, who could agree upon interpretations of your poetry. More than this, you could not find a handful even of careful readers who would think that it was a serious effort. Pardon me if I say this. I am talking quite seriously, and am trying not to be critical but to be reasonably helpful. . . ."

In the end he did suggest testing one poem. He would print it and let "*The Atlantic's* public be judge and jury." But, upon further consideration, he did not carry out his own suggestion, perhaps because he felt that a presentation of Miss Stein's work would add little to an issue of his magazine.

Hemingway, however, seemed to share Gertrude Stein's own estimate of her work. He told her and several other people that *The Making of Americans* was a great book. Soon, too, he convinced Ford Madox Ford that this enormously long manuscript should be published serially in *The Transatlantic Review,* a magazine which Hemingway helped Ford to edit. Hemingway told her that Ford thought she received substantial payments for her work whenever she could be talked into allowing a magazine to publish any of her writing. He had been careful not to challenge this idea, Hemingway said, but had promised to try to convince her that she should in this case accept thirty francs a page. Without hesitation, the oft-rejected Miss Stein indicated she would settle for that amount. With this detail taken care of, Hemingway laboriously proceeded to make a copy of the manuscript for the printer. It was as a result of this chore, Gertrude Stein felt, that her protégé first learned the value of repetition in writing.

In such close work, she observed, "you learn the values of the thing as no reading suffices to teach it to you."

Clearly, Hemingway was more than pleased by his relationship with Miss Stein. As the critic, John Malcolm Brinnin, has commented, the youthful writer hungered for her approval: "Like a child showing off before an only half-attentive parent, he was, on the one hand, continually calling her attention to his exploits in boxing, bullfighting, skiing and fishing and, on the other, telling her how mightily he was struggling with creative problems and how much, under her guidance, he was learning . . . He sent her word-counts of his progress, reported in detail the all-night writing hours he kept, and analyzed for her every shift in his creative impulse . . ."

Hemingway was, in fact, soon boasting to Sherwood Anderson of his close friendship with Miss Stein, and he wrote her a series of boyish thank-you notes. He had never realized how bad his writing was before he met her, he said. Not that it was good yet—but, he said, he had learned enough from her so that he was now conscious of his faults. Previously, he said, writing had been easy. But that was before he had begun to realize how much of what he had been doing was wrong.

Although he was writing steadily, much of Hemingway's time was taken by his work as a European correspondent for the *Toronto Daily Star,* and this disturbed his mentor. ". . . look here," she said to him one day, as she later reported in *The Autobiography of Alice B. Toklas.* "You say you and your wife have a little money between you. Is it enough to live on if you live quietly. Yes, he said. Well, she said, then do it. If you keep on doing newspaper work you will never see things, you will only see words and that will not do, that is of course if you intend to be a writer."

Again Hemingway listened to her advice and seemed ready to accept it.

But an unanticipated development changed his plans.

"He came to the house about ten o'clock in the morning," Gertrude Stein wrote later, in describing what must have been an exasperating moment for the young Hemingway, "and he stayed . . . all afternoon, he stayed for dinner and he stayed until about ten o'clock at night and then all of a sudden he announced that his wife was enceinte and then with great bitterness, and I, I am too young to be a father. We [Miss Stein and Miss Toklas] consoled him as best we could and sent him on his way."

The expected child kept Hemingway from following Gertrude Stein's instructions immediately. But he had made up his mind. He saved as much money as he could, and within a year he had given up newspaper work and was settled in Paris, writing full time. He listened to Gertrude Stein, to the editor Ford Madox Ford, and to the poet and literary pioneer Ezra Pound; and he accepted much of the advice they offered him.

Toward Sherwood Anderson, however, he began to grow increasingly critical. To Edmund Wilson he wrote that Anderson's writing had gotten very bad indeed, perhaps because too many literary people were too willing to praise automatically anything he published. Yet Anderson himself seems to have had no hint of the change in the attitude of the young writer he considered something of a protégé.

It was Gertrude Stein, not Sherwood Anderson, who was beginning to take a closer look at Hemingway. She was, for example, intrigued by the contrast between his determination to appear rugged and his apparent physical softness.

". . . Hemingway although a sportsman was easily tired," she recalled later. "He used to get quite worn out walking from his house to ours." And, somewhat waspishly, she also recorded a remark by another close acquaintance of Hemingway's. ". . . Ernest is very fragile," this acquaintance had pointed out. ". . . whenever he does anything sporting something breaks, his arm, his leg, or his head."

Sometimes Gertrude Stein discussed the mystery of Hemingway with Hemingway himself.

". . . Hemingway," she was to say to him one day after a long talk, according to her report in the *Autobiography,* "after all you are ninety percent Rotarian. Can't you, he said, make it eighty percent." Her answer, as recorded in the *Autobiography:* "No, said she, regretfully, I can't."

Later, she was to talk with Sherwood Anderson at great

length about the engima of Hemingway. Both of them felt they had molded this youth as a writer, though he was to turn so violently against Anderson—and, later, against Gertrude Stein herself.

There was another friend of Hemingway's early days who was later to puzzle over the man's abrupt reversals in his attitude toward those who had helped him. This was Harold Loeb, the rich young man whom Hemingway was to portray so savagely as Robert Cohn in *The Sun Also Rises*. At this time, Loeb was in Europe editing the little magazine *Broom*. But his first novel, *Doodab*, had been accepted by the New York publishing firm of Boni & Liveright.

One day Loeb advised the still-unsuccessful Hemingway, as he reports in his autobiography: "What you've got to do, I suggested, is bring in women. People like to read about women and violence. You've got plenty of violence in your stories. Now all you need is women."

Hemingway showed little respect for this advice, but he did follow another of Loeb's suggestions.

If Boni & Liveright were ready to publish his own book, Loeb said, maybe the firm would also publish one by Hemingway. Perhaps Hemingway could assemble some of his sketches, stories, and poems—enough to make a small volume —and send them to Loeb's publishers. Loeb himself was planning to go to New York soon to talk over the editing to be done on *Doodab*, and while he was there, he could look in on the editor who was reading Hemingway's manuscript.

After some hesitation, apparently because of his reservations about Loeb's judgment, Hemingway agreed.

Once in New York, Loeb was at first caught up in his own affairs. But a letter from Hemingway soon reminded him of his promise.

"I was conscience-stricken," Loeb recalled in his reminiscenses of the 1920's entitled *The Way It Was*. "I had been in New York over two weeks and had done nothing about Hem's manuscript beyond asking [Isidor] Schneider [an editor] about it. Isidore [sic] had said that it was with one of their readers, and then, when I asked again, he had told me that no decision had been reached."

Probably no friend was to prove of more practical assistance to the youthful Hemingway than Loeb.

"I rushed down to the office," he recalled. "Liveright was busy but Isidore suggested that I speak to Beatrice Kaufman. It seemed a good omen that a friend of mine had it. She was at her desk when I asked her about the manuscript. She said: 'What a coincidence. I was just sending it back.'

"Then she picked a package addressed to Hem from the outgoing mail basket.

"'Don't,' I said. 'You'll live to regret it. You are missing a tremendous opportunity. He can write. One paragraph will tell you that. And his next is going to be a novel. I was a bookseller once and I know how tough it is to sell a book of short stories. But you've got a writer there. Take another look.'

"She gave me an Assyrian smile, and placed the package carefully on top of the pile beside her. . . ."

After a week Loeb returned to ask Beatrice Kaufman about Hemingway's book, and she told him that the firm had agreed to publish it.

Loeb cabled the news to Hemingway.

"A few days later," he has recalled, "another letter came from Hemingway. It had been written in Austria on February 27, the day he had received my cable. It told how they all had been up at the Madleurer [sic] Haus—1987 meters—when the two cables came up, one from me, one from Don [writer Donald Ogden Stewart]. Hem couldn't fully realize it at first and then he couldn't sleep . . .

"He wanted to know what the dope on it was. Would it be a fall publication, along with my book? What would he have to cut? How much money would he get?"

Later, Hemingway was to repay his friend Loeb by using him as a model for the "miserable character" named Robert Cohn in *The Sun Also Rises*. The parallels between Loeb and the fictional Cohn were difficult to miss for anyone who knew Loeb. Hemingway wrote that Cohn was "a member, through his father, of one of the richest families in New York, and through his mother of one of the oldest." Like Loeb, Cohn had "discovered writing." Wrote Hemingway: "He wrote a novel, and it was not really such a bad novel as the critics later called it, although it was a very poor novel." By Hemingway's account, Cohn's novel was "accepted by a fairly good publisher," and he went to the United States, as Loeb had done, to see his publishers. Then Hemingway observed: "The publishers had praised his novel pretty highly and it rather went to his head." Hemingway also gave Cohn interests which were strikingly similar to those that filled the rich young Loeb's days in Paris ("He read many books, played bridge, played tennis, and boxed at a local gymnasium"). And he reconstructed with considerable fidelity—but some distortion—a trip to the bull fights in Pamplona which he and Loeb had once taken together.

Later, Loeb was to ascribe the abrupt ending of their relationship to the fact that his own sympathy during this trip was reserved for the bulls rather than the matadors. It was this, he felt, that had irritated Hemingway. But there were others who observed the two men during this period and felt that Loeb's friendship with Hemingway had already been doomed, simply because Loeb had given the young newspaperman help in finding a publisher. There can be little doubt that Hemingway seemed determined to prove to the world he needed no one's help. In addition, Loeb was guilty of being insufficiently impressed by Hemingway's supposed toughness.

Whatever the explanation, the man who had rescued the manuscript of *In Our Time* from the rejection pile at Boni & Liveright was to suffer for years from a "vindictive" portrayal of himself in *The Sun Also Rises*.

In the meantime, Hemingway had become more and more deeply convinced that the reputation of his old mentor, Sherwood Anderson, had grown far out of proportion to Anderson's actual talent. And now, even before he finished *The Sun Also Rises,* he decided to try his hand at deflating that reputation.

The result was a spirited lampoon of Anderson's novels, which Hemingway published under the title of *The Torrents of Spring.* Of this parody, one critic said: "Hemingway has caught a glint of Anderson's professional naiveté. Beyond that, however, parody is a gift of the gods. Few are blessed with it. It missed Hemingway. . . ." But almost all reviewers detected the echoes of Anderson's style, including his mock simplicity, his awkwardness, and his use of senseless repetition, and the New York *Times* felt that the book revealed the writer's "gift for high-spirited nonsense."

Perhaps the most effective scenes in *The Torrents of Spring* burlesqued what Ernest Hemingway considered the simple-mindedness of many Anderson heroes. To this end, the parodist created as his protagonist a sentimental wanderer named Scripps, who, in an early scene, rescues a half-frozen bird from the snow and, in order to revive it, tucks it inside his shirt.

A few minutes later, Scripps reaches the railway station of a small town named Petoskey.

Wrote Hemingway, with mock simple-mindedness:

"... Scripps read the sign again. Could this be Petoskey?

"A man was inside the station, tapping something back of a wicketed window. He looked out at Scripps. Could he be a telegrapher? Something told Scripps that he was.

"He stepped out of the snow-drift and approached the window. Behind the window the man worked busily away at his telegrapher's key.

" 'Are you a telegrapher?' asked Scripps.

" 'Yes, sir,' said the man. 'I'm a telegrapher.'

" 'How wonderful!'

"The telegrapher eyed him suspiciously. After all, what was this man to him?

" 'Is it hard to be a telegrapher?' Scripps asked. He wanted to ask the man outright if this was Petoskey. He did not know this great northern section of America, though, and he wished to be polite."

Hemingway then used the kind of blunt dialogue that was to make him famous.

"The telegrapher looked at him [Scripps] curiously [wrote Hemingway].

" 'Say,' he asked, 'are you a fairy?'

" 'No,' Scripps said. 'I don't know what being a fairy means.'

" 'Well,' said the telegrapher, 'what do you carry a bird around for?'

" 'Bird?' asked Scripps. 'What bird?'

" 'That bird that's sticking out of your shirt.' "

Then the writer reverted to his pseudo-Andersonian style.

"Scripps was at a loss. What sort of chap was this telegrapher? What sort of men went in for telegraphy? Were they like composers? Were they like artists? Were they like writers? Were they like the advertising men who write the ads in our national weeklies? Or were they like Europeans, drawn and wasted by the war, their best years behind them? Could

he tell this telegrapher the whole story? Would he understand? . . .

" 'My wife left me,' Scripps said abruptly.

" 'I don't wonder if you go around with a damn bird sticking out of your shirt,' the telegrapher said."

Throughout most of *The Torrents of Spring*, Hemingway
criticized Anderson's writing by using the weapon of parody.
But in one curious section, he denounced directly Anderson's
treatment of a subject Hemingway already considered his
own. That subject was war. Now Hemingway wrote:

"This chap in the book by Anderson. He had been a
soldier, too. He had been at the front two years, Anderson
said. What was his name? Fred Something. This Fred had
thoughts dancing in his brain—horror. One night, in the time
of the fighting, he went out on parade—no, it was patrol—in
No Man's Land, and saw another man stumbling along in the
darkness and shot him. The man pitched forward dead. It had
been the only time Fred consciously killed a man. You don't
kill men in war much, the book said. The hell you don't,
Yogi thought, . . .

"Afterward, killing this man haunted Fred. It's got to be
sweet and true. That was the way the soldiers thought,
Anderson said. The hell it was. . . ."

A little later, all pretence of speaking through his characters was dropped, and the forthright Hemingway challenged
Anderson sharply. "Nobody had any damn business to write
about it [war], though, that didn't at least know about it from
hearsay," wrote Hemingway at this point.

After *The Torrents of Spring* had appeared, Hemingway
wrote Anderson a letter. It was, Anderson says, "certainly the
most self-conscious and probably the most completely patronizing letter ever writen. . . .

"He spoke of the book as something fatal to me. He had, he

said, written it on an impulse, taking only six weeks to do it. [Actually, Hemingway said he wrote *The Torrents of Spring* in ten days.] It was intended to bring to an end, once and for all, the notion that there was any worth in my own work. This, he said, was a thing he had hated doing, because of his personal regard for me, and he had done it in the interest of literature. Literature, I was to understand, was bigger than either of us.

"There was something in the letter that was gigantic. It was a kind of funeral oration delivered over my grave. It was so raw, so pretentious, so patronizing that in a repellent way it was amusing, but I was filled with wonder. Just what I said to him, in return, I don't remember. It was something to the effect that I thought it foolish that we writers should devote our time to the attempt to kill each other off. In the letter he had used a prize-fighting term, speaking of the knockout blow he had given me, and in my answer I think I did say that I had always thought of myself as a pretty good middleweight and I doubted *his* ever being able to make the heavyweight class."

As Hemingway became more and more successful, he was frequently to be seen shadow-boxing as he walked along the streets of Paris, and he often insisted that his new acquaintances punch him in the stomach. He also spent hours in the ring with other amateur boxers. Some of his friends were amused by this adolescent posturing, but others were impressed. One of those who was impressed was the novelist of "flaming youth," F. Scott Fitzgerald, and it was in Paris in the summer of 1928 that Fitzgerald's romanticized faith in Hemingway's ability as a fighter led to one of the most farcical of disputes between writers.

Fitzgerald had learned that Hemingway and the Canadian writer, Morley Callaghan, sometimes met to box at a nearby gymnasium, and when he asked if he could watch one of these informal matches, he was reluctantly invited to do so by Hemingway. But, as long as Fitzgerald was present, Hemingway decided that he should serve some function. He asked Fitzgerald to be timekeeper for the bout, explaining carefully to him that each round should last precisely three minutes, with one-minute rests between rounds.

Fitzgerald nodded in understanding.

When the first round began, he concentrated on his watch, and at the end of three minutes he shouted, "Time," and the two boxers sat down beside him on a bench.

Fitzgerald was surprised that Hemingway had permitted the short and rather flabby Callaghan to get in some blows during the opening round, according to the expatriate publisher Robert McAlmon, who later talked to all three of the writers about the fight. But upon reflection Fitzgerald decided that Hemingway was simply playing along with Callaghan, hoping to "let him down easily without showing him up in a mortifying way."

But the man who was mortified as the fight went on was Hemingway himself. In the second round, Callaghan fought fiercely and effectively, and Fitzgerald was astonished to see blood on Hemingway's mouth. It was only after Callaghan had actually knocked Hemingway down that Fitzgerald remembered he was supposed to call time—and the round by then had run "on and on," far beyond the agreed three minute limit.

Hemingway apparently "thought Scott forgot to call time purposely," McAlmon wrote.

To others who had heard of the results of the bout, Hemingway offered his own explanation for his poor showing. His story, McAlmon recalled, "was that he had been drinking the night before and was boxing on three pick-me-up whiskies so that his wind gave out."

The incident was to have repercussions a few months later, when Callaghan returned to Toronto. Shortly after that, the New York *Herald-Tribune* published an inaccurate story about the summer afternoon in Paris. The *Herald-Tribune* story said that Hemingway had challenged Callaghan to a fight and that Callaghan had knocked him out in one round. Equally inaccurately, it said Hemingway had told Callaghan that a story he had written about prize-fighting was no good and that Callaghan knew nothing about prize-fighting. This, said the newspaper, had been the reason for the fight.

When Callaghan read this version in the *Herald-Tribune* he wrote immediately to the newspaper, denying the story. But his letter had not yet appeared when he received a collect cablegram from Scott Fitzgerald demanding that he deny it.

The offended Callaghan, who felt that Fitzgerald was accusing him of placing the inaccurate account in the *Herald-Tribune*, sent him an angry reply.

Then he learned that the cable had been sent by Fitzgerald at Hemingway's order—and only after Fitzgerald had tried to talk Hemingway out of making such a move.

There followed an exchange of challenges between Hemingway and Callaghan. But the two men were on different continents, and after a while Hemingway wrote to Callaghan to suggest that they both had better things to do with their time than to keep in peak physical condition just to be prepared in case of a future accidental meeting. Callaghan agreed —and he never heard from Ernest Hemingway again.

In 1933, another old Hemingway friend, Max Eastman, who, like Gertrude Stein and Sherwood Anderson, had observed Hemingway for years, published an essay entitled "Bull in the Afternoon" in the *New Republic*. The essay dealt with the paradox of Hemingway's character, and touched on his most cherished illusion: that he was the tough, unsentimental man he had spent years trying to be.

"It is of course a commonplace that Hemingway lacks the serene confidence that he *is* a full-sized man," Eastman wrote. ". . . But some circumstance seems to have laid upon Hemingway a continual sense of the obligation to put forth evidences of red-blooded masculinity. . . . This trait of his character has . . . moreover begotten a veritable school of fiction writers—a literary style, you might say, of wearing false hair on the chest."

For four years Ernest Hemingway brooded over these words. Then, in 1937, he, for the first time since the appearance of that essay, ran into Eastman, in the New York offices of Charles Scribner's Sons. Each had dropped by to see Maxwell Perkins, the famous editor who worked with both writers.

Eastman, who had made an appointment with Perkins, was already there when Hemingway appeared at the office door. What followed has been disputed by the two participants themselves.

" 'Hello, you great big son-of-a-bitch,' " Hemingway greeted Eastman, according to Eastman's own account.

Eastman looked up. He thought the greeting was robust but friendly.

" 'Hello, Ernest!' " he said. And then he added:

" 'Big? Why you're twice as big as you used to be!' "

And to indicate how impressed he was, he went through the adolescent gesture of feeling Hemingway's arm muscles.

The two men discussed the civil war in Spain for a few minutes, and Eastman said he was sorry he had missed seeing Hemingway in Key West the previous winter.

" 'Yes,' " Hemingway said, " 'I was very sorry too.' "

Suddenly, then, to Eastman's surprise, Hemingway began unbuttoning his shirt. " 'I want to show you something,' " he said.

Eastman saw some dark, coarse hair on Hemingway's chest.

" 'Is that false hair?' " demanded Hemingway.

As Eastman tried to think of an adequate reply, Hemingway, he says, reached out and began unbuttoning Eastman's shirt. The essayist's chest was by comparison practically hairless.

Now Eastman, laughing at the absurdity of the scene, said:

" 'I guess you've got me there!' "

Both Hemingway and Perkins joined in the laughter. But then, again according to Eastman's account, Hemingway's mood changed for the second time.

" 'Look here,' " he said, " 'what did you say I was sexually impotent for?' "

Startled, Eastman replied: " 'Ernest, you know damn well I didn't say that or anything like it. . . .' "

" 'Yes, you did,' " Hemingway insisted, according to Eastman, " 'and you played right into the hands of the gang that were saying it.' "

But Eastman stood his ground.

" 'I never heard it said. I never dreamed anybody ever said it. . . .' "

Now Hemingway veered to another subject.

" '. . . Moreover,' " he said, " 'you tried to kiss my wife in a taxicab in Paris.' "

Eastman was stunned.

" 'I never was in a taxicab with your wife,' " he insisted, " 'and never had an impulse to kiss her.' "

" 'Yes, you did,' " Hemingway asserted, " 'and you go around saying things behind my back. If I had your essay here, I'd show you what you said.' "

Fortunately or unfortunately, a book by Eastman in which the essay in question had been reprinted happened to be on

Maxwell Perkins' desk, and Eastman handed the volume to Hemingway.

" 'Here it is,' " Eastman said. " '. . . Show me—show Max, and let him judge whether I said or insinuated that you are impotent.' "

After first accusing Eastman of deleting from this book version of the essay the most insulting paragraph, Hemingway found the statement that " '. . . some circumstance seems to have laid upon Hemingway a continual sense of the obligation to put forth evidences of red-blooded masculinity.' "

Eastman now denied that he had meant to imply what Hemingway thought he had implied.

But Hemingway was not to be put off.

" '. . . You know damn well what you meant,' " he shouted, and thrust the book in Eastman's face.

The two men grappled indecisively. Eastman says he managed to throw Hemingway on his back across Maxwell Perkins' desk. But Hemingway later told a *Times* reporter that Eastman " 'jumped at me like a woman—clawing, you know, with his open hands' " and that he simply held Eastman off, since he didn't want to hurt him.

" 'I didn't really sock him,' " Hemingway said. " 'If I had I might have knocked him through that window and out into Fifth Avenue. . . . That would have got me in wrong with my boss . . .' "

Maxwell Perkins managed to talk the two into stopping their fight. Then the two began picking up the pencils and books they had pushed off the desk.

" 'You don't need to pick up those things, boys,' " Perkins now said. " 'The girls can do that.' "

" 'I'm glad, . . . because I'm winded, . . .' " Eastman said.

But Hemingway, according to Eastman, shouted a few more words, and then Eastman said quietly, " 'Ernest, I think you're a lunatic . . .' "

Though this remark almost brought on a second set-to, East-man—according to Eastman—stopped the bickering by re-minding Hemingway that he had interrupted Eastman's ap-pointment with Perkins.

" 'All right,' " Hemingway is reported to have said, " 'I know. I'll get out.' "

He did, according to all versions of the incident, and the great battle was ended.

It would be difficult to decide which of Hemingway's two original mentors, Sherwood Anderson or Gertrude Stein, re-vealed the more appropriate reaction to their pupil once he had become famous, for each reacted characteristically.

For years following the publication of *The Torrents of Spring*, as Sherwood Anderson later recorded in his memoirs, Hemingway avoided meeting the man he had so harshly lampooned when Anderson made occasional visits to Paris. Then, one day, the two saw each other one final time.

". . . there was a sudden knock on the door of my hotel room," Anderson (who loved to create dramatic effects), has written, in a perhaps slightly overdrawn account, "and there Hemingway was.

"He stood in the doorway.

" 'How about a drink?' he said, and I followed him down a stairway and across a street.

"We went into a small bar.

" 'What will you have?' [Hemingway asked.]

" 'Beer. And you?'

" 'A beer.'

" 'Well, here's how.'

" 'Here's how.' "

There was no other conversation.

Wrote Anderson: "He [Hemingway] turned and walked

rapidly away. He had, I dare say, proved his sportsmanship to himself."

It was, appropriately, Gertrude Stein who, speaking again through Alice B. Toklas, recalled a revealing analysis which she and Sherwood Anderson had made of the writer they had first known when he was so young. Wrote Miss Stein:

"Gertrude Stein and Sherwood Anderson are very funny on the subject of Hemingway. The last time that Sherwood was in Paris they often talked about him. Hemingway had been formed by the two of them and they were both a little proud and a little ashamed of the work of their minds. Hemingway had at one moment, when he had repudiated Sherwood Anderson and all his works, written him a letter in the name of american literature which he, Hemingway, in company with his contemporaries was about to save, telling Sherwood just what he, Hemingway thought about Sherwood's work, and, that thinking, was in no sense complimentary. When Sherwood came to Paris Hemingway naturally was afraid. Sherwood as naturally was not.

"As I say he and Gertrude Stein were endlessly amusing on the subject. They admitted that Hemingway was yellow, he is, Gertrude Stein insisted, just like the flat-boat men on the Mississippi river as described by Mark Twain. But what a book, they both agreed, would be the real story of Hemingway, not those he writes but the confessions of the real Ernest Hemingway. It would be for another audience than the audience Hemingway now has but it would be very wonderful. And then they both agreed that they have a weakness for Hemingway because he is such a good pupil. He is a rotten pupil, I [Miss Toklas] protested. You don't understand, they both said, it is so flattering to have a pupil who does it without understanding it, in other words he takes training and anybody who takes training is a favourite pupil. They both admit it to be a weakness. Gertrude Stein added further, you see he is like Derain. You remember Monsieur de Tuille said, when I did not understand why Derain was having the success he was having that it was because he looks like a modern and he smells of the museums. And that is Hemingway, he looks like a modern and he smells of the museums. But what a story that of the real Hem, and one he should tell himself but alas he never will. After all, as he himself once murmured, there is the career, the career."

Hemingway responded to this summation of himself by referring to Gertrude Stein in his *Green Hills of Africa* as "some female" he had helped "get published." He further commented that all Gertrude Stein's talent had "gone to malice and nonsense and self-praise. It's a god-damned shame, really," he quoted himself as saying in a conversation with his second wife, Pauline, about Miss Stein. "It's a shame you never knew her before she went to pot. You know a funny thing; she never could write dialogue. It was terrible. She learned how to do it from my stuff and used it in that book. She had never written like that before. She never could forgive learning that and she was afraid people would notice it, where she'd learned it, so she had to attack me. It's a funny racket, really. But I swear she was damned nice before she got ambitious. . . ."

Curiously enough, Hemingway thought her hostility toward him had arisen from her need to prove that he had exerted no influence upon her writing or her career—precisely the explanation many observers have given for Hemingway's own later hostility toward Sherwood Anderson, Harold Loeb, and Gertrude Stein herself.

A few years later, in *For Whom the Bell Tolls*, Hemingway, in retaliation, had his hero, Robert Jordan, say, just for good measure: " 'An onion is an onion is an onion' "; and then think: ". . . a stone is a stein is a rock is a boulder is a pebble."

It was a remark which was not lost on Miss Stein. But back in Paris she had by this time discovered a game she delighted in playing with her dog. Pretending to be a matador, she would wave a delicate lady's handkerchief in front of her pet, saying all the while in great good humor to the dog: "Play Hemingway. Be fierce."

11

Mr. DeVoto & Mr. Sinclair Lewis call each other Fools & Liars.

WHEN things seemed too quiet in the literary world of the 1950's, the benign Harrison Smith, the president of the company which publishes *The Saturday Review*, would wander into the office of one editor or another and say: "What this magazine needs is another good feud." Nostalgically, then, Mr. Smith would recall the literary feuds which had taken place in the pages of *The Saturday Review* during the previous decade, notably the argument over the sources of Thornton Wilder's hit Broadway play, *The Skin of Our Teeth,* or the far better-known feud between the Nobel prize-winning novelist, Sinclair Lewis, and the Pulitzer prize-winning critic and historian, Bernard DeVoto.

The controversy over Thornton Wilder's drama had been heated but short-lived. It had begun in December of 1942, when readers of the magazine, then known as *The Saturday Review of Literature,* had opened a pre-Christmas issue to discover a surprising article entitled "The Skin of Whose Teeth?"

In this article, Joseph Campbell and Henry Morton Robinson called Wilder's play "an Americanized re-creation, thinly disguised, of James Joyce's 'Finnegans Wake,' " and asserted that the playwright had taken much of his plot, some of his dialogue, most of his major themes, and many of his characters from the widely discussed but little-read novel by Joyce.

"It is a strange performance that Mr. Wilder has turned in," they wrote. "Is he hoaxing us? On the one hand, he gives no credit to his source, masking it with an Olsen and Johnson technique. On the other hand, he makes no attempt to conceal his borrowings, emphasizing them rather, sometimes even stressing details which with a minimum of ingenuity he could have suppressed or altered."

Campbell and Robinson seemed particularly irritated by critics who "dismissed 'Finnegans Wake' as a literary abortion not worth the modern reader's time, yet today hail with rave-notices" the Wilder play based on Joyce's book. "The banquet was rejected," they wrote, "but the Hellzapoppin's scrap that fell from the table they clutch to their bosom."

The controversy quickly spread to other magazines and to newspapers. Wilder, on active duty as an officer in the Army, said nothing, but here and there he found a defender. Bennett Cerf wrote in his column in *The Saturday Review of Literature:* "It's our theory that anybody who can turn that sort of thing into a smash hit on Broadway is entitled to everything he can get."

Tallulah Bankhead, who was appearing in the play, was baffled by the argument over the character Sabina, who was supposedly based on a "Sabine" woman in *Finnegans Wake*. "Who the hell am I supposed to be, anyhow?" she asked. And an anonymous letter writer to the magazine asked: "What are you trying to do—drive people into reading Joyce? Has everyone gone stark mad?"

In February, 1943, the industrious Campbell and Robinson published "The Skin of Whose Teeth?: Part II." After more detailed study of the play, they cited such parallel passages from Joyce's book and Wilder's play as these:

" 'There are certain charges that ought not to be made, and I think I may add, ought not to be allowed to be made.' (From *Skin of Our Teeth*, page 5).

" 'There are certain statements which ought not to be, and one should like to hope to be able to add, ought not to be allowed to be made.' (From *Finnegans Wake*, page 33)."

After making many specific comparisons, they said: "Open the work [*The Skin of Our Teeth*] to any page and echoes vibrate from all directions."

Edmund Wilson wrote that "The Messrs. Campbell and Robinson are, of course, quite right," but indicated that he did not share their indignation, since Wilder was simply following an old and honorable literary tradition in basing one work upon another.

A while after the public accusation of Wilder, Campbell and Robinson published their *Skeleton Key to Finnegans Wake* to guide earnest readers through the Joycean maze. Some suspicious readers of *The Saturday Review of Literature* then began to suspect that the two articles had been written chiefly to gain advance publicity for the book. The controversy subsided, without any rebuttal by Wilder.

A little more than a year later, Bernard DeVoto and Sinclair Lewis staged one of the great public brawls in literary history in the pages of the same magazine. Their raucous feud is still remembered by all connoisseurs of the fine art of literary mayhem.

The assailant was DeVoto, a former teacher who had become a literary critic. At the time of the dispute, he was leading a strange double life. Under his own name Mr. DeVoto spent much of his time telling such novelists as Ernest Hemingway, John Dos Passos, William Faulkner, Thomas Wolfe, and Sinclair Lewis what was wrong with their books. At the same time, under the pseudonym of John August, DeVoto was turning out a series of potboilers which were so undistinguished that a reviewer in the Boston *Transcript* was moved to comment: We read John August's campus 'thriller' a long time ago in Colliers' [sic]. At the time we thought it was pretty bad. Rereading doesn't help much . . ."

In 1944, the undaunted Mr. DeVoto transcribed some lectures he had delivered a few months earlier at the University of Indiana and proceeded to use them as the basis for a contentious book of criticism entitled *The Literary Fallacy*. His chief target in *The Literary Fallacy* was his fellow critic, the widely respected Van Wyck Brooks. But he also attacked most of the major American writers of the post-World War I period, including Sinclair Lewis. It was largely due to Mr. Brooks's misleading advice, DeVoto asserted, that the most influential novelists of the postwar decades had wasted their time and confused their readers. As a result, he said, these writers were writing about the wrong things and presenting a false picture of life and moral values in the United States.

"Never in any country or any age had writers so misrepresented their culture, never had they been so unanimously wrong . . . ," the pontifical Mr. DeVoto declared. These writers had, he said, portrayed American life as "malformed, tawdry, and venal." Why, he asked, did they insist on featuring unworthy heroes? Why did they not write about "the man who is loyal to his friends, believes in his country, is a good citizen, loves his wife, works for his family, brings up his children, and deals resolutely with the vicissitudes, strains, anxieties, failures, and partial successes that compose our common lot?"

Mr. DeVoto then lodged specific charges against Sinclair Lewis and the characters to be found in Lewis's novels—including those in *Arrowsmith,* the novel in which the central figure was a great scientist.

"As a mind," wrote DeVoto, "Martin [Arrowsmith] suffers from arrested development, as a scientist he is a *fool.* . . . Is not the same true of Mr. Lewis's characters in general? Leora Arrowsmith is emotionally underdeveloped. Ann Vickers is an immature mind and her emotions are child-like. Dodsworth is so simple a personality that one doubts if he could have managed a corporation . . . The lives explored are uncomplicated, the experience revealed is mediocre . . . The critics have never been sure whether Mr. Lewis was trying to truly represent the life of his time or to caricature it, and it seems likely that Mr. Lewis has shared their uncertainty."

He expressed a fear that many readers had been misled into believing that the world portrayed in books by Lewis and by other major writers of the 1920's was the actual American world of that time. And he even offered a rather startling solution to the problem he had posed: If Lewis and other writers did not reform, he suggested, then the next step should be taken by readers. They should, he declared, revolt.

"Writers must be content to hold their peace until they know what they are talking about," DeVoto said. "Readers must be willing to hold them to the job if they refuse to hold themselves. An uninstructed gentleness toward writers has been the mistake of readers in our time. Words like 'fool' and 'liar' might profitably come back to use. . . ."

Mr. DeVoto failed to remind those who read the magazine's excerpt from his book that he had not always been so critical of Mr. Lewis. In fact, in earlier years, he had frequently praised him. In 1925, for example, immediately following the publication of one of the very novels he was now denouncing, DeVoto had written that *Arrowsmith* was "the most American novel of the generation," and he had predicted it would "endure with a few other great novels of America . . ." Later, in the early 1930's, when other critics were detecting a serious decline in Lewis' work, DeVoto had also publicly declared that *Ann Vickers* was as good as *Arrowsmith* and that Lewis was "the finest American novelist of his period . . ."

DeVoto and Lewis had met each other from time to time, and, in 1933, DeVoto had invited Lewis to speak at the Bread Loaf Writers' Conference at Middlebury College in Vermont, even though a previous appearance by Lewis at the conference had ended in near disaster because of his drinking.

It was apparently during the 1933 conference that DeVoto first began to change his mind about his one-time hero. DeVoto was then at work on a novel entitled *We Accept with Pleasure,* and he introduced a Lewis-like charcter in the book under the name Frank Archer. Archer, as described in the novel, had "the mind of a cheer leader. Ploughboy gaping at the eternal dawn. Diurnal wonder of the tremendous platitude. Periodical discovery of the utterly apparent."

One conversation between the "world-famous" novelist Archer and a younger writer in DeVoto's novel seemed to foreshadow DeVoto's open criticism of Lewis in *The Literary Fallacy.*

"It's a docile public," DeVoto's young writer, Ric Barreda, says to Frank Archer in *We Accept with Pleasure,* "but it can be pushed too far. You've been telling it that its great men were crooks and fools. You've been calling its gods Baal—no, Moloch. You've informed it that its beliefs were absurd and its desires trivial. Worst of all, you've been telling it that its genuine loves, the things it really lives by outside your fantasies, Frank, are old-fashioned and childish and absurd

. . . Well, it's a docile public . . . But it's getting fed up, Frank . . ."

And Barreda, speaking in the same smug tone that DeVoto was to use a decade later, offered Archer almost the same formula for his future novels that DeVoto was to offer Sinclair Lewis:

"[Your] new book," says Barreda, "should tell how Frank Archer rebelled against the old-time morality and prudery and unwholesome middle-class repression of his parents. He went to the Village, about when you did, and met Sonia and struck up a fine, free, fearless love. Then grief came upon them, and loss, and old jealousies and older pain, and in the darkness their hearts were humbled. So they married and went back to Illinois, where Frank worked in his father's office and the children came and he and Sonia faced middle age. They had learned that old ways are best. . . ."

Fascinated by his own words, Barreda apparently found it difficult to stop. ". . . give us Dobbin instead of America's Family Car," he told Archer. "Give us elms on a village green . . . Give them softer women, women in crinolines, who are wooed, not taken . . . give them summer evenings in the small towns that all Americans know . . . Above all, give them heroes. They want men, not dwarves, Frank . . . Give them the flag . . ."

Archer interrupts to ask:

"Whose guitar is that?"

"Mine," a character named Ted replies.

"Play it," Archer says. "Drown out Barreda."

But once Ted begins playing, as the novelist DeVoto notes with satisfaction, Archer as well as the others ask for songs that express "the simpler sentiments that Ric demanded."

We Accept with Pleasure had hardly given an adequate picture of the irascible, red-headed Sinclair Lewis.

But it had been cast in the form of fiction, and now, in the pages of *The Saturday Review of Literaure* in 1944, Mr. DeVoto was criticizing Sinclair Lewis and his fellow writers forthrightly—and in nonfiction. The editors of the magazine, apparently detecting the seeds of controversy, now made sure that Lewis received an advance copy of *The Literary Fallacy,* which made it possible for them to publish in the very next issue Mr. Lewis' reply to Mr. DeVoto.

The reply was probably the most violent denunciation of one writer by another in the entire history of literary feuds. Making use of Mr. DeVoto's own words, Lewis bluntly wrote:

"I denounce Mr. Bernard DeVoto as a fool and a tedious and egotistical fool, as a liar and a pompous and boresome liar.

"He is a liar in his statement of the purposes of *The Literary Fallacy,* and a fool in his repetitious announcements that he is the one authority on the American frontier, psy-choanalysis, family life, the literature of geology, the technic of biography, the treatment of burns, and on Mark Twain, and all New England writers whatsoever."

Angrily, he then turned his attention to DeVoto's attack on Van Wyck Brooks.

". . . What he [Mr. DeVoto] really says," wrote Lewis, ". . . is merely that Mr. DeVoto is an incalculably wiser and nobler man than Mr. Van Wyck Brooks.

"This is the third or fourth book, now, in which DeVoto has led a frantic one-man revolution with the slogan, 'Brooks must go!' I do not believe that Mr. Brooks has ever answered or ever will answer. He is too gentle, too just, too scholarly—and perhaps too pitying."

In the midst of his counterattack, Lewis decided it was necessary for him to explain how he happened to know De-Voto, since he had clearly managed to convey the impression that his antagonist was not a man whom an intelligent writer would seek out.

"My first encounter with DeVoto," he wrote, "was on a train to Philadelphia, years ago. He timidly introduced himself as a teacher who was trying to write for *The Saturday Evening Post*. I had never heard of him but I was interested in that froglike face, those bright eyes, that boyish and febrile longing to be noticed."

Majestically, Mr. Lewis summarized for the ages his attitude toward Mr. DeVoto:

"I was reasonably polite to him," he said, "and he was grateful. I saw him several times afterward, but his screaming, his bumptiousness, his conviction that he was a combination of Walter Winchell and Erasmus, grew hard to take, and it is a long time now since I have seen him. . . .

"The man must be studied," he continued. "Like his fellow ornaments of New England, Lydia Pinkham, William Dudley Pelley, and Phineas T. Barnum, he has by brashness and self-advertisement pushed himself into notoriety, and since no serious critic, . . . has thought it worth while to deflate him, many innocent and youthful believers still listen to him. . . ."

DeVoto's chief literary activity, Lewis argued, was shouting to his fellow critics: " 'Look at me! How much smarter I am than any of you! You never heard of that! Yah, yah, yah!' "

But, he revealed to those readers who were unaware of the fact, this same critic of modern fiction also from time to time offered questionable contributions to the world of letters. Recently, for example, as Lewis pointed out, Mr. DeVoto had published a novel called *The Woman in the Picture*. Modestly enough, however, as Lewis now sarcastically explained, DeVoto had not signed this volume with his own name.

"Certainly not," Lewis said. "It is signed with his pen name,

'John August,' and a damn silly pen name it is, too. 'Sarda-napalus September' would have been much more convincing.
. . ."

Much of the remainder of Lewis's counterattack was devoted to a satirical study of this flavorless dime novel.

"The hero," wrote Lewis, "has to drive the heroine halfway across the country, spending most of his time peeping at her bare legs and bosom, as enthusiastically reported by Mr. De-August, with a ten-year-old, behind-the-barn eroticism which has now been discarded by most of the pulps. There is also in the story the standard B-picture equipment of airplanes, automatic revolvers, telegraph codes, and gentlemen constantly getting themselves tied to logs, boxcars, telegraph poles, . . . coincidences, and lapses in the plot. . . ."

The deflation of Bernard DeVoto seemed complete.

"You put that poor devil through such a wringer that you have squeezed tears out of me," one especially interested reader of the essay wrote to Sinclair Lewis. This was Van Wyck Brooks, and he added: "It is simply a masterpiece of demolition,—I don't see how he can appear in print again."

But Mr. Brooks, like many other readers of *The Saturday Review of Literature,* had underestimated the self-esteem of Mr. Lewis' victim, who did indeed continue to appear in print, and whose far more notable works in the field of history won him a nomination in November, 1944, to the National Institute of Arts and Letters.

Curiously enough, the National Institute was one of the very few organizations in which Lewis himself had shown sustained interest; and members of New York's literary world wondered what Lewis' reaction would be to the proposal to honor his most virulent critic.

To the surprise of almost everyone—probably including Bernard DeVoto—Lewis made an enthusiastic speech seconding the nomination. As unexpectedly as it had begun, one of the most abusively personal of all literary battles had ended. And a little later when Lewis and DeVoto met on a New York street which was crowded with Christmas shoppers, they chatted pleasantly a few moments and then went their separate ways.

MR. NORMAN MAILER

challenges all the talent in the room.

A T A PARTY in his Greenwich Village flat in 1959, Norman Mailer took his friend and fellow writer Calder Willingham to one side. He asked Willingham if he would like to read a brief section of his recently completed but not yet published book, *Advertisements for Myself*.

Willingham, who had achieved early fame as the author of *End as a Man*, read in an exaggerated Southern drawl from printer's proofs an "evaluation" by Mailer of Willingham as a writer:

"Calder Willingham is a clown with the bite of a ferret, and he suffers from the misapprehension that he is a master mind. He has written what may be the funniest dialogue of our time, and if *Geraldine Bradshaw*, his second novel, had been half as long, it would have been the best short novel any of us did. But it is hard to bet on Calder, for if he ever grows up, where will he go? He lacks ideas, and is as indulgent to his short-comings as a fat old lady to her Pekingese . . ."

Willingham recalled in 1962: "I chuckled over Norman's criticisms of me, since they seemed to me rather funny. I didn't discuss his comments with him then, and I haven't since."

But he added:

"I did suggest to him in a letter that he might better spend his time writing stories, rather than criticism, since I feel that a creative talent is rarer than an ability to write criticism."

Of the seventeen young writers Mailer appraised in *Advertisements for Myself*, most appeared to agree with Willingham that Mailer should devote his energies to fiction. For in the section entitled "Evaluations—Quick and Expensive Comments of the Talent in the Room," only five of Mailer's contemporaries came off well. These were Truman Capote, Anatole Broyard, Myron Kaufmann, Ralph Ellison, and Chandler Brossard.

The others in Mailer's gallery found themselves and their work under scrutiny so critical that it shadowed their relationships with Mailer for decades.

These "Evaluations" became the basis for the liveliest and most far-ranging of all post–World War II literary feuds:

J. D. Salinger: "I seem to be alone in finding him no more than the greatest mind ever to stay in prep school."

Saul Bellow: "To tell the truth I cannot take him seriously as a major novelist. I do not think he knows anything about people, nor about himself."

James Baldwin: "Too charming a writer to be major. Even the best of his paragraphs are sprayed with perfume."

Gore Vidal: "In his fiction it seems difficult for him to create a landscape which is inhabited by people. At his worst he becomes his own jailer and is imprisoned in the recessive nuances of narcissistic explorations which do not go deep enough into himself, and so end as gestures and postures."

William Styron: "I wonder if anyone who gets to know him well could wish him on his way. I will try to be fair to his talent, but I do not know if I can, because I must speak against the bias of finding him not nearly as big as he ought to be."

James Jones: "Jones has sold out badly over the years [because he is] trying to be the first novelist to end up as a multi-millionaire."

Herbert Gold: "I have a terrible confession to make. I have nothing to say about any of the talented women writers who write today. Out of what is no doubt a fault in me, I do not seem to be able to read them. At the risk of making a dozen devoted enemies for life, I can only say that the sniffs I get from the ink of the women are always fey, old-hat, Quaintsy Goysy, tiny, too dykily psychotic, crippled, creepish, fashionable, frigid... [and] the little I have read of Herbert Gold reminds me of nothing so much as a woman writer."

Before *Advertisements for Myself* was published, rumors about Mailer's wholesale assault upon the post–World War II generation of writers reached James Jones in Paris. After receiving an advance copy of the book, Jones invited James Baldwin and William Styron, both of whom were then living in France, to come to his flat and to join him in reading Mailer's comments on them and their work.

They read passages aloud to each other, and Baldwin considered sending Mailer a cable to protest the attacks. Then he changed his mind. Mailer was probably hoping for an angry response, he decided, and therefore it would be better not to react in the way Mailer expected.

Jones could find little comfort in Mailer's praise for *From Here to Eternity* after reading that his second novel, *Some Came Running*, was a "debacle" and his third, *The Pistol*, "a dud."

But at least Mailer had concluded: "If Jones gives up the lust to measure his talent by the money he makes; if he dares not to castrate his hatred of society with a literary politician's assy cultivation of it, then I would have to root for him because he may have been born to write a great novel."

There was no such hopeful forecast for Styron's future work. But Mailer did predict that the not-yet-completed *Set This House on Fire* would receive a very favorable reception for dubious reasons. The reaction of the critics could serve as "a study in the art of literary advancement," Mailer wrote. "For Styron has spent years oiling every literary lever and power which could help him on his way, and there are medals waiting for him in the mass-media."

When he returned to New York a few months later, James Baldwin decided to discuss his reactions to the "evaluations" with Mailer in person.

The Actor's Studio was offering a dramatization of Mailer's *The Deer Park*, and Baldwin went to the studio, feeling certain that Mailer would be there for the performance. At the end of the play, he stood quietly at the edge of the crowd, and Mailer noticed him.

Baldwin told Mailer he wanted to talk to him, and Mailer did not seem surprised. They went to a nearby bar.

As they began talking, Baldwin was pleased to realize that he felt no anger at all toward his old friend. He was merely curious, and asked Mailer directly why he had felt it necessary to make the comments he had.

Mailer, speaking in what Baldwin took to be his Texas accent (one of several he sometimes uses), said that he felt that Baldwin "had it coming" to him and added that he considered the judgments given in *Advertisements for Myself* fairly accurate. But as they continued talking, Mailer expressed some regret for this one evaluation and said he might phrase it somewhat differently if he were writing the section now.

It was the end of the discussion.

While other victims were cursing or writing angry letters, Gore Vidal found himself in the enviable position of being able to respond in *The Nation*.

In his article Vidal recalled that he himself had been a widely-praised novelist of twenty-three when Truman Capote passed along to him a report about Mailer's huge—and then unpublished—*The Naked and the Dead*. This news had "promptly aroused my competitive instincts. I remember thinking meanly: so somebody did it. Each previous war had had its big novel, yet so far there had been none for our war, although I knew that a dozen busy friends and acquaintances were grimly taking out tickets in the Grand War Novel Lottery. I had debated doing one myself...

"I did not suspect then that the ambitious, rather cold-blooded young contemporary who had set out to write the big war novel and who pulled it off would one day be in the same fix I was."

This "fix," according to Vidal, was: "Not safe. Not wise. Not admired."

Vidal then set forth for the readers of *The Nation* his own "evaluation" of Mailer.

When *The Naked and the Dead* appeared in 1948, he recalled, his first reaction had been: "It's a fake. A clever, talented, admirably executed fake." He had, he confessed,

never finished reading the book, but he had "read a good deal
of it." He had felt then and he felt now that the novel contained "made up, predictable characters taken not from life,
but from the same novels all of us had read..."
In 1954, he finally met Mailer. "I liked Mailer," he recalled, "though I am afraid my first impression... was somewhat guarded: I am suspicious of people who make speeches
at me. And he is a born party-orator...."
After reviewing Mailer's rather stormy career, Vidal
summed up his famous rival:
"Mailer does not begin to know what he believes or is or
wants. His drive seems to be toward power of a religio-
political kind. He is a messiah without real hope of paradise
on earth or in heaven. I am not sure, finally, that he should
be a novelist at all, or even a writer, despite formidable gifts.
He is too much a demagogue..."

One paragraph in Vidal's analysis in *The Nation* brought an
immediate reply from Mailer. In it Vidal accused Mailer of
opportunism.
"I am fairly certain," he wrote, "[that] Mailer will survive
everything. Despite a nice but small gift for self-destruction,
he is uncommonly adroit, with an eye to the main chance...
I noted with some amusement that, despite the air of candor,
he makes no new enemies in this book. He scores off those
who are lost to him anyway."
Mailer responded:
"Only a fool brags of making new enemies, but I was
bruised to the bone by this quick assertion, and when Vidal
called a few days later to discover my reaction to his piece, I
gave documents to the man, page and paragraph, about the
new enemies I had made, and by God yes I think even Gore V.
would admit this day he was hasty."

Some months after *Advertisements for Myself* appeared Norman Mailer became embroiled in three incidents which gave the editors of the tabloids an opportunity to sneer at him in print. On November 14, 1960, he had an argument over a bill for $7.60 in a New York night club. The excited club manager brought a charge of disorderly conduct against him. While this trivial dispute was being featured in the papers, the second far more serious episode occured as the aftermath of a party which Mailer and his wife, Adele, gave at their Manhattan flat. Two or three hours after their guests had departed, Adele Mailer was taken to the University Hospital, suffering from several cuts which she told doctors she had received after slipping and falling on broken glass. Then, the following day, she gave a detective a different explanation of her injury. Mailer, she said, had stabbed her.

Mailer was committed to Bellevue Hospital for observation, and later, after pleading guilty to a charge of simple assault, was placed on probation for six months.

While he was still awaiting trial in the assault case, Mailer was invited to give a poetry reading at a Young Men's Hebrew Association meeting in New York. As he was reciting one of his poems, a YMHA representative rang down the curtain on him. Some of Mailer's verses, said the YMHA official, were "a raw recital of filth."

During this troubled time Mailer found in his mail a Christmas card from Vance Bourjaily, with whom he had also dealt rather negatively in *Advertisements for Myself.* Though Bourjaily had intended the card to serve as a gesture of reconciliation, he later regretted sending it. He feared that Mailer may have read it as a rather cruel effort at irony — a fear that is symptomatic of the delicate stage the Mailer free-for-all had reached.

When I began work on this book in 1962, I decided to interview both Mailer and his victims. Mailer was the first to respond:

"I'm perfectly willing to talk to you," he wrote after I described the book I had in mind, "but I think if I'm going to be quoted by you it would be better to give a short but formal answer to the questions in your letter because my style in talking seems to be sufficiently vague or at any rate ambiguous to cause me much grief afterward. Most often I have the impression I was misquoted."

Then he laid down some ground rules:

"To save us from this, why don't you wait until you've heard from all the writers you've written to, get together all your questions, let me know how long a reply you would want from me and I'll keep to the limit you set. It would be understood, of course, that you will quote everything I say, not two-thirds or one-third or a phrase. Since I've no desire to dictate the proportions of your article I'm perfectly willing to keep my answers extremely short, five words to the subject or ten, I don't care, but I'm sure you can understand that I would not want to be quoted partially."

I accepted Mailer's offer, and also promised to quote in full the letters of others who made the same request.

One early reply was from William Styron. Mailer had erroneously predicted success for Styron's third novel, *Set This House on Fire*. Styron wrote:

". . . both Mailer's honesty and his gift for prophecy are contained in his statement 'For Styron has spent years oiling every literary lever. . . and there are medals waiting for him in the mass-media.' As anyone who read the reviews of *Set This House on Fire* can recall, the medals were made of solid lead."

He concluded:

". . . any 'feud' which exists has always, for some queer reason, seemed far more important to Mailer than it has to me."

Mailer replied:

"Betting blind, I honestly thought Styron had written a good book which would be called a great book. How was I to know he had written a limp book, a floppy book, which the critics were kind enough to call mediocre? I think Styron is right, I am a poor prophet. It's a mistake to take young Southern novelists on their own terms."

Herbert Gold launched a counter-offensive:

"Poor Norman," he wrote, "he yells so loud because he's deaf. I don't think it makes sense to try to outyell him. . . . We were unfriends around Manhattan while I was living there, though I didn't dislike him, just thought him sad. Now he's found a way to make the scene without doing the usual hard work of thinking & writing. Well, let him make it his way. I don't like the noise."

Gold concluded:

"He did have a gift."

To this letter, Mailer's response was unyielding.

"Herbert Gold used to be a mosquito," he wrote. "Now he is an angry mosquito. I better get my ass covered."

Although Gore Vidal had already had the opportunity to answer Mailer at length in *The Nation*, yet two years later he still had a great deal to say.

"From [Mailer's] point of view, I suppose his analysis [of my work] is understandable," Vidal said, recalling the accusation that he was "narcissistic." "But then he did not read *The Judgment of Paris*, the best of the novels, nor much else. Yet he is a good intuitive critic, and I never disregard any of his commentary. "'Narcissistic' is a popular cant word to describe any kind of homosexuality," Vidal continued. "Since I have written a good deal at times about that subject my writing must then, to complete the ponderous syllogism, be narcissistic. I think otherwise. I should have thought the viewpoint a cold and realistic one, 'uningratiating' as Muriel Spark wrote in praising my short stories."

He then said that Ernest Hemingway was an example of a truly narcissistic writer.

"What is Mailer?" Vidal then asked. ". . . a romantic who wants to be what he is not, tall blond handsome, a ruthless goy like Sergius. Mailer is closest in temperment to Scott Fitzgerald."

Then he commented on the literary scene of the 1960s, and found it "a confused one at present because there are no critics in a position to set standards, right or wrong. The result is anarchy in which a Salinger is overvalued. I am undervalued. Mailer is valued irrelevantly as a kind of deranged celebrity who could just as easily be a jazz singer or movie star."

He added:

"No one reads him. They hear of him." Nevertheless he offered as his final estimate of Mailer's talent: "He is, all in all, very good."

In this case, Mailer was moved to write a detailed answer, explaining first of all that his use of the word "narcissistic" had been misinterpreted.

"Vidal ought to know me well enough," he wrote, "to know that when I use a word I use it because I think it is the best word available to me and not because people will thereby be encouraged to suppose I mean another word. When I implied that Gore's worst vice as a writer might be narcissism I was not talking about homosexuality. He has written very well about that particular subject, modestly, soberly and with instinctive good taste."

He continued his explanation at length.

"It is," he wrote, "precisely in his more ambitious books like *The Judgment of Paris,* some of which I did read and did like, that this narcissism is most present and most defeating to the potential reach of his talents which are considerable. The difficulty of writing in a narcissistic vein is that one's heroes are hermetically sealed in upon thmeselves. They may rant, rage and roar, or stand aside burnishing their wit, but either way nothing dramatic passes between them and other persons in the novel. The result is inevitably a study of lonely decomposition. One may attempt to struggle against this."

He agreed with Vidal about Hemingway.

"Hemingway, who was a terribly narcissistic writer," he said, "was forever violating the hermetic logic of his characters and so dropping them into love affairs which were unbelievable and all too often seriously maudlin. Certainly this is true of all the romances written after *To Have and Have Not.* Gore in his turn avoids this trap and remains true to the logic of the characters which is that they have a tendency to find less and less happening to them as their adventures continue. It is a truthful way of writing and one could say that Vidal was reflecting the time except that I've always found him disproportionately fond of the way in which his characters are isolated."

He offered an example:

"If a man stops to pick a rose in his garden every morning, this is probably as respectable an action as taking a brisk ten-minute walk, but when the man who picks the roses says, 'I am the only gardener in this part of the world who knows a good rose when he sees one,' then the beginning of a small distaste may be legitimate."

He turned to other points of contention. Of him, Vidal had written in *The Nation* article:
"He is a messiah without real hope of paradise."
Mailer replied:
"On the contrary, I do think there is paradise. On earth, in heaven. If one is exceptional, if one ends up being more honest, more noble, more brave than others might expect, one finds that—but, do the work yourself."
In the same article, Vidal had also called him a "demagogue."
"As for being a demagogue, don't know," Mailer now wrote. "Sounds like an attractive career. Don't know I have the right sort of loutishness to carry it off."
Then he quoted verbatim Vidal's final charge.
" 'No one reads (Mailer),' " he said. " 'They hear of him.' "
On this point, he defended himself.
"Nobody Gore knows reads me," he explained. "That's true."
Then, perhaps with Vidal's commercial successes in mind, he added:
"Nobody in Hollywood, Broadway or Washington has been reading me for the last ten years. When occasionally they stumble across a magazine piece they are overcome. 'Why, he's such a good writer,' they say. But then each to his different audience. Sometimes I like to think I am read fairly carefully by some of the people who go to college now and take the writing courses, or at least that is my illusion. Any established writer who wishes to continue a feud or perchance start one with me is advised to attack on this line. It is the weakest link in my military dispositon."
Of the entire *Nation* article, Mailer wrote in summary:
"Wouldn't call Gore's piece a counter-attack. Would call it a good, intelligent critical review. Indeed I think it is one of

the best pieces he has written. I disagree with almost all of it, from beginning to forgotten end, but Gore did set out his point of view so very well that if I were thus attacked, it was a pleasure. Tovarich."

In *Advertisements for Myself*, Mailer had decided that the first two novels of his off-and-on friend, Vance Bourjaily, were "insignificant." He had also said that Bourjaily was a writer who had survived because of his "really nice gifts as a politician."

". . . I kept expecting him to go Madison Avenue," he had written. "I was certain he would sell out sooner or later. Instead he did the opposite, wrote a novel called *The Violated*, which is a good long honest novel . . . He is the first of my crowd to have taken a major step forward, and if his next novel is as superior to *The Violated* as was *The Violated* to his early work, he could end up being champion for a while . . ."

He had then added:

"But I doubt if he could hold the title in a strong field, for his taint is to be cute."

Bourjaily had been in South America at the time *Advertisements for Myself* appeared. When I was working on the first edition of *The Fine Art of Literary Mayhem* in 1962, I asked him for comment on Mailer's evaluation. He wrote a very long, detailed reply and requested that it be published in full.

I did quote the full letter in the first edition. It covered four pages. While revising the book in 1982, I requested permission to make some cuts, and Bourjaily responded:

"Let's simplify things. I find my 20-year-old letter almost too tedious to reread. There's one paragraph I'd like you to keep . . ."

Bourjaily then offered this briefer general comment on his relationship with Mailer and his estimate of Mailer's talent:

"There was never a breach [between Mailer and me]. Consequently, it seems (and seemed) inaccurate to me for the first edition of *The Fine Art of Literary Mayhem* to use the phrase 'a gesture of reconciliation'. The following paragraph from my old letter—in which I first describe having been 'fairly sore' and having got over it—may be worth keeping for clarification:

> At the time of Norman's greatest difficulties, I felt very strongly urged to do or say something sympathetic, and handled it badly; it was Christmas time and I sent a Christmas card to him and Adele, having seen in the papers that they were back together. I think Norman took the card as an attempt at irony at his expense, for which I was very sorry; but it was my own fault. I ought to have been able to think of the decent thing to say in the circumstances and couldn't and hoped the card would convey it.

"I still respect Norman as a writer, and think of him as a friend. If we rarely see one another these days, lay the blame on geography. Occasionally we exchange letters, if there's something to write about, and when I write him one soon congratulating him on his Nobel prize, the answer will be prompt. As for his prediction about my own stuff, I still don't seem able to find the way to Madison Avenue; is it just over the hill from Parnassus?

"Best wishes for the new edition."

One other comment by Bourjaily from his 1962 letter I would like to preserve:

"It seems to me that literary feuding is one of a number of fairly silly things which writers do when they're not writing well, whether for financial reasons or psychic ones. It comes from a feeling of being in competition with one another, a sort of athletic metaphor for our real situation and a very inaccurate one. I do not honestly know if I'm a better writer than anyone else, and when things are going well it doesn't concern me much; what concerns me is whether I'm a better writer than I was. The real competitor, and we all know it, is interior, and there's feud enough to keep one agile and anguished forever. Or, to straighten out the athletic metaphor, it's the interior competitor who's the real, red-dogging son of a bitch, who always foresees what play one is going to try next, where its weakness is, where to crash in to try to stop it. I wish all your feudists luck with that one; what they say about or do to one another doesn't matter, even slightly."

When I sent a copy of Bourjaily's letter to Mailer, he wrote: "Read Bourjaily's letter with interest. It is too long to answer properly."

Then, in a new Mailer evaluation, he added:

"One can say, however, that Vance is a rare breed: good writer, gentleman."

What was Norman Mailer's feeling about the section in *Advertisements for Myself* that stirred up such a prolonged literary row? Had he hesitated at all before publishing those candid estimates of the talents of his contemporaries?

When I asked him that in 1962, he wrote me:

"I worked on the 'evaluations' during odd moments for all of three months and re-read them more perhaps than any other part of *Advertisements* — so the answer would be that yes I certainly did hesitate, on ground of caution, and on some of the more speculative moral grounds, for on the better levels one doesn't know if one has the right to do that sort of thing. Pip, pip! At any rate, I did it, and better levels to the side, don't think I regret it."

He did observe, however, that he still had not heard from his old friend, James Jones, one of the writers he had dissected at greatest length in *Advertisements for Myself*.

"For a while people would bring me messages from him," Mailer wrote. "He would send his love. I never took it too seriously, because there is now something Italian about Jones. He only sends his love to people he has decided to kill."

Postscript, 1982: Echoes of a Distant Battle

While revising this chapter for the new edition, I wrote to several of the surviving participants in this great literary brawl.

I had hoped that Gore Vidal might contribute a thoughtful analysis, but he was conducting a mildly amusing campaign for the U.S. Senate in California, and my letter was directed to his campaign headquarters. I have an idea one of his aides may have discarded it as soon as he discovered that it contained no campaign contribution.

As always, Norman Mailer responded promptly:

> Dear Myrick Land,
>
> I'm in the ongoing act of finishing a novel that I've been working on for ten years about ancient Egypt, so there's no time to do anything else at all. I stopped long enough to reread your chapter and laughed a little as I did. Let it stand as it is. Some of the opinions hold up, some do less well, but it would take a week to get into thinking how I would add to it today, and I just don't have the time. I'd like to see the book when it comes out, though. It's well worth reprinting.
>
> Cheers,
> Norman

Vance Bourjaily also replied, and I have incorporated his letter into the revised chapter. And when I asked Herbert

Gold for his reflections on Mailer and Mailer's comments, his one-line reply indicated that all is quiet on the literary battle-fronts occupied by the novelists who emerged just after World War II. Offered a chance for a last word, Gold, who was one of the principal targets of Mailer's evaluations, responded serenely:

> Dear Mr. Land:
>   New times, new interests in life.
>
> Best wishes,
Herbert Gold

"Gentlemen! Gentlemen! Let's Not Call Names!"

WHILE no single literary free-for-all of the 1960s, 1970s, or early 1980s has led to the sustained uproar traceable to Norman Mailer's *Advertisements for Myself*, at least four encounters of recent years have contributed colorful episodes to the long history of literary feuding.

The first of these involved C. P. Snow, whose transitory reputation as a great novelist came under an extraordinarily violent attack by the critic F. R. Leavis.

While the aftershocks of that assault were still being felt, the young, irreverent Tom Wolfe mocked *The New Yorker* as

"The Land of the Walking Dead" and offered a caricature of William Shawn, the magazine's editor, that gained the wrathful attention of many of *The New Yorker*'s famous contributors.

A long-simmering feud between the conservative writer-editor-columnist William F. Buckley, Jr., and the liberal novelist-essayist-controversialist Gore Vidal reached a climax before an audience of millions when the ABC television network brought them together to comment on the 1968 party conventions.

Much more quietly Edmund Wilson continued a troubled friendship with the Russian-born novelist Vladimir Nabokov, but the strain became too great and finally they too clashed publicly, partly because Wilson found it difficult to take Nabokov's most successful novel, *Lolita,* seriously.

Each of these four encounters seems to me to deserve brief examination.

"He can't be said to know what a novel is."

By the early 1960s the British novelist C. P. Snow had become Sir Charles Snow and was well on his way to becoming Lord Snow—one of the few writers ever to achieve such eminence.

Every year or so the industrious Sir Charles would add a new volume or two to his long row of books, but he still found time for an occasional stroll along "the Corridors of Power." He offered advice on scientific matters to the cabinet, and his opinions on both literature and various public questions were often sought by the BBC and the Sunday papers.

Snow's novels often focused on young careerists who achieved great power in the academic world—Cambridge is the setting for at least two novels—or in the greater world outside the university. The novels gained great popularity in Britain and the United States and many critics solemnly analyzed Snow's work.

One critic, the notoriously ill-tempered Cambridge don F. R. Leavis, observed the rise of Sir Charles with some astonishment. Leavis, who had led a long, heated, successful campaign for the recognition of the genius of D. H. Lawrence, periodically settled upon other writers as targets of his unrestrained attacks. In the early 1960s he focused his disapproving gaze on Sir Charles, whose existence he had tolerated without public comment for decades.

Leavis's general impression was that Sir Charles was being extravagantly overpraised both as a novelist and as a Wise Old Man whose views of public questions should be treated with special respect.

His reservations seem to have grown much stronger because of the extraordinary success of a lecture given by Snow at Leavis's own university—Cambridge.

In this lecture—"The Two Cultures and the Scientific Revolution"—Snow argued that scientists should no longer isolate themselves from the study of literature and that non-scientists (including members of the literary establishment) should overcome their lamentable ignorance of scientific theories and discoveries.

When the Cambridge University Press published Snow's widely discussed lecture, Leavis was interested enough to wander down to the showroom maintained by the Press to glance at a copy. But he "had no inclination to lay down three-and-six-pence" for it, he recalled later, so he did not read it. He apparently expected the little book to disappear after a few months.

But as time went by he watched with increasing bafflement as Snow's small volume "took on the standing of a classic. It was continually being referred to—and not only in the Sunday papers—as if Snow, that rarely qualified and profoundly original mind, had given trenchant formulation to a key contemporary truth. What brought me to see that I must overcome the inner protest, and pay my three-and-six-pence, was the realizing, from marking scholarship scripts, that sixth-form masters were making their bright boys read Snow as doctrinal, definitive, and formative—and a good examination investment."

Reluctantly Leavis exchanged his coins for the book, which by then was in its sixth printing.

"I was then for the first time in a position to know how mild a statement it is to say that 'The Two Cultures' exhibits an utter lack of intellectual distinction and an embarrassing vulgarity of style," Leavis told startled listeners during a lecture at Cambridge. Snow's famous lecture had so many examples of "bad writing," Leavis said, that there would be some excuse for a schoolmaster to use it "as a text for elementary criticism." But it wasn't just the stylistic faults that disturbed him—it was "the thought, the essence, the pretensions."

After labeling Sir Charles' general analysis "intellectual nullity," Leavis then turned to the novels that had gained Snow an appreciative worldwide audience and a considerable volume of praise from other critics.

Snow's naive belief in himself as a novelist "of high order (of world-class even, to adopt his own idiom)" was completely unjustified, Leavis said.

". . . as a novelist he doesn't exist; he doesn't begin to exist. He can't be said to know what a novel is."

Every page of Snow's published work revealed that he was a literary "nonentity," the critic said. Then he added:

"I am trying to remember where I heard (can I have dreamed it?) that [the novels] are composed for him by an electronic brain called Charlie, into which the instructions are fed in the form of chapter-headings . . ."

If Snow did indeed depend on the assistance of "Charlie," Leavis said, the electronic brain had failed him.

"When the characters are supposed to fall in love you are told they do, but he can't show it happening. Abundant dialogue assures you that this is the novelistic art, but never was dialogue more inept . . .

"Among the most current novels of Snow's are those which offer to depict from inside the senior academic world of Cambridge, and they suggest as chararacteristic of that world lives and dominant interests of such unrelieved and cultureless banality that, if one could credit Snow's art with any power . . . one would say that he had done his university much harm . . ."

He then focused on one bestselling Snow novel, *The Affair*, which concerns a case of academic fraud at Cambridge. He called the book a "feeble affair" and said it exhibited no more skill than would be found in the work of "a very incompetent manufacturer of who-dunnits . . ."

Many British critics and reviewers were startled by the savagery of Leavis's assault on Snow, and several of them came to Sir Charles' defense. Unfortunately for Sir Charles, one of those attracted by the sounds of violence was the acerbic and unpredictable Malcolm Muggeridge.

Muggeridge, who had often spoken rather sharply about other writers, began calmly enough by indicating that he thought Leavis had gone a bit too far in his attack on Snow. But with that matter out of the way, Muggeridge then turned his full attention to the works of Sir Charles and to Sir Charles' limitations as a man and as a novelist.

Snow, he said, was "ponderous," "humorless," and "naive," and had an "endearingly innocent" view of the the world and a deluded idea about the extraordinary power wielded by a few doddering old men.

Muggeridge then turned to one of Snow's novels, *Corridors of Power*, to illustrate this weakness. He quoted a sentence from that novel:

> During the winter the gossip began to whirl out from the clubs and the Whitehall corridors.

Mockingly, Muggeridge then asked:

"But wait a minute—what clubs? What corridors? The Athenaeum, perhaps, where seedy clerics and atrocious dons desperately wash down bad food with bad wine? Or the Carlton, home of outmoded Conservative politicians in black coats hoping against hope for a telephone call that never comes to summon them to be under-under-parliamentary-secretary at the Ministry of Nothing? Or Whites whose red-faced members suck down their tenth Bloody Mary, still keeping a weather-eye open for Lord Boothby, or even Randolph Churchill. Or the Garrick, dear God, the Garrick, frequented by noisy lawyers, moronic actors, and American newspaper and television correspondents who manage to persuade themselves that they are consorting with the mighty in their seats . . .

"As for the corridors, we journalists who have paced them often and long enough in search of a story; who have visited those sad, sad knights in their ministries, looked at them across their desks; grey, listless men with black briefcases stamped with the Royal Arms (ministerial equivalent of the airlines bag) which they take with them, to and fro, between Whitehall and their homes in Putney or Wimbledon—we just can't accept the swirling rumors. What wouldn't we have given for just one tiny swirl to take back to the office . . ."

After dismissing "the imbecility of Snow's vision of power,"

Muggeridge observed that journalists know too much to take Snow's novels about those who rule Britain seriously. He himself had spent more time than he should have with Sir Charles' books, he said, and could not face the frightening prospect of plowing through the others the hard-working Snow was certain to produce in the years ahead. "I give up," he concluded wearily.

Sir Charles did not respond directly to either the Leavis assault or the supposed defense by Malcolm Muggeridge. He did observe sadly that a few—"very few"—of the criticisms he had been subjected to in the 1960s "have been loaded with personal abuse to an abnormal extent..."

At first the Leavis lecture seemed to have little effect upon Snow's reputation. Reviewers continued to praise him for his "mature knowledge of men and affairs," his "intelligent view of society," and his ability to "draw the reader into the gentle activity of reason." Some still compared him favorably with Charles Dickens, Jane Austen, and other great British novelists.

But slowly the respectful treatment began to change. A reviewer in The New York Times Book Review seemed to yawn his way through one of Snow's books, then referred to the style as "Late Victorian Humdrum" and observed that Snow "sluggishly unfolds a story patched together from conventional plot elements." D. J. Enright said, "With the worst will in the world I cannot believe that the rich and leisured are as consistently tedious and nerveless" as Snow made them appear. "Is Britain run by zombies?" he asked. Julian Moynahan called Snow's prose style "usually turgid and occasionally slipshod to the point of unintelligibility."

Writing in The New York Review of Books, Russell Davies commented, "If honors, age and output added up to reputation, Lord Snow ought by now to be the Grand Old Man of the British novel. But he is not."

While Leavis's violent attack had at first brought out some defenders who felt Snow had been unfairly dealt with, the questions raised by the angry critic were later echoed by others, and the long-range effect has been insidious. By the early 1980s, few seemed ready to proclaim Lord Snow as one of the immortals.

A visit to "The Land of the Walking Dead"

The first major American feud of the 1960s began with the publication of a rather obscurely worded advertisement in the *New York Herald Tribune,* which was then using controversy as a weapon in its war for survival.

Readers were confronted by this puzzling announcement:

> And, suddenly, after 40 years, it all adds up. Whispering, inconspicuous—formal, efficient—but the perfect qualifications for a museum custodian, an undertaker, a mortuary scientist. Thirteen years ago, upon the death of Harold Ross, precisely that difficult task befell William Shawn: to be the museum curator, the mummifier, the preserver-in-amber, the smiling embalmer—for Harold Ross's *New Yorker* magazine.

Those convoluted sentences were meant to arouse interest in a forthcoming Sunday feature—an attack upon the very mild, almost invisible editor of *The New Yorker,* William Shawn.

The assailant was 34-year-old Tom Wolfe, who had already attracted some notice for his baroque style, his use of typographical tricks, and his marked disrespect for the literary establishment. *Time* magazine noted that his articles were "filled with grunts and guffaws" and that his plentiful supply of metaphors were "launched, mixed, and sometimes hopelessly scrambled."

Shawn received an advance copy of the first part of Wolfe's two-part article, and responded with uncharacteristic anger. The normally retiring editor first placed a midnight telephone call to John Hay (Jock) Whitney, the publisher of the *Herald Tribune*. This was followed by a flurry of other calls, including four to the newspaper's editor, James Bellows.

When these seemed to accomplish nothing, Shawn wrote a desperate, last-minute plea to Whitney:

"Tom Wolfe's first article on *The New Yorker* is false and libelous . . . a vicious, murderous attack on me and on the magazine I work for. It is a ruthless and reckless article; it is pure sensation-mongering. It is wholly without precedent in respectable American journalism—in one stroke it puts the *Herald Tribune* right down in the gutter. . .

"For your sake and for mine, and, in the long run, even for the sake of Wolfe and his editor, Clay Felker (God help me for caring about them), I urge you to stop the distribution of that article."

But the presses were already running for the newspaper's Sunday magazine, *New York,* and on Sunday morning, April 11, 1965, about 450,000 *Herald Tribune* readers were confronted by Wolfe's mocking headline:

TINY MUMMIES! THE TRUE STORY OF THE
RULER OF 43RD STREET'S LAND OF THE
WALKING DEAD!

Wolfe, leader of a revolution against traditional newspaper or magazine style, plunged into his article by indicating that *The New Yorker* editors had tried to handicap him by imposing a vow of silence on the staff:

> *Omerta!* Sealed lips! *Sealed lips,* ladies and gentlemen!
> Our thing!.... For weeks the editors of *The New Yorker*
> have been circulating a warning among their employees
> saying that someone was out to write an article about *The
> New Yorker.* This warning tells them, remember: *Omerta!*
> Your vow of silence...
>
> One wouldn't even have known about the warning...
> except that they put it in writing, in memos. They have a
> compulsion in *The New Yorker* offices, at 25 West 43rd
> Street, to put everything in writing. They have *boys* over
> there on the 19th and 20th floors, the editorial offices,
> practically caroming off each other... because of the fan-
> tastic traffic in memos.

It was the kind of beginning Wolfe's readers had come to
expect—lively, unorthodox, irreverent. But staff members at
The New Yorker immediately challenged every detail in those
two paragraphs except the street address.

They had not been warned about Wolfe's plans to write
about the magazine, they said, and had never seen the memos
he mentioned. And they were baffled by his assertion that the
editors had "a compulsion... to put everything in writing."
Actually the editors were notoriously reluctant to communi-
cate through memos, they said, and therefore the picture of
the "boys" caroming off each other "because of the fantastic
traffic in memos" was pure fantasy.

These were mere quibbles, of course, but as those who
were familiar with *The New Yorker* examined Wolfe's articles
closely they picked out dozens of obvious errors. "His research... wouldn't get by the editor of a high school year-
book," wrote Dwight Macdonald in a lengthy reaction. "He
seems to be honestly unaware of the distinction between fact
and fabrication."

One of the many "inside" details about *The New Yorker*

Wolfe revealed was that the editors had gotten into the odd habit of choosing new staff members on the basis of their size.

"[Lately] *The New Yorker* has settled upon small people," he wrote, "small physically that is, who can preserve through quite a number of years that tweedy, thatchy, humble style of dress they had in college."

Macdonald and others puzzled over this bit of secret intelligence. Macdonald observed that recent arrivals had in fact been "of assorted sizes," including one who was quite tall and one who was "gigantic."

While much of the criticism of Wolfe's articles focused on his rather casual attitude toward facts, it was his caricature of William Shawn that aroused the strongest reaction.

Although Wolfe had never met Shawn, he had no hesitation about offering a quick sketch of the editor:

> He always seems to have on about 20 layers of clothes, about three button-up sweaters, four vests, a couple of shirts . . . a dark shapeless suit over the entire ensemble, and white cotton socks.

With that out of the way, Wolfe then repeated whatever he had heard about Shawn's fear of elevators, his claustrophobia, his reluctance to talk to strangers, and his tendency to whisper. The habit of whispering had spread through the magazine's staff, Wolfe indicated, and no one ever spoke in a normal voice in the vicinity of the editor's office. He referred to that area as "The Whisper Zone."

After referring to many manifestations of Shawn's phobias, Wolfe offered a theory to explain the editor's behavior.

Someone had told Wolfe that Richard Loeb and Nathan Leopold, the wealthy Chicago youths who murdered young Bobby Franks in 1924 simply to discover what it felt like to kill someone, had briefly considered killing young William Shawn instead.

The "evidence" he was able to provide in support of the theory might have seemed flimsy to even the most casual and inexperienced reporter:

> [Leopold and Loeb] went over about six names, the first one of which was "William." The court records do not give a last name . . .

Since the court records were that vague, Wolfe decided to fill in the last name himself: "Shawn." After all, young William Shawn *did* live in Chicago at the time of the murder, and he *did* attend the school which the victim, Bobby Franks, also attended.

Having made the leap from the little that was known to the limitless details that could be provided through speculation, Wolfe then traced editor William Shawn's phobias to the traumatic boyhood experience of being chosen as a potential murder victim:

> [Shawn] must have felt as if the intellectual murderers . . . had fixed their clinical eyes upon him at some point . . . How could anybody in God's world be safe if there were people like Leopold and Loeb going around killing people just for the . . . *aesthetics* of the perfect crime. The whole story, and others about Shawn, supposedly help explain why Shawn is so . . . *retiring,* why he won't allow interviews . . . why it *pains* him to ride in elevators, go through tunnels, get cooped up—why he remains anonymous, as they say, and slips *The New Yorker* out each week from behind a barricade . . .

Along with this psychoanalysis-through-rumor Wolfe offered readers his own estimate of *The New Yorker*'s contribution to twentieth-century literature: "For forty years it has maintained a strikingly low level of literary achievement."

He then provided documentation for this surprising statement—and again proved himself a rather casual researcher. As a writer in *The New York Times* later observed, Wolfe's two articles were "chockablock with details" about *The New Yorker*, but "a number of them were wrong—ranging from trivial facts like where the magazine was printed to more serious errors such as an inaccuarate list of writers Wolfe compiled to support a contention that the best writers were no longer publishing in *The New Yorker*."

The response to the two pieces was immediate and scathing. E. B. White, widely credited with a major role in the creation of *The New Yorker*, said Wolfe had set "some sort of record for journalistic delinquency." J. D. Salinger, who like Shawn jealously protected his own privacy, called the articles "unrelievedly poisonous." Other commentators used the words "vicious" and "contemptible," and Murray Kempton expressed his strong reaction to Wolfe's assault on Shawn:

> Journalism has always sinned by invasion of personal privacy. But I do not think it has before now been a canon of even the worst journalism that someone otherwise inoffensive has offended just by being jealous of his privacy.

Wolfe's articles "set literary jowls aquiver from Morningside Heights to Greenwich Village, and threw *New Yorker* staffers into a spate of semi-public wig flippings that are still going on," *Time* magazine reported.

Some *New Yorker* contributors began carving up the Wolfe pieces paragraph by paragraph. The most detailed public refutation was prepared by Dwight Macdonald, who had occupied an office at the magazine for 13 years and could easily demolish whole segments of "TINY MUMMIES!"

In *The New York Review of Books* Macdonald asserted that

Wolfe had used a "bastard form" that combined "the factual authority of journalism and the atmospheric licence of fiction."

After noting Wolfe's problem in distinguishing between facts and unfacts, Macdonald then fired off this salvo:

> The errors are of two kinds: innocent and tendentious. The former is the kind of mistake any sloppy reporter might make, such as omitting the third editorial floor, the 18th, giving the wrong address for Shawn's home at the time of the Loeb–Leopold murder and the wrong floor for his present apartment, and stating the change of printers took place "several years ago" instead of one year before his articles appeared. Since no special point depends on any of these errors, I call them "innocent," due to mere ignorance or sloth. By "tendentious" mistakes, I mean the uncritical acceptance of whatever rumors, unverified impressions, anonymous anecdotes, and old wives' tales fit his thesis.

After citing and responding to many of the mistakes (such as the age of the "boys" who carry copy from writers to editors and from editors to writers at *The New Yorker*), Macdonald then concentrated on one of the "tendentious" errors— Wolfe's long account of the Loeb–Leopold episode.

Macdonald spent six hours "searching for 'William' through the 4,713 pages of the [court] record," he said, but found nothing that even vaguely confirmed Wolfe's assertion that young Shawn was a potential murder victim. "The names of a number of what the defendants airily called 'prospects' are given, but none of them was named 'William' and none of their last names . . . was Shawn . . ."

After a careful review of contemporary accounts of the trial, Macdonald concluded: "So there seems to be nothing in it."

Wolfe responded calmly to his famous critics.

The New Yorker "has become a Culture totem for bourgeois culturati everywhere," he said. "Its followers—marvelous!—react just like those of any other totem group when somebody suggests that their holy buffalo knuckle may not be holy after all. They scream like weenies over a wood fire."

Although the controversy died down after a few months, it has had one long-range effect. Each of Wolfe's books published since 1965 has been widely discussed and widely read. But for 18 years his existence has gone unnoticed in the Whisper Zone. Not one of his books has ever been mentioned in the book review pages of *The New Yorker*.

And Wolfe himself, although he has gathered almost all of his magazine work in a series of volumes, seems for some reason reluctant to republish

TINY MUMMIES! THE TRUE STORY OF THE
RULER OF 43RD STREET'S LAND OF THE
WALKING DEAD!

"Gentlemen! Gentlemen! Let's not call names!"

A television network's battle for higher ratings led to one of the noisiest of recent literary feuds.

ABC hoped to increase its share of the audience during the 1968 party conventions by matching a widely known conservative commentator with an equally famous liberal.

The conservative was chosen first—William F. Buckley, Jr. While he was discussing the proposal with ABC executives, Buckley was asked whether he could suggest an adversary. He recalled later that he offered the names of Arthur Schlesinger, Jr., John Kenneth Galbraith and Norman Mailer.

Asked if there was anyone he would refuse to debate with,

Buckley recalls that he replied:

"I wouldn't refuse to appear alongside any non-Communist
... as a matter of principle; but I didn't want to appear opposite Gore Vidal." He told ABC that he had had "unpleasant
experiences" with Vidal in the past and did not trust him.

With that helpful reminder from Buckley, ABC naturally
proceeded to select Vidal as the liberal commentator.

"It was a question of who would best play off against
Buckley," an ABC executive explained.

One critic called this "the vaudeville-team approach to in-
terpretative journalism" and others were equally critical of
the intrusion of a showbusiness attitude toward the presentation of a major news event.

Shortly after Vidal and Buckley undertook their television
assignments the insults began. The mutual hostility seemed
to increase night after night, and sometimes all pretense of
concentrating on the convention was dropped. Finally, in one
long, disjointed argument, this exchange occurred, while the
noted television commentator Howard K. Smith attempted
heroically to restore some semblance of order:

> VIDAL: As far as I am concerned, the only crypto Nazi I
> can think of is yourself...
> HOWARD SMITH: Now, let's not call names.
> BUCKLEY: Now listen, you queer. Stop calling me a
> crypto Nazi or I'll sock you in your goddamn face and you'll
> stay plastered...
> SMITH: Gentlemen! Gentlemen! Let's not call names...
> BUCKLEY: Let Myra Breckenridge go back to his pornog-
> raphy and stop making allusions of Nazism.

In August and September 1969, Buckley and Vidal both
had a chance to replay this scene and other encounters in
articles each wrote for *Esquire*.

Buckley again focused on Vidal's personal life and Vidal
seemed to imply rather strongly that Buckley was anti-black,

anti-semitic, pro-war, and, incidentally, a "crypto-Nazi." At one point Vidal compared Buckley to Adolf Hitler, but observed that he lacked Hitler's charm.

When Buckley's charge and Vidal's counter-charge appeared in print, both men went looking for lawyers. Buckley sued both Vidal and *Esquire* for libel; Vidal aimed only at Buckley.

Esquire expressed some surprise at being caught in the crossfire. After all, each writer had been given equal freedom to speak. The editor asked *Esquire*'s readers just what he and the other editors *should* do "when two writers for the same magazine choose to annihilate each other . . ."

Three years after the first of the Buckley–Vidal articles appeared, a Federal judge decided that the Buckley case could go to trial but that Vidal's counter-suit could be dismissed.

Faced with that decision, *Esquire* paid Buckley enough money to cover his legal costs ($115,000, according to some reports), and he withdrew his libel action.

The magazine also offered an apology:

"*Esquire* is utterly convinced that Mr. Buckley is not 'anti-black,' 'anti-semitic,' a 'war-monger,' or, in any respect whatsoever, 'pro-crypto-Nazi,'—all of which charges were made in the Vidal article."

The magazine added that it was happy to renew its "long-standing and cordial relationship with Mr. Buckley."

There was no word about its equally long-standing and perhaps equally cordial relationship with Mr. Vidal.

And Mr. Vidal himself was uncharacteristically silent.

The nymphet Lolita ends a long friendship

For more than a decade the novelist Vladimir Nabokov sent many of his works-in-progress to the critic Edmund Wilson for comment, but he did not follow that custom with *Lolita* when he completed the manuscript in 1954.

Nabokov had some unresolved questions in his mind about the novel that was to make him famous. He had even considered destroying the manuscript, but had been dissuaded by his wife. Later he thought it might be best to publish the book under a pseudonym because of his fear that the story of the pursuit of the nymphet Lolita by the obsessed Humbert Humbert might be judged pornographic by narrow-minded readers, and that this might endanger his career as a lecturer at Cornell.

His doubts may have been compounded by his experiences with four American publishers who rejected the novel. They responded to *Lolita* "with fright and incomprehension," according to Nabokov's biographer, Andrew Field. One such response came from a publisher who had allowed Wilson to read the manuscript even though, Field says, Nabokov had submitted it with the "strict instructions that the manuscript was not to be shown to anyone." Field adds:

> Wilson wrote to Nabokov (November 30, 1954) and told him that he liked it less than anything else of his which he had read. The situation seemed to him to be too absurd to be tragic and too unpleasant to be funny, and he felt that the novel had too much background and description of places . . .
>
> Wilson enclosed two notes with his letter. One was from Mary McCarthy—she was writing to Wilson, not Nabokov—and she took what she termed a midway position. There were various things in the book she liked, but she concluded by saying that she thought the writing was terribly sloppy throughout, worse perhaps in the second part. The other note was from Wilson's fourth wife, who wrote that she could not put it down and thought it a very important book.

Nabokov was outraged by the publisher's failure to follow his instructions and also by Wilson's casual gesture of passing the novel around to his various wives. He later became convinced that Wilson had read no more than half of *Lolita* before rendering his verdict.

Dismayed by the rejections of his twelfth novel by U.S. publishers, Nabokov submitted it to the Olympia Press in Paris. From somewhere he had the impression that Maurice Girodias, the head of Olympia, specialized in fine editions. Actually, Girodias was best known for such works as *White Thighs, Until She Screams,* and *The Sexual Life of Robinson Crusoe*—books which nervous travelers once went to great trouble to sneak past disapproving customs inspectors.

Under the imprimatur of the Olympia Press *Lolita* seemed destined for failure. It could not compete with *White Thighs* for the attention of Girodias's faithful customers, and not a single review of the book appeared during the first six months after publication.

Then Graham Greene called it one of the best books of the year during an interview with *The Times* of London. Reviewers, their attention belatedly attracted by Greene's enthusiastic comments, agreed or disagreed, and there was enough heat in the exchanges to entice readers to buy the novel. *Anchor Review* published a long excerpt in 1957, and Putnam's issued the book in 1958 after reaching an agreement with Olympia.

Although the book was widely denounced, the administration at Cornell (where Nabokov had been teaching) received only one letter of protest:

> Frankly, we have forbidden our youngster to enroll in any course taught by Nobkov, and we would be in fear for any young girl who consulted him at a private conference or ran into him after dark on the campus!
> —Two Concerned Parents

Wilson observed the extraordinary success of *Lolita* with some astonishment, and wrote a mockingly congratulatory letter:

> I hope that *Lolita*, as a study of amorous paternity and delinquent girlhood, will touch the American public to the point of making your fortune. If you can get her married to Pnin [another Nabokov character] in Alaska and bring them home to life tenure and the American way of life in some comfortable American university, you may be able to compete in popularity with *Marjorie Morningstar* and be lecturing on young people's problems from Bangor to San Diego.

The strain in the Wilson–Nabokov relationship was obvious in the months following the emergence of Nabokov as a famous writer, but the final public quarrel was still some years away.

Nabokov was grateful for the many favors Wilson had done for him since their first meeting in 1940. The Russian-born writer was then an almost-penniless immigrant, and Wilson was one of the few Americans who knew of his achievement. Wilson was then studying Russian to equip himself to study the Russian classics without depending upon translations, and he read some of Nabokov's then untranslated novels.

Even during their earliest meetings there were occasional awkward moments. One day while they were strolling together Wilson suddenly asked Nabokov if he believed in God.

"Do you?" Nabokov asked.

"What a strange question!" Wilson muttered, and abandoned the exploration of Nabokov's religious convictions.

But there were also many long, mutually enjoyable conversations about Russia, about literature, and about life in America. and Wilson set about industriously finding bits of financial assistance for Nabokov and his wife. As literary editor of *The New Republic*, Wilson assigned Nabokov some reviews which brought modest but helpful payments—twelve dollars or so for each review. He also spoke of the Russian writer to other editors, and this led to the appearance of translations of two of Nabokov's short stories in *The Atlantic Monthly*.

Wilson and Nabokov agreed that a university appointment would give him the assured income he needed. Nabokov decided a 50-minute lecture, fully written out, would run about 20 typewritten manuscript pages. He wrote out close to 2000 pages—enough to be broken into one hundred lectures on Russian literature.

He used those pages several times over the years before *Lolita* freed him from the classroom. He later told his biographer:

> The labor [of writing the 100 lectures] was tremendous, but I had no labor after that. I could think about something totally different while I was delivering the lectures.

He realized that students also might be thinking of something else during the 50 minutes, and developed a method of testing their alertness. He would choose a natural place for a pause in his presentation, then skip back to the first page and begin re-reading the precise words with which he had begun the day's lecture.

He would watch sardonically as the students bent over their desks, recording this repeated material, phrase by phrase. This sometimes continued for as long as two minutes, he told Andrew Field. Then one by one the students would look up from their busy note-taking, suddenly realizing that the canny professor was up to one of his tricks.

Nabokov's university appointments were usually conditional and tentative. Both he and Wilson felt that Harvard was the most promising institution for a tenured professorship, and some members of the Harvard faculty who were aware of his work agreed. While he did not possess the usual academic degrees, they said, the university should recognize that he was a distinguished novelist and was therefore particularly well equipped to lecture on comparative literature. Roman Jakobson, a noted linguist, responded to this argument:

> Gentlemen, even if one allows that he is an important writer, are we next to invite an elephant to be Professor of Zoology?

Others beside Jakobson questioned whether Nabokov was quite what the university was seeking. When he delivered a long, fierce attack on Cervantes during one of his lectures, a Harvard professor dismissed the criticism with a single sentence:

> Harvard thinks otherwise.

Throughout this period Wilson was continuously helpful to the still-obscure Nabokov. His endorsement undoubtedly helped Nabokov when he applied for a Guggenheim fellowship, and he introduced the Russian to editors at *The New Yorker,* and they became enthusiastic about his "casuals" for the magazine.

Wilson proposed that Nabokov collaborate with him on a book growing out of their mutual interest in Russian writers, but this project fell through after the contract was signed. Year after year Wilson spoke of his plan to devote a major essay to Nabokov's novels, but other authors seemed to take precedence. There is some question of whether he ever managed to read all of Nabokov's novels, or even a majority of them, despite repeated attempts.

Then, in 1965, Nabokov published a four-volume translation of Pushkin's *Eugene Onegin*. Suddenly he had Wilson's
full attention, as the July 15, 1965, issue of *The New York
Review of Books* revealed:

> This production, though in certain ways valuable, is some-
> thing of a disappointment; and the reviewer, though a
> personal friend of Mr. Nabokov—for whom he feels a
> warm affection sometimes chilled by exasperation—and
> an admirer of much of his work, does not propose to mask
> his disappointment.

Wilson then focused on one of his old friend Nabokov's less
appealing characteristics:

> Since Mr. Nabokov is in the habit of introducing any job of
> this kind that he undertakes by an announcement that he
> is unique and incomparable and that everybody else who
> has attempted it is an oaf and an ignoramus, incompetent
> as a linguist and a scholar, usually with the implication
> that he is a low-class person and a ridiculous personality,
> Nabokov ought not to complain if the reviewer, though
> trying not to imitate his literary manners, does not hesitate
> to underline his weaknesses.

And Wilson did not hesitate. He called the translation
"bald" and "awkward" and said parts of it were "banal." He
compared it with a previous translation that Nabokov had
denounced as disastrous and then said that Nabokov's own
rendering of *Eugene Onegin* was "more disastrous."
"As a translator into English," Wilson said, "Nabokov has
one great flaw. He translates into English words most readers
have never seen and will never again have occasion to use."
Then he offered examples from the four volumes—English words that would baffle most readers of English:

curvate
dit
shippon
rememorating
sapajous
mollitude
dulcitude

The work was also marred by lesser flaws, he observed. Some passages were "vulgarly phrased," others "appear grotesque," and the entire work was presented in an "unnecessarily clumsy style."

He also noted that Nabokov obviously did not understand the work he had spent months translating: "[He] missed a fundamental point in the central situation."

Then there was the appendix — a section of a book not often singled out for special mention by reviewers. This one deserved attention, Wilson said, because it was "tedious and interminable."

Finally Wilson found something to praise — a feature that Nabokov could take no credit for. The actual volumes, however defective in content, "have been admirably produced," Wilson wrote.

Attached to the devastating review was a note about Nabokov's other works. Biographer Andrew Field calls the note "hideously superficial," and then adds:

> Seven novels are mentioned, several of them tossed away in a line or two, and only *Lolita* is praised. Wilson acknowledges at the beginning of his note that he has been moved to write it in order "to correct any possible injustice that I might have seemed to have done to Mr. Nabokov's work in other departments of literature than the scholarly . . ." He calls attention to and is obviously made awk-

ward by Nabokov's latter-day fame, but his remarks only add up to an ill-tempered, somehow half-hearted, and yet frequently successful attempt to shoot a few arrows *ad hominem*...

Wilson's envy of a protégé who suddenly gained worldwide fame and enormous wealth has sometimes been offered as an explanation for the change in their relationship. This may have been an element, but there seem be be other factors that led to their estrangement.

Nabokov once said that Wilson believed that "he knows Russian history better than I because of his Marxism, and that he knew at least as much about Russian literature as I." At times, Wilson also contended that he knew more about the Russian language than Nabokov. He sometimes quoted dictionary definitions to instruct the Russian in the proper use of his own tongue.

Another more basic disagreement may have been over the significance and value of Nabokov's work. While Wilson respected Nabokov's literary *efforts*, there is little to indicate that he considered the Russian's *achievements* as anything remarkable. He liked the obscure and struggling Nabokov, but he may have been first surprised and then baffled by the extraordinary change in the writer's fortunes.

After angry public debate over *Eugene Onegin*, the friendship was over. But Wilson had not forgotten the younger Nabokov, an enthusiastic collector of butterflies. Field recalls a final gesture:

> Wilson's Christmas card to Nabokov included on two occasions a paper butterfly powered by a rubber band. I happened to be present when the last butterfly from Wilson arrived in Montreux in 1968. It thrummed inelegantly straight to the floor, twitched a few times, and was still... and that was that.

Acknowledgments

SEVERAL distinguished scholars, who are also the authors of major literary biographies, gave me generous help while I was working on this book.

I am grateful for the comments and suggestions offered by Avrahm Yarmolinsky, the biographer of Ivan Turgenev and Fëdor Doestoevski; Gordon N. Ray, the biographer of William Makepeace Thackeray; Hesketh Pearson, the biographer of George Bernard Shaw; Rupert Hart-Davis, the biographer of Hugh Walpole; Carlos Baker, the biographer of Ernest Hemingway; and Louis Kronenberger, editor of a selection of the works of Dr. Samuel Johnson and James Boswell.

All were of enormous help in guiding me through several centuries and the lives of many famous writers. Often when I was confronted by conflicting accounts of a particular episode I was able to consult them while determining which witness was more reliable or which report was more credible.

I also wish to record my appreciation to my literary agent and friend, Nannine Joseph, whose genuine enthusiasm for books and writers was a factor in the birth of many volumes over four decades; to Robert Lescher and James Whitfield Ellison, who first decided there was a book in the subject of literary feuds; to Richard Hanser, whose own survey of this field in an article entitled "A Plea for Literary Mayhem" suggested my title; and to John Haverstick and Louise Waller, who gave freely of their time and their unusual skill in helping me shape most of these chapters into their present form.

Grateful acknowledgment is also made to the following agents, executors, and publishers for permission to reprint from their publications.

Sir Irving Albery, surviving executor of the will of Sir Charles Wyndham, for the letter from Sir Charles Wyndham to Henry Arthur Jones.

Arco Publications, for passages from *Turgenev: The Man, His Art, and His Age* by Avrahm Yarmolinsky, copyright © 1959 by Avrahm Yarmolinsky.

The Atlantic Monthly, for quotations from two Ellery Sedgwick letters to Gertrude Stein.

Quotations from *Portrait of Max* by S. N. Behrman, first published by Random House, copyright © 1960 by S. N. Behrman, reprinted by permission of Brandt & Brandt Literary Agents, Inc.

Cambridge University Press for quotations from *The Savage Pilgrimage* by Catherine Carswell.

Jonathan Cape, Ltd., and Charles Scribner's Sons for brief quotations from *The Torrents of Spring* by Ernest Hemingway. Copyright © 1926 Charles Scribner's Sons; copyright renewed 1954 Ernest

Angelo Ravagli and C. Montague Weekley, as Executors of the Estate of D. H. Lawrence. Reprinted by permission of Viking Penguin Inc.

Random House, Inc., and Calman A. Levin of Levin, Gann & Hankin, for quotations from *The Autobiography of Alice B. Toklas* by Gertrude Stein, copyright © 1933 by Alice B. Toklas, copyright renewed 1960 by Alice B. Toklas; Random House, Inc., for excerpts from the Introduction to *Cakes and Ale* by W. Somerset Maugham (Modern Library Edition) copyright © 1950 by Random House, Inc.; and for excerpts from *Fools, Liars and Mr. DeVoto* by Sinclair Lewis, copyright © 1944 by The Saturday Review Associates, Inc., reprinted from *The Man from Main Street*, edited by Melville H. Cane and Harry E. Maule.

The Society of Authors and the Public Trustee, London, for extracts from the letters of George Bernard Shaw to Henry Arthur Jones, previously published in *Taking the Curtain Call* by Doris Arthur Jones.

The University of Illinois Press, Champaign, Illinois, for the texts of the letters from Henry James and H. G. Wells.

Letters from Vance Bourjaily, Van Wyck Brooks, Herbert Gold, Aldous Huxley, Norman Mailer, W. Somerset Maugham, William Styron, Gore Vidal, Rebecca West, and Calder Willingham, responding to questions by the author, are quoted by permission.

Every effort has been made to locate the copyright owners of material quoted in this volume. In the very few cases where we have been unsuccessful, the source has been carefully acknowledged.